Choice,
Growth and
Development

José Encarnación

Choice, Growth and Development

Emerging and Enduring Issues

Essays in honor of
José Encarnación

Edited by
Emmanuel S. de Dios
Raul V. Fabella

Published by the University of the Philippines Press
and the School of Economics
University of the Philippines

Cataloging-in-Publication Data
Choice, growth and development: emerging and enduring issues:
essays in honor of José Encarnación / edited by Emmanuel S. de
Dios, Raul V. Fabella. — Quezon City: University of the Philippines
Press: School of Economics, c1996.
xxxvii, 322 p.; 23 cm.
Includes list of publications by José Encarnación.
ISBN 971-542-058-3

1. Economics. 2. Economic Development. 3. Decision-making—
Mathematical models. 4. Encarnación, José, 1928-
I. de Dios, Emmanuel S. II. Fabella, Raul V. III. Title: Essays in honor
of José Encarnación.
HB 171 C35 1996

Production Supervision:	*Laura L. Samson*
	Emmanuel S. de Dios
Cover Design:	*Sandy Salurio and Tonton Santos,*
	The Creative Response Co., Inc.
Layout Artists:	*Alfonso Apollo Cortez*
	Lilian A. Jimenez-Marfil

CONTENTS

FOREWORD

The School of Economics of the University of the Philippines welcomes the opportunity to honor José (*Pépe*) Encarnación with a *Festschrift* containing contributions by recognized international scholars in economic science.

Serving as dean over many years until his retirement from the University, Professor Encarnación was largely responsible for the growth of the U.P. School of Economics (founded in 1965) and for shaping its view of its role in society. A good part of Professor Encarnación's influence, however, derives from his personal example as an indefatigable scholar who preaches and practices the tenet that science knows no national boundaries and that researchers in universities in developing countries must show their worth by publishing in international journals. For him, living in a developing country has never been an excuse for failing to keep abreast of the frontiers of one's field. He may not have predicted it, but Southeast Asia's march towards globalization and rush to meet global standards are now proving him right.

"Choice," as well as "development" are fundamental concerns in economics, and in both instances, emerging issues are varied and exciting, while profound questions endure. "Choice" is a keystone of high theory, while "development" economics is the starting point of much of what is now known as "policy-oriented" research. The breadth of Professor Encarnación's scholarly involvement is revealed by his active interest in both. And we are the richer for it. Involved though he may be with issues of the day, he has never lost sight of his lifelong pursuit of fundamental relations, perhaps dating from his days as a young philosophy instructor.

Ultimately this *Festschrift* reminds us just how fortunate we are to have been associated with him, and how we continue to be enriched by the experience. This is a sentiment shared, I am sure, by his friends and colleagues who contributed to this volume. As many of his students and colleagues have found out, to discuss with *Pépe* is to be immediately forced to raise one's standards of precision and rigor, be it in the use of language, or in the search for necessary and sufficient conditions for one's conclusions to hold. In such discourses, only ideas and the search for truth matter; bankbooks, rank, and awards are of second-order importance. For *Pépe*, the results of teaching and research have always been their own reward. For all of us, on the other hand, the chance to be student or colleague has been nothing less than a rare privilege.

Thanks, *Pépe*.

Felipe M. Medalla
Dean
School of Economics
University of the Philippines
June 1995

INTRODUCTION

It will at first seem ironic, in the light of a later career challenging orthodoxy, that Professor José (*Pépe*) Encarnación's origins are thoroughly mainstream. He was born on 17 November 1928 in a Manila that was still the small town of the country's social and intellectual elite, shortly before large-scale in-migration transformed it irreversibly into an anonymous mega-city. His parents were mainline *Tagalog*, the dominant and most urbanized language community; both were connected with prominent and well-known families. Viewed more closely, however, these beginnings were not incongruous, and *Pépe* Encarnación's openness to what is new and unorthodox is not far-fetched. His father's province, Cavite, was the seat of the Philippine revolution for independence at the turn of the century. (His first cousin, Nemesio Prudente, would be jailed under the Marcos regime for alleged armed partisan activity.) Relations on his mother's side trace themselves to José Rizál, a namesake[1]. This, after all, has not been the first time (think of Keynes) that those who are thoroughly immersed in the mainstream, and who have not needed to struggle for legitimacy, have also been the first to gain the confidence and self-assurance to question it.

---

[1]Rizál, the country's national hero and a martyr of the anti-colonial struggle against Spain, was a medical doctor, writer, scholar, and polyglot. Much of the national premium given to educational excellence dates from his influence and example as a role model.

Pépe Encarnación's lifelong connection with academe, the University of the Philippines (U.P.) in particular, was both obvious and direct. His father, the elder José Encarnación was a physician and professor on the medical faculty of the University of the Philippines (then in the City of Manila proper), and the young *Pépe* led a life close to the campus and revolving around the University and its activities. As the eldest child among three, *Pépe* was accustomed to the deference and allegiance of his siblings, tempered by the stern discipline of his father.

High school was interrupted by war and the Japanese occupation. His father's assessment that the war would soon end—and that therefore any schooling under enemy occupation would be futile, since it would be invalidated—proved too optimistic. The war dragged on and, with the evacuation of Manila, the younger Encarnación ended up spending three years in the province in a self-study of the classics, particularly Plato and Aristotle. This was, upon hindsight, arguably a better education than he could have gotten anywhere in the country under the circumstances. Barely escaping death as a teen-ager in a massacre of all able-bodied men of his village by a retreating enemy, he returned to school at war's end, older and more precocious than most of his peers.

Pépe Encarnación took his first degrees in philosophy (B.Phil. and M.Phil.), and a teaching career was almost inevitable. He was soon part of a circle of bright young instructors on the University of the Philippines department of philosophy with a common interest in the ideas and programme of Bertrand Russell. "Working like a dog," pounding first-course logic into undergraduates, the instructor Encarnación nonetheless quite enjoyed the reputation of *enfant terrible*. He was brilliance combined with looks and physique, with the obvious self-assurance of one who would not suffer fools among students, colleagues—or even his superiors.

In 1958 his first publication appeared in the philosophical journal *Mind*, a small note on the Liar Paradox. There he argued that what one author considered an exception to Russell's theory of types was in fact not so. In method and tone, the insistence on precision, logical consistency, and a fair interpretation of the work of others would foreshadow many of his later contributions in economics. In the meantime, of course, all this was high theory in the province and the first publication by any member of the philosophy faculty in a reputable international journal. The young instructor was palpably surprised and dismayed by the lukewarm reception it received from his seniors. This circumstance would do much to determine his decision to change fields.

At the same time, the type of bold philosophical inquiry going on in the department was ill-suited to the ruling tastes and politics of the times. Bertrand Russell's atheism and open admiration for socialism were, after all, well known. By illogical extension, his local adherents and admirers were suspect in the eyes of both government and religious authorities, during a time the Philippines was undergoing the throes of its own version of McCarthyism.

At the beginning of the 1950s, the university decided to send a number of its younger faculty members on foreign scholarships to develop faculties in other fields. Fittingly for what the ancients regarded as the queen of sciences, a good number of those who later became the country's leading scholars in the social sciences came from the brilliant but troublesome young men of the philosophy department. Understandably, however, the philosophy department found it difficult to withstand this loss and still has to regain its former glory. At the same time, whether by accident or design, it cannot have failed to have been a source of satisfaction to a few in authority that the irreligious and difficult young philosophers were sent away to involve themselves in what were thought to be less dangerous pursuits. His other colleagues were sent off on scholarships to study psychology, sociology, and other social sciences: Encarnación left for Princeton to study economics.

Economics and Princeton were different, but not foreign. After all, following Russell, mathematics was merely applied logic, and economics at the time was still in the first blush of its love-affair with mathematical technique. Mathematics did need to be learned, but then again, it was nothing foreign to one who had already glimpsed the foundations. There might be larger and smaller nuts, but none impossible for a logician to crack. Upon hindsight, the confidence *Pépe* Encarnación has always felt in his grasp of the purely formal and logical aspects of a problem has certainly allowed him to concentrate on studying what mattered most: economic sense.

Of his stay in Princeton, *Pépe* Encarnación has always had only the fondest memories. One of the lasting impressions Princeton left on him as a student was the "publish-or-perish" rule, emphasized by his adviser Professor W. J. Baumol. It was a dictum *Pépe* would carry home and impress on his colleagues and students. The pressure in Baumol's class, it was said, had been so great that, as a result, fully a quarter of the students had published before finishing graduate work. *Pépe's* first economics publication (1958) was a note clarifying the meaning of "consistency" between Say's Law and the Cambridge equation. He had spotted a flaw in the usual proofs of inconsistency. This was the logician still at work; language and conventions might be different, but underneath, mistakes were still mistakes in whatever guise.

While in the United States, he married Patricia Kearney, a bright and creative art historian with whom he has four children. Having completed his studies, he returned to the Philippines with his wife (by freighter!) to resume his teaching career. At home, a wave of nationalism and student unrest had begun to sweep the campuses, especially the U.P. Through most of this, however, Encarnación would remain largely aloof, immersing himself in research and publishing instead. His first spate of publications came thick and fast. His reputation at university was now less that of an *enfant terrible* and increasingly that of a precocious eminence. Students stood in awe (at times in fear) of the intellectual authority of the stern young professor with an athlete's physique, a flair for dress, and uncompromising academic standards.

The idea most identified with Professor Encarnación is, of course, hierarchical or lexicographic preferences. The concept was already contained in his dissertation at Princeton (1960), which posed the following question: in planning investment, what are the goals governments seek to achieve? He noted that criteria for investment, as variously stated and practised, differed according to the preferences or priorities of governments. Objectives were patently multiple, and there was a problem of how to interpret or elicit government priorities at any given time. He formally described what was in essence a gradient interpretation of the weights in a government's utility function but in the end proposed a "quasilexicographic" formulation of government's preferences, a concept that up to that point was apparently lacking a genealogy.[2] He argued that in planning investments, governments would in practice attend to goals successively, e.g., first employment, then, consumption, and finally savings (or growth).

Later, his first postulative (as distinct from his critical or diagnostic) economics article (Encarnación 1964) appeared, a lexicographic interpretation of Baumol's notion of the sales-maximizing firm. Baumol had maintained that firms were observed to maximize sales—or in a dynamic context, growth—subject to profits not falling below a certain level. In essence, therefore, the pursuit of profits was a first priority but only up to a point, typically in order to keep shareholders content. Beyond that point, however, sales became the overriding concern.

The observation that the firm pursued different multiple objectives was really part of a broad emerging unorthodox

---

[2]It is certain he was influenced by Baumol (1959), who used the same principle in an applied context, in his suggestion of a sales-maximizing firm.

tradition that questioned the neoclassical "blackbox" view of the firm as global profits-maximizer. Basing themselves on a strong empirical tradition, economists such as Hall and Hitch, Berle and Means, Herbert Simon, Cyert and March, Nelson and Winter, and subsequently Oliver Williamson, observed that, contrary to the neoclassical presumption, managers and entrepreneurs did not maximize profits but instead followed other "rules of thumb," such as mark-up pricing, sales or market-share maximization, etc. These observations led to two branches of inquiry: *first*, it became clear that in the modern corporation, there was no complete congruence of interest between shareholders and managers, and that this was one source of the existence of multiple, sometimes changing and conflicting objectives in the firm. This branch would be revived in later years and become the basis for theories regarding the internal organization of the firm, e.g. the problem of agency (e.g. Jensen and Meckling 1976) and more generally transaction costs associated with various forms of governance (Williamson 1975, 1985).[3]

The *second* branch of the literature that emerged, however, was a questioning of the limits of actual decision-making itself. Quite apart from the internal organization of the firm, the prevalent use of "rules of thumb" that were at most locally optimal was seen to pervade *all* decision-making situations. Rules of thumb were an interaction between endemic uncertainty (as distinct from risk) and the limited human data-processing capacity. Important developments of these have been Herbert Simon's concept of "satisficing" and "bounded rationality" as distinct from global optimizing; Richard Day's concept of "cautious suboptimizing"; and Nelson and Winter's "evolutionary adaptation." Hence the second stream of inquiry, to which Encarnación belongs, sought a more fundamental understanding of the decision process itself.

---

[3]Encarnación, however, has never emphasized the idea of a potential conflict among different *groups* within a firm. He has always tended to view institutions as going concerns and, for this reason, paid less attention to the problem of *how* the multiple objectives became established in the first place.

Encarnación was increasingly convinced that the principle of lexicographic ordering pervaded *all* choice situations. The idea was straightforward and, more importantly, corresponded with the manner in which people ordinarily described the way they made decisions. The objects of choice—goods, actions, or prospects—manifested certain characteristics that were the real points of interest. In the language of the early utility theorists, goods fulfilled certain distinct "wants" or "needs." But the importance of each characteristic (or set of characteristics) accorded with a definite hierarchy of priorities. An alternative x is superior to another, say y, if it scores higher on a more important characteristic, even if y is better on lower priority ones. The color of a prospective car is probably less important than its price, so one would pick a price-worthy car with the wrong color, over one whose color was preferred but whose price was inappropriate. Similarly, x would be preferred to y if they tied on the most important criteria, but x was better on a less important one. If two cars ranked the same in terms of price, then color would be the decisive factor in choice.

The lexicographic idea also seemed ideal in capturing the fact that in many important decisions, some criteria loomed largest and could not be "traded off" against others. In many contexts, choices involving physical safety and survival, honesty, or integrity, are absolute imperatives, demanding minimum levels to the exclusion of all other criteria.

More succinctly, let the vector $u(x) = [u_1(x), u_2(x), \ldots]$ represent the scores $u_i(x)$ of an alternative denoted by x on the various characteristics or criteria $i = 1, 2, \ldots$, arranged in decreasing order of importance. Define $u(y)$ similarly. Then x is better than y if the first nonzero component of the vector difference $u(x) - u(y)$ is positive. The term "lexicographic" refers to the fact that dictionaries also order words by their successive components, i.e. letters. (The mathematician Hausdorff had first used the term in 1914 in a formal context to describe the ordering of decimal numbers.) In economics, lexicographic preferences first entered the literature as an aberration: Debreu in 1954 cited lexicographic preferences as an instance where real-valued utility functions failed to exist.[4] But for Encarnación what was initially regarded as a curiosum increasingly seemed to be the general case.

Encarnación obtained important sources of support and vindication for this idea: the first he discovered in Nicholas Georgescu-Roegen's classic 1956 article "Choice, utility, and measurement," which showed how the original ideas of the founders of utility theory (especially the Austrians) were diluted by the modern representation of utility as a catch-all function. Georgescu-Roegen argued that consumer choice was to be understood as the successive attention to satiable wants, arranged according to a definite hierarchy. He found further support in John Chipman's classic article of 1960 on the foundations of utility, which concluded that "(u)tility, in its most general form, is a lexicographic ordering, represented by a finite or infinite dimensional vector ...." Preferences may be ordered along the real line only if the additional "Axiom of Archimedes" is accepted. This strongly suggested that both formally and in the evolution of thought, vector-valued preferences were the more general class and real-valued utility the special case. What was incomprehensible was how the majority of the profession could persist in the widespread employment of what was, at bottom, merely the special case.

The standard objections fell into two categories. Even if the structure of preferences were indeed lexicographic, it was argued, the only ever *observable* criterion would be the first (Houthhaker 1961). Behaviourally, therefore, agents would act as if they had been maximizing a real-valued function, namely the first component of the vector $u(x)$. Encarnación supplied an answer to this in a small but important note (1964) recalling and developing the notion of "thresholds" introduced by Georgescu-

---

[4]Let X denote the choice set, I an indifference relation defined on X, and X/I the set X partitioned into indifference classes. The requirement for preferences to be representable by a real-valued function is that X/I be *order-dense*.

Roegen: each want in its turn, is finally satiable, and this fact causes attention to turn to the next want in the hierarchy.

This same thinking was also to be found in Herbert Simon's idea that behaviour was "satisficing," rather than maximizing. If $u_i(x)$ represents the degree of achievement in criterion i when in possession of x, a threshold level u_i^* may be defined corresponding to a satisficing level. The novel idea is that further increases in u_i beyond u_i^* do not matter. The importance of an alternative x with respect to the ith criterion may then be written as $v_i(x) = \min(u_i(x), u_i^*)$. Hence, ordering wants or criteria in decreasing order of importance, define the vector $v(x) = [v_1(x), v_2(x), ...]$. Then in the familiar vector comparison, x is preferred to y if the first nonzero component of the vector difference $v(x) - v(y)$ is positive. The point is that, unlike simple lexicographic ordering, higher-order components of v come in consideration, since, beyond a certain point, alternatives are equally satisfactory with respect to more important priorities. To differentiate it from the canonical example of lexicographic preferences, Encarnación called this structure an "L^*-ordering," which has been associated with his name ever since.

The second typical objection was actually related to the first. Are there in fact phenomena that cannot be described just as well by *assuming* that behaviour follows from a real-valued utility function? To answer this objection adequately, however, would require investigating actual behaviour that could not be represented other than by lexicographic ordering. What has been remarkable in this connection is the growing literature on experimental tests of the subjective expected-utility theory (EU). Experiments and examples following the famous early ones by Allais (1953), Ellsberg (1961), such as those of Tversky and Kahnemann, Loomes and Sugden, Machina, etc. demonstrated behaviour that in many cases represented substantial violations of EU theory. Hey (1991:92) who gives a recent survey of the gamut of experiments in expected-utility theory points to the growing tentative consensus that "no one theory explains everything."

For Encarnación, however, the paradoxes in choice theory based on EU came as no surprise but rather as a vindication somewhat overdue. That the criteria for judgement apparently often change simply points to the oversimplification involved in seeking to reduce the basis of choice to a single function; it merely showed that preferences must be represented not by one but by several criteria in turn.

In 1965 his description of the structure of the lexicographic choice under uncertainty was straightforward. Let $x = (x_1,..., x_n)$ be a set of prospects that may be realized under various states of the world $1,...n$, with corresponding probabilities of being realized, $0 < p(x_k) < 1$, $k = 1,...n$, and $\Sigma_k p(x_k) = 1$. Define $\pi_i(x, u_i^*) = \Pr(u_i(x) > u_i^*) = \Sigma_k p(x_k)$ where $u_i(x_k) > u_i^*$ for all k. Then $\pi_i(x, u_i^*)$ is the probability that x fulfills the ith criterion, $i = 1, 2, ...$ Further let π_i^* be a satisfactory level of probability of this happening. An L^*-ordering under uncertainty may then be given by $v(x) = [v_i(x)]$, where $v_i(x) = \min [\pi_i(x, u_i^*), \pi_i^*]$. Again, x is preferred to y if the first non-zero element of the vector difference $v(x) - v(x)$ is positive. In essence, $\Pr(u_i(x) > u_i^*)$ may be interpreted to mean that x is evaluated only for those of its possible realizations x_k where $u_i(x_k) > u_i^*$. A direct descendant from this family is the idea of "lexicographic safety-first," which was later found fruitful in applications modelling the risk aversion of farmers (e.g. Roumasset (1976); also Roumasset, this volume).

A more general presentation is possible, however. Let $w_i = w_i (x, p(x))$ be the ith utility from a vector of prospects $x = (x_1, ..., x_k, ...)$ which has associated probabilities $p(x) = (p_1(x_1), ..., p_k (x_n))$. Note that the criterion function w_i depends explicitly not only on x but on the probabilities associated with x.[5] One may then define w_i^* as the satisficing level of w_i and proceed to define lexicographic preference in the customary manner, with $v(x) = [v_1(x), v_2(x), ...]$ and $v_i(x) = (w_i(x, p(x)), w_i^*)$ for all i. It is

---

[5]The same point is made by Menger (1973). This is interesting considering the links Georgescu-Roegen drew between the early-Austrian theory and lexicographic preferences.

straightforward to reproduce expected utility as a particular case by defining some primitive utility function u (.) that depends only on the individual x_k. In this case, one may write $w_1(x, p(x)) = p(x) \cdot u(x)$, where $u(x) = [u(x_1), u(x_2), ...]$ and set w_1^* sufficiently high to obtain SEU. If other criteria were allowed to come into play, on the other hand, different possibilities arise. For example, for some i, w_i may depend only on the *probability* of ruinous levels of x, or on the *maximal values* of x.

Encarnación used a form of this in a 1987 article in an ambitious attempt to reconstruct and explain *all* these apparent "paradoxes" in choice theory. Apart from lexicographic comparisons the new element introduced into the structure was the notion of significant differences in the values of criterion functions. Choice between two uncertain alternatives x and y, he suggests, turns on whether they differ *significantly* on the following lexicographically arranged criteria: (1) expected value, (2) the possibility of a large loss, (3) the possibility of maximal gain, and finally (4) expected value once more. Unlike his earlier 1964 formulation, however, this one allows for intransitivity.

Interestingly enough, similar questions regarding the foundations of choice theory have been taken up again in recent years (e.g. by Sen (1993), Anand (1993) and Sugden (1985)). The abovementioned questioning of subjective expected utility theory, for example, has merely continued from the past. This is hardly surprising, since the kinds of questions raised in the 1960s failed to be resolved satisfactorily, but were rather brushed aside as minor aberrations in the otherwise triumphant march of "positive economics." But as economics and economists have become more established and less paranoid about proving themselves, they have been more willing to pose awkward questions. (It has been scarcely noticed that Samuelson (1983) himself, for example, subsequently expressed some doubts regarding subjective expected utility theory.)

In more recent garb, the resumption of some of these doubts has taken the form of "context-dependent" preferences. The general pattern is formally captured by the following canonical example: when the set of feasible choices consists solely of x and y, the individual prefers x to y. But when the choice is between x, y, and z, y is preferred to x. The implication for subjective utility theory is immediate. A simple but pointed example is as follows: in general, you would rather read newspaper x than newspaper y, which is also available, and you would rather read a newspaper than do without one (alternative z). But if only x were available, you would rather read no newspaper at all. The "sure-thing principle" requires that if $u(x) > u(y)$, as posited, then $\theta u(x) + (1 - \theta)u(z) > \theta u(y) + (1 - \theta)u(z)$ where θ is the probability of z occurring. But "context-dependent" choice would allow for the opposite to occur as well, simply because the preferences defined over the set S differ from those defined over T, even if the latter contains the former. In this and similar traditions, therefore, observed behaviour which received theory brands as "irrational" turns out to be fully comprehensible. It is not behaviour that is "irrational"; it is received theory that is unreasonable.

Apart from the theory of choice, Professor Encarnación's interests have ranged far and wide to cover such fields as econometrics, demography, growth theory, and macroeconomics. His work on demography is particularly interesting in suggesting some econometric results on classificatory variables and the modelling of regime-changes, similar to the regime-switching techniques made subsequently fashionable by disequilibrium theory. But the greater part of Professor Encarnación's theoretical work—certainly that part he seems to value most—has been devoted to attempts to demonstrate the fecundity and wide application of the idea of vector-valued utility, a concept that Encarnación (in the words of Richard Day in this volume) "almost single-handedly defended and developed." Through the years, a succession of papers of his has followed which have sought to elaborate the usefulness of lexicographic preferences in various contexts. The most important ones have included papers on reconstructions of explanations of paradoxes of choice (1987); consistency of choice (1984, 1993); consumer theory (1990); portfolio choice (1991); arbitration (1986); and group and social decision-making (1983, 1992), among others.

Considering his major involvement with theory, Professor Encarnación's insistence on the need to begin from observed behaviour is interesting. Economists often wear the blinders of normal science and tend to work on problems only their existing theories can solve, while neglecting inconvenient questions and phenomena that do not fit their framework. Encarnación, by contrast, has always been uncompromising in insisting that it is theory that must adjust to reality, not the other way around. On a broader scale, this is in fact the principle underlying his persistent championing of the lexicographic cause; the conclusions reached by real-valued and expected utility are markedly inapplicable to *many* aspects of reality. Similarly in the choice of questions to put forward, the most important method is not merely to pose questions that are logically possible, but more important, to understand what is observed.

Some hint of this view is found in his article "Social values and individual choices" (1983). The tribute and (inverted) reference to Arrow's classic (1963) book is obvious. This notwithstanding, Encarnación indirectly suggests that the paradox of social choice is something of a false problem, for organizations and societies do in fact engage in social choices, many of which do *not* degenerate into the traps that had caused Arrow's apprehension. The reason, he argued, was that in fact, groups could be presumed *a priori* to have a set of common values that prevented cycles. What he thought important was not the demonstration that logical contradictions would prevent a democracy that possessed all the "desirable" qualities; more important was to understand how actual governments could and did survive. The gentle point being made was that it is not theory's principal role to depict why things could not exist, but how and why they did.

On one occasion, one of the editors of this volume expressed some marvel over the negative result by Debreu, Montel, and Sonnenschein that market demand functions may not be "well-behaved" even if individual demand functions were (Shafer and Sonnenschein 1985). Characteristically, Encarnación replied that, on the contrary, it was more important for economists to find out why most observed market demand functions *were in fact* well-behaved, notwithstanding the negative theoretical results. For a person given over mostly to theoretical work, Professor Encarnación, it will surprise many to know, has consistently advocated the view that economics is mainly an applied and empirical science. He has always regarded it as an unfortunate trend that increasingly "mathematicians have invaded the discipline." This is mostly because of the temptation to generate problems that may be formally interesting or novel but with thin content or little appeal to economic intuition. A "model," in mathematical logic, is merely an interpretation of a formal language; the latter may exist even apart from its interpretation, or appplication. In the social sciences, on the other hand, "models" are valid only to the extent that they correspond plausibly to reality.

Still and all, and notwithstanding Encarnación's own hard work, it must be conceded that the idea of lexicographic ordering has thus far failed to become a serious formal rival to rules based on standard expected utility. Understanding the profession's slow and lukewarm response to alternative viewpoints such as lexicographic preferences is revealing, and is probably sufficient in itself to warrant a separate study in the evolution of thought. This is, of course, not the occasion to do so. It should simply be pointed out that in the case of lexicographic preference theory, at least on the face of it, there seem to be no issues of a purely *ideological* or *methodological* nature involved. The notion of lexicographic preferences *is* a branch of neoclassical theory in its insistence on rationality, methodological individualism, even subjective optimization. If anything, it differs from the latter only in that it takes the call for "positive economics" to heart and takes observed behaviour seriously. In the same manner that studies of identical twins dispose of intervening factors such as genetics, a comparison of the differing fortunes of orthodox real-valued and vector-valued preferences would probably reveal less about economic theory itself than about the sociology of economics.

No doubt sheer inertia in the profession has been a most important factor. *Dogmengeshichte* is replete with seminal ideas that have been pushed to the side, simply because they have not been expressed in a manner to which the majority of the profession has been accustomed. For this same reason, in the period before the discipline was mathematized, Carl Menger's literary exposition of subjective value theory was more influential than the mathematical presentations of Walras and Jevons. Some economizing is undoubtedly at work: if the bulk of the profession has already made large sunk investments in certain tools, retooling will usually be viewed as costly or risky (think of the likely objective function of young Ph.D.s up for tenure) without the likelihood of large payoffs in the form of significantly different propositions. At the margin, therefore, only so much adjustment and innovation in methods is likely to be undertaken as is needed to explain "significantly different" phenomena.[6] There are good reasons to suspect, therefore, that at any one time, economic theory does not push itself up to the frontier of what is explainable.[7]

It is also tempting to think of sociological or at least circumstantial reasons. Owing largely to his conscious decision to make a career in his own country, and partly to his rejection of the peculiar rigors of Philippine travel formalities (including a stubborn refusal to appear personally to apply for foreign visas)

---

[6]This observation applies not only to events that Kuhn calls "paradigm-shifts" but to what he would call the progress of "normal science" as well.

[7]This would be true of any science, even the "hard sciences." But it is likely to be even more of a problem in fields where the pressure for empirical verification is not as compelling, nor the criterion for falsifiability as unambiguous.

Professor Encarnación's communications with the profession in the rest of the world have occurred almost entirely through the journals. His trips outside the country have been comparatively rare, the only extended ones being to Stanford, where his hope of collaborating with Arrow failed to materialize, and to Wisconsin, where he formed enduring ties with a kindred spirit, Richard Day. Professor Day's own work on "cautious suboptimizing" was fully parallel to Encarnacion's own thinking, and Day and Robinson (1973) would subsequently publish an important paper setting out sufficient conditions for the kind of continuity required by general-equilibrium for demand and supply correspondences generated by lexicographic preferences.[8]

All things considered, the extent to which Professor Encarnación's work is known outside the Philippines is remarkable. One may wonder, of course, how much *larger* a hearing he would have obtained if he had instead chosen to "do" the circuits of major economics conferences, collaborated with other prominent colleagues, and so on. Some personal elements will be involved as well, not the least of which is Professor Encarnación's distaste for either self-promotion or solicitation in the matter of ideas. This is reflected in his writing style, which is beautifully austere and concise, with a hint of delight in understatement. In a similar vein, his graduate students will attest that Encarnación has never imposed his own ideas, but has rather always fairly and fully presented those contrary to his own, leaving students to judge the relative merits for themselves. His is the proud attitude of an older school that did not talk down to anyone, but did not bow for anyone else either.

Outside observers may perhaps find curious the high esteem with which Professor Encarnación is held in his country. His efforts notwithstanding, after all, the idea of lexicographic

---

[8]This is extended in Day's excellent contribution to this volume. Encarnación was also associate editor of the *Journal of Economic Behaviour and Organisation,* with Day as editor.

preferences may still be regarded as something exotic, not the least in the Philippines, where problems of development tend to dwarf the finer points of choice theory. Such a view fails to take into account his profound influence on the development of the economics profession in the Philippines, however. Directly or indirectly, Encarnación as teacher has exercised his influence on several generations of Filipino economists over the past three decades.

The decision to stay and develop the economics profession in his country was clear from the start, interesting offers from abroad notwithstanding. Soon after his return, he had been sought for recruitment by a foreign university. He admits to a foolishness upon hindsight in not rejecting their offer outright but rather quoting a reservation price that had seemed exorbitant to him at the time. To his dismay, however, this price was matched. In a bind, he sought help from then U.P. president, Carlos P. Romulo, and the latter obliged by ordering him to wire the foreign university, to the effect that he, Encarnación, would be unable to accept the offer at the last moment, upon orders by "General Romulo" who had directed him to start the Ph.D. program in economics for the university. The device worked.

Until the mid-1960s, economics in the Philippines had barely extricated itself from management and finance. The economics faculty was merged with those teaching business administration. In the public perception, the distinct relevance and contribution of economics as a a discipline was even more vague, with lawyers, businessmen, journalists, and other sorts of what Keynes called "practical men" all presuming themselves equally qualified to give advice on and to make economic policy. This was soon to change, however, as Encarnación and the first batch of professionally trained economists returned to the country to constitute a critical mass for the profession, and a demand for quality economic research and policy advice began to arise, initially from official agencies. A watershed of sorts was marked by his review of an existing local economics textbook written by the older school. This "review" consisted of nothing more than a list of the eccentric (to put things kindly) economic definitions from the book. The reviewer Encarnación then simply dispatched these with the withering conclusion that the authors had been too modest in their claim of not wishing to add anything novel to economic theory.

By necessity, *Pépe* Encarnación's generation of professional economists had to plunge into almost all fields simply because the dearth of people prevented any narrowing of specializations. As a result papers followed, authored or co-authored, that dealt with monetary theory, public finance, growth, investment programing, econometrics, population and demography, all in relation to development. A number of these were simply thrust upon him by circumstances, and some topics were obviously closer to his heart than others. In reading any of these papers, however, the qualities of careful attention to data and well-considered judgement consistently shine through, the hallmark of the true scholar and professional.

Pépe has always been the embodiment of the academic ethos. The excitement he derives at a discovery is contagious. His knack for putting a finger on the core of the issue is uncanny. Once after the usual U.P.School of Economics Friday Seminar, Professor James Roumasset was excitedly detailing the subtleties of computable general equilibrium analysis. *Pépe* raised his eyes to the ceiling and with a naughty smirk blurted out "Witchcraft!".[9] This was the classic *Pépe*: deliciously brief, clinically correct and supremely confident. Age has not dimmed his curiosity, and he has never had to draw from past triumphs for intellectual authority.

Pettiness and partiality are common pitfalls among academic institution-builders. The malaise typically sets in when research work has long ceased and one's authority hinges on political maneuverings and financial considerations. The inevitable result

---

[9]See Chipman's contribution to this volume.

is a diversion of energies and rankle in the ranks over favors unearned. No fortress can long endure with its defenders at each other's throats. *Pépe*, however, never allowed triviality or unfair preference to cast their shadow during his watch, a good part of the reason his moral authority was never undermined. He pursued fairness almost to a fault and did not shy away from ruthlessness to attain it. As Shakespeare so aptly put it, "Nothing so encourages sin as mercy." For fools and for sloppy logic, the younger *Pépe* simply had no mercy. Vintage Encarnación has even less.

Now and in the future, Professor Encarnación's chosen path will continue to raise profound questions about the proper role of an economist in a less-developed country. His example breaks the pattern of scholars from developing countries who win international renown for theoretical contributions only as expatriates, and whose adult connections with their native countries extend little beyond circumstances of birth or a post-eminent desire to assist the old country. This rule, of course, is no accident: after all, high theory should not be expected particularly to flourish in the periphery. It is therefore the view of "practical men" that the pursuit of theory and excellence in the periphery is something of a misguided choice, a use of resources that rubs against the grain of comparative advantage. Not only does the rareness (and difficulty) of *Pépe* Encarnación's example suggest this, it would also seem supported by positive experience.

Developing-country economists *in situ* who do manage to catch the world's attention have almost always been associated with positions of policy influence in countries enjoying episodes of economic success. Some obvious examples are S.C. Tsiang and T.C. Liu, who bucked the intellectual tide of import substitution in the 1950s and made export promotion the engine of Taiwan's economic miracle. Rolf Ludders and the "Chicago Mafia" played a similar part in Pinochet's Chile in the late 70s, political objections to that regime notwithstanding. Indonesia too had its Berkeley Mafia. Domingo Cavallo in Argentina may be another credible candidate to this exclusive club. Much, much earlier, in postwar and economically prostrate Germany, Ludwig Erhard and his colleagues from Freiburg brandished the view of the *soziale Marktwirtschaft* with astounding success. When such events do occur, the rest of the world typically demands no further evidence that academics can and do at times contribute substantial value-added. Such positive examples do seem to suggest the way for the majority of academics to concentrate on policy and be co-opted into policy-making.

Unfortunately, however, achievements of this sort and of such visible proportions are themselves rare exceptions rather than the rule. In practice, the majority of academics called on to serve policy in developing countries will likely have little more to show for it than an additional line in their vitae, some fond memories of close encounters with the high and the mighty, and possibly a subsequent comfortable job with a multilateral agency. In less developed countries, such career-paths no longer raise eyebrows and are well accepted, perhaps even envied. That such circumstances may fulfill the individual professional's ends (including subjectively altruistic ones) is not in question; what *is* at issue is whether it can stand as a prescription, an existential "ought." For, in the meantime, even as academics may accept government positions for their own objectives, the state may proceed according to a dialectic quite its own.

Governments will pursue their own objectives in recruiting academics, only part of which is an honest search for expertise and knowledge. Another part will be dominated by the equally important imperative of legitimation. The premium for an academic derives from his being widely perceived to be the advocate of the fair, the consistent, and the (constrained) best. There is at least an initial suspense of public disbelief that the academic could consent to being a mere pawn of vested interests. Academic economists have an additional role in this respect, owing to an LDC government's need to work on a second audience, namely external lending agencies who need reassurance that the moneys they advance will be used as promised. In this context, the glitter of economics Ph.D.s from prestigious U.S. universities—not to mention shared interests in squash and Rose Bowl match-ups—can and does disarm even the sternest loan officers. It thus becomes easy for academics to slip into the comfortable role of manservant or handmaid.

Serviceable as he is, however, the academic in government cannot be *too* inflexibly committed to standards of scholarly merit, lest he prove to be a nuisance, or—with sufficient obduracy and public support—even a threat. This is especially likely for those whose professional reputations precede and exceed the derivative splendor of a bureaucratic position. Mindful of this danger, governments do not often recruit academics at random: the candidate must share the dominant ethos (good or ill); he or she must understand why being out-of-play on matters at the edges is justified by being in-play on matters at the core, as well as accepting the leadership's shifting definition of what is at the "core" and what is on the "edge." Of course, since information and quality control are imperfect, mistaken appointments do at times occur; but even here the damage can be minimized by a simple quarantine and the forced "voluntary" resignation. Faced with such prospects, it is no wonder that, notwithstanding undoubted examples of clear value-added by academics as policy-shapers, many who experience the true joys of a scholar's life view the prospect of getting sucked into the policy maelstrom with deep unease.

Many of these apprehensions will sound arcane in developed societies and economies where politics and social divisions are less extreme. In such circumstances, the choice between pursuing truth (however this may be subjectively perceived) and serving the powers-that-be is one that is much less of an existential struggle, considerably less taxing morally. Then people may indeed move freely between faculty lounges and halls of power without closing doors.

This was not the case, however, for a good part of *Pépe* Encarnación's stewardship. Where the state is far from being the disinterested Leviathan and is more of an arena of patronage and plunder, there is good reason to think an academic's best contribution may be found in academe itself.

Under such circumstances, however, even a retreat into academe does not totally end existential choices. The potential and actual exercise of freedom in an academic milieu may be viewed with suspicion by a state sensitive to criticisms of its own legitimacy. At this point, either political correctness may be rudely enforced, or academe may be insidiously co-opted. At the University, after the initial repression of the early 1970s, the wooing of the academe began in the form of numerous new special-purpose institutes and financially rewarding consultancies. The arena of debate then shifted from ideas and discoveries to power and privilege. As a science professor moaned at the time, "Science in the Philippines is 90 percent politics." Even worse, the texture of debate itself deteriorated. The new methodological credo was aptly summed up by yet another scholar: "These are the conclusions upon which I will base my facts." Especially where scholastic traditions are porous, academe is always in danger of succumbing to the dominant outside ethos. Through control of the purse strings and the investiture of revolving-door ministerial positions, the state may slowly recreate the University in its own image.

Ironically, however, not only political co-option by the state threatened academe and helped along the collapse of scholarship but, to a lesser extent, resistance to authoritarian tendencies as well. As opposition to government became more widespread in the mid-1980s, it became possible and expedient to soften the borders of intolerance for loose scholarship to accommodate political zealotry. Once lines have been drawn for a political showdown, a clear show of partisanship may at times appear more important or urgent than correct reasoning and a careful consideration of the facts.

A university actually leads a dual life, as *ecclesia* and *agora*. The *agora* encourages and thrives in logodiversity and debate. The *ecclesia*, however, has only intolerance and contempt for heedless argument and for persuasion by any other authority than reason and evidence. The academe needs both. Without free discourse, disciplined reason and logic become mere affectations. Without disciplined reason, on the other hand, free debate becomes a babel of tongues, superficially entertaining but ultimately a huge waste of time. For a time, fear and autocratic patronage, on the one hand, and a contrarian populism, on the other, made for a strange elixir that further weakened the academic ethos. It was in this double eclipse of the academe that the economist as academic in *Pépe* Encarnación shone most brightly. His imperative was and still remains preserving and nurturing the seeds of scholarship threatened by creeping politicization.

Pépe Encarnación's relationship to politics during this long and difficult period will seem enigmatic to those unable to appreciate the priorities he considered truly important. Those merely looking in from the outside will either dismiss him as being politically naïve or aloof, on the one hand, or a willing party to co-option, on the other. The situation was, in fact, far more complex. For most of this period, *Pépe* Encarnación made it a point to keep his political opinions to himself for a simple reason: to preserve the School of Economics and the quality of its work. On several occasions, he succeeded in fending off attempts to subsume the School's research agenda to external "direction" of any sort, or to turn the School into an institute of official consultants, advocates, and firefighters. This was a prodigious task, considering the government's sway over university budgets.

To protect the standards and integrity of the School of Economics, he was not beneath using his charm, wit, intellectual and social influence, or even somewhat disingenuously playing the role of a detached scholar, too lost in the mists of theory and academic matters to know much of practical affairs. In that earlier period, he walked a tightrope between allowing the faculty the intellectual freedom it needed and preserving the School from outside retaliation.

In 1984, after the assassination of Benigno S. Aquino, a group of faculty members signed and published what became known as the "White Paper," a critical report, subsequently widely publicized, that analyzed the mistakes and abuses of economic policy-making under authoritarianism. Soon after, however, the School's performance and budget were up at some meeting with government functionaries, and the rankling criticism of government policies by the "White Paper" was inevitably brought up. At that point, *Pépe* Encarnación as dean maintained that the offending report was signed only by a minority of the School faculty. He was, of course, technically correct: the faculty at the time consisted of twenty-one members, and the ten signatories were one shy of a majority. What he conveniently neglected to mention of course was that he, *Pépe*, had in fact participated most actively in all the discussions and the writing of that report and fully shared the assessment it contained, although he ultimately did not sign it.

To what end? Ultimately, to maintain academic integrity and standards, and safeguard the survival of the institution. In essence, *Pépe* saw the need to suppress his own preferences to preserve the integrity of the institution; in a difficult situation, he felt, he could not afford publicly to have his own opinions. In the end, of course, even this enforced prudence in the institution's behalf could not withstand the strength of his own beliefs or the pressure of events. In the period leading up to the 1986 EDSA Revolution, a threshold was exceeded, and *Pépe* participated fully and openly in the University's mobilization, an unprecedented event which surprised many of his colleagues. Even today he feels proud of having bought his first pair of athletic shoes since decades, for the sole purpose of joining a march to EDSA.

In the meantime, before that, owing in no small measure to *Pépe*'s efforts, the School was preserved. If the world was intolerant, the School provided (and still provides) a haven for the pursuit of inquiry and the co-existence of the most diverse trends of thought. Neoclassicals, new classicals, Marxists, Keynesians, and neo-Keynesians, institutionalists, and plain eclectics found a home in Encarnación's strange academic menagerie. Though an enigma to the outside world, *Pépe* Encarnación's aims and priorities were never in doubt among his colleagues at the School. He placed no demands for conformity, only for excellence. Where the status quo no longer regarded standards and rigor alone as bankable, or even necessary, *Pépe* relentlessly pushed his people to seek self-reaffirmation and vindication in international scholarship. An existential nuance was attached to the phrase, "Publish or perish" which he learned from Baumol's class and took to heart. This was a lifeline *Pépe* himself valued highly, and he led by example. His frequent admonition to aim at standards set by the refereed journals had a larger social significance, namely to imbue his faculty with a sense of worth that transcended the perks and power of a position of influence.

It has always been *Pépe*'s deepest conviction that it is academic institutions and the search for knowledge they nurture that truly endures. Though its dominance may seem interminable, the latest fad, vested interest, or political expedient that holds politicians and "practical people" in thrall is always bound to pass. It is for that reason that the integrity and continuity of the academe must be preserved, for the day it can come into its own. It takes time and foresight, far beyond seeing the exigencies of the moment, for the value of this to be apppreciated. "Next year in Jerusalem" was for a thousand years only a dream kept alive by true believers—a pipe dream to others. At the height of Nazi power in Germany, *soziale Marktwirtschaft* was the antithesis of the pervasive regulatory and command environment then prevailing. Who then could say if and when the country would ever emerge from its moral and cultural hibernation? Perhaps not till the end of the thousand-year Reich. But the fires were stoked quietly, constantly, indeed foolishly it then seemed. When finally Nazi Germany collapsed, however, "social market economy" provided the vision and the roadmap to an economic miracle. At that point, Erhard and his fellows knew exactly how to proceed.

What has been said of Samuelson may also be said of Encarnación: he did not found a school of thought; instead he founded a *real* school, the U.P. School of Economics, the institution he would lead as dean for two decades from 1974 until his retirement in 1994. Through that time, the School would acquire a faculty with a reputation for quality teaching and solid and independent-minded scholarship. It would be superficial to measure Professor Encarnación's influence as a teacher simply by the following his particular ideas have gained, as, say the "Austrian School" or the "Chicago School" may be associated with particular approaches or ideas in economics. Instead, his students and colleagues have learned things that are much more fundamental and valuable: high moral principles; a striving for excellence in scholarship; basic fairness; generosity; and a quiet, pragmatic commitment to improving people's lives. It is these lessons, if any, that are to be learned from Encarnación's "school" of economics. In this sense, the school *Pépe* founded is an anomaly. In ethos, in procedures, in standards, it is "in" a developing country but not quite "of" it, as currently constituted. Such is *Pépe* Encarnación's legacy as an economist and academic: he belongs not only to the Filipino but to the world.

Raul V. Fabella
Emmanuel S. de Dios
School of Economics
University of the Philippines

References

Allais, M. (1953) "Le comportement del'homme rationnel devant le risque: Critique des postulats et axiomes de l'école Americaine," *Econometrica* 21: 503-546.

Anand, P. (1993) "The Philosophy of Intransitive Peferences," *Economic Journal* 103, March: 337-346.

Arrow, K. (1963) *Social Choice and Individual Values.* 2nd ed. New York, London: Wiley and Sons.

Baumol, W. (1959) *Business Behavior, Value, and Growth.* New York: Macmillan.

Berle, A. and G. Means (1932) *The Modern Corporation and Private Property.* New York: Macmillan.

Cyert and March (1963) *A Behavioural Theory of the Firm.* Englewood Cliffs, New Jersey: Prentice-Hall.

Chipman, J. (1960) "The Foundations of Utility," *Econometrica* 28: 193-224.

Day, R. and S. Robinson (1973) "Economic Decisions with L**-Utility," in J. Cochrane and M. Zeleny eds. *Multiple Criteria Decision-making.* Columbia: University of South Carolina Press.

Debreu, G. (1954[1983]) "Representation of a Preference Ordering by a Numerical function," reprinted in *Mathematical Economics: Twenty papers of Gerard Debreu.* Cambridge: Cambridge University Press.

Ellsberg, D. (1961) "Risk, Ambiguity, and the Savage Axioms," *Quarterly Journal of Economics* 75: 643-669.

Encarnación, J. (*Please refer to the list of publications by José Encarnación at the end of this volume.*)

Georgescu-Roegen, N. (1956) "Choice, Expectations, and Measurability," *Quarterly Journal of Economics* 58:503-534.

Hall, R. and C. Hitch (1939) *Price Theory and Business Behavior.* Aldershot, U.K.: Elgar.

Hey, J. (1991) *Experiments in Economics*. Oxford and Cambridge MA: Blackwell

Houthhaker, H. (1961) "The Present State of Consumption Theory," *Econometrica* 29: 704-740.

Jensen, M. and W. Meckling (1976) "Theory of the Firm: Managerial Behavior, Agency Costs, and Capital Structure," *Journal of Financial Economics* 3: 305-360.

Loomes, G. and R. Sugden (1983) "A Rationale for Preference Reversal," *American Economic Review* 73: 428-432.

Machina, M. (1982) "'Expected Utility' Analysis without the Independence Axiom," *Econometrica* 50: 277-323.

Menger, K. (1973) "Austrian Marginalism and Mathematical Economics," in J.R. Hicks and W. Weber, eds. *Carl Menger and the Austrian School of Economics*. Oxford: Clarendon Press.

Nelson, R. and S. Winter (1982) *An Evolutionary Theory of Economic Change*. Cambridge, Mass.: Harvard University Press.

Roumasset, J. (1976) *Rice and Risk: Decision-making Among Low-incomeFarmers*. Amsterdam: North-Holland.

Samuelson, P. (1983) *Foundations of Economic Analysis*. Second Edition with Appendix. Cambridge, Mass.: Harvard University Press.

Sen, A.K. (1993) "Internal Consistency of Coice," *Econometrica* 61(3), May: 495-521.

_____ (1988) "Freedom of Choice: Concept and Content," *European Economic Review* 32: 269-294.

Shafer, W. and H. Sonnenschein (1985) "Market Demand and Excess-Demand Functions" in K. Arrow and M. Intriligator, eds. *Handbook of Mathematical Economics* Vol. 2. Amsterdam: North-Holland: 671-693.

Simon, H. (1957) *Models of Man: Social and Rational*. New York: Wiley and Sons.

Sugden, R. (1985) "Why be Consistent? A Critical Analysis of Consistency Requirements in Choice Theory," *Economica* 52: 167-183.

Tversky, A. and D. Kahnemann (1981) "The Framing of Decisions and the Psychology of Choice," *Science* 211: 453-458.

Williamson, O. (1975) *Markets and Hierarchies: Analysis and Antitrust Implications*. New York: Free Press.

_____ (1985) *The Economic Institutions of Capitalism*. New York: Free Press.

Satisficing Multiple Preferences In and Out of Equilibrium

*Richard H. Day**

Introduction

The way people think, argue over goals, and seek accord within groups is reflected by popular and scholarly commentaries on political and economic problems. These are frequently couched in terms such as "setting" or "reordering" priorities, as, for example, in the series of volumes entitled *Setting National Priorities* that were initiated years ago by Schultze *et al.* Psychologists, such as Maslow, have long considered human behavior to be driven by various needs and wants that have an order of precedence. Ethologists, such as Leyhausen, have carefully documented similar mechanisms in animals.

Decision-making when goals, objectives or preferences are ranked and considered in a sequence is formalized in the theory of lexicographic preferences expounded by Georgescu-Roegen in his 1954 article, "Choice, Expectations and Measurability." Drawing on the works of the neoclassical founders of utility

*Professor of Economics, University of Wisconsin, Madison. This paper is dedicated to José Encarnación who has almost single-handedly kept alive this important and relevant, yet much neglected topic.

theory (Jevons, Menger, Marshall, Walras), Georgescu-Roegen observed:

i) "The reality that determines the individual's behavior is not formed by utility, or optimality, or any single element, but by his wants, or his needs."

ii) "It has long since been observed that human needs and wants are hierarchized."

iii) "This principle clearly implies that [individual] wants are finally satiable."

iv) "Choice aims at satisfying the greatest number of wants, starting with the most important and going down the hierarchy."

In the same place Georgescu-Roegen and subsequently Chipman investigated lexicographic utilities in the context of consumer theory. Simon, Cyert and March, and Ferguson studied business behavior with hierarchies of goals. In a series of papers Encarnación explored a class of "L^*" lexicographic orderings in a variety of applications in microeconomics. His treatment of L^* preferences provides a formalization in utility terms of Georgescu-Roegen's satiation property (iii). It is, in effect, equivalent to Simon's concept of satisficing in which individual goals are not pursued "to the max" but until a satisfactory or "satisficing" level is attained.

Motivated by this observation, Steve Robinson and I showed that with certain reasonable restrictions on the structure of preferences, the behavior of agents generated by L^* behavior exhibited the continuity requirements needed for the existence of competitive economic equilibrium, and that such behavior could be rationalized by means of a single function, thus establishing a link between some of the principles of behavioral economics and general economic equilibrium. Our treatment incorporated *state dependence* of preferences and feasibility domains which makes it possible to consider the implications of L^* behavior in an adaptive, disequilibrium context of the kind I discussed in Day (1971, 1975). This paper gives an elaboration of these findings. In particular, I sketch the proof of competitive equilibrium in the Arrow-Debreu framework when households have L^* preferences, consider the existence of viable trajectories for an abstract adaptive society with L^* agents, and discuss some of the implications of the L^* approach for interpreting economic change. Throughout I shall use the term "criterion" for utility, preferences, needs or wants interchangeably for the analysis can be made to apply to decision making in many different contexts.

Illustration

The lexicographic approach can be illustrated with the usual two-good consumer choice problem as in Figure 1.

The steep, curved lines represent indifference curves of a preference ordering determined by a first, most important want. Satiation of this want is reached when $\varphi_1(x) = \sigma_1$. The flat curves represent indifference curves of a second want. For this want, satiation is reached when $\varphi_2(x) = \sigma_2$. Or, we could say that satisficing is attained for the first preference ordering when $\varphi_1(x) \geq \sigma_1$ and for the second when $\varphi_2(x) \geq \sigma_2$.

For a given budget and given prices, choice is based on a first preference ordering until a satisficing level is reached. Then, subject to the additional constraint that this level is maintained, the next criterion in the hierarchy is considered until it is satisficed, and so on until a final choice or a final set of choices is reached within which the decision maker is indifferent. The exact manner by which a decision maker gropes toward eventual satisfaction of a given criterion is, of course, a behavioral and dynamic question. In order to simplify the discussion, let us set aside the cognitive procedures involved in answering it and assume for convenience that for any given set of preferences and constraining limitations, a best feasible choice is attained. The

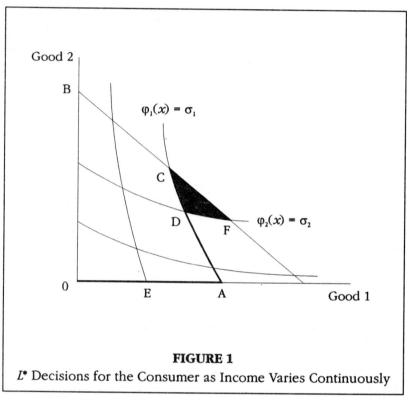

FIGURE 1

L^* Decisions for the Consumer as Income Varies Continuously

heavy, connected, kinked lines show the locus of these maximal choices as income is varied continuously with prices fixed (Figure 1) and as the price of good 1 is varied continuously when income and the price of good 2 is fixed (Figure 2). These lines eventually cross the shaded region of equally good choices within which both criteria are satisficed.[1]

Two important facts immediately stand out. The first is the kinked, irregular shape of the expansion paths. This implies a richness of demand and expenditure patterns not ordinarily associated with utility maximizing behavior. The second is, that despite this increased complexity, the induced behavior is

---

[1]Encarnacion (1964b), Ferguson (1965), and Day (1979) present similar graphical examples drawn from the theory of the firm.

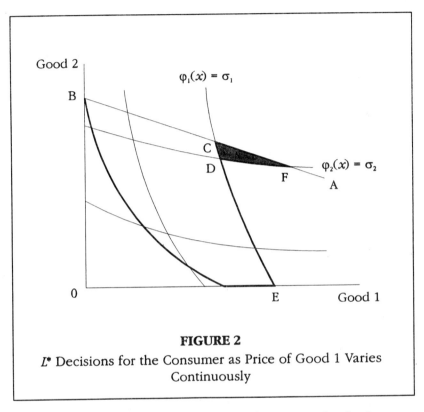

FIGURE 2

L^* Decisions for the Consumer as Price of Good 1 Varies
Continuously

clearly continuous; that is, a small change in the budget set
induces a small change in behavior. It is this property that plays
such an important role in further theorizing.

Continuity of Satisficing Choices

Now consider the theory in a general form. Begin with
optimizing choices. Let x be a choice variable or vector in a
choice space **X** and let w be a datum or parameter in an
information space **W**. A slight generalization of a standard result
for optimal solutions of constrained maximizing problems is
needed which allows both preferences and feasible regions to

vary parametrically. Given a datum $w \in \mathbf{W}$, preferences and feasible alternatives are perceived (or "felt" intuitively) and the (rational) problems of comparing alternatives with a view to selecting the best one can be formulated.

The *feasibility correspondence* is a multivalued map $\Gamma: \mathbf{W} \to 2^{\mathbf{X}}$, the *utility function* is a single-valued function $\varphi : \mathbf{X} \times \mathbf{W} \to \mathbb{R}$. The *indirect utility function* is a single-valued map $\pi : \mathbf{W} \to \mathbb{R}$ defined by

$$\pi(w) := \max_{x \in \Gamma(w)} \varphi(x, w) \tag{1}$$

The *choice correspondence* is a multi-valued map $\Psi: \mathbf{W} \to 2^{\mathbf{X}}$ defined by

$$\Psi(w) := \operatorname{Arg} \max_{x \in \Gamma(x)} \varphi(x, w) \tag{2}$$

The Maximum Theorem. *Assume that* $\mathbf{X}$ *and* $\mathbf{W}$ *are topological spaces. If* Γ *is nonempty and continuous on* $\mathbf{W}$ *and if* φ *is continuous on* $\mathbf{X} \times \mathbf{W}$, *then* π *is continuous and single-valued on* $\mathbf{W}$ *and* Ψ *is upper semicontinuous on* $\mathbf{W}$.

Proof. Following Berge (1963:115, 116), Theorems 1 and 2, we observe that if Γ and φ are continuous, so is π. The (*weakly*) *better-than* correspondence is a multi-valued map $M : \mathbf{W} \to 2^{\mathbf{X}}$ defined by

$$M(w) := \{x \in X \mid \varphi(x, w) \ge \pi(w)\} \tag{3}$$

The complement of the graph of M is

$$\{(x, w) \mid \varphi(x, w) - \pi(w) < 0\}$$

which is open by the continuity of θ and π. Hence, M is closed. As $\Gamma(w)$ is continuous, it is also closed. It is clear that $\Psi(w) = \Gamma(w) \cap M(w)$. The intersection of closed sets is closed, so this implies, by Theorem 7 (Berge 1963: 112), the upper semicontinuity of Ψ.[2]

---

[2]Our version is slightly more general than Hildenbrand (1970).

Remark 1. If $\varphi(x,w)$ is quasi-concave for each w, then $M(w)$ is a convex set. Therefore, if $\Gamma(w)$ is a convex set for each w, the $\Psi(w)$ is, also.

Now consider the utility function defined by

$$\varphi(x, w) = \min \{\mu(x, w), \sigma(w)\} \quad x \in \mathbf{X}, \, w \in \mathbf{W} \qquad (4)$$

where $\sigma : \mathbf{W} \to \mathbb{R}$ is a real single valued *satisficing function*. Robinson and Day showed that Ψ is continuous when φ is given by (4) if the underlying functions μ are strictly quasi-concave in x for each w.

Theorem 1. *Let* $\mathbf{X}$, $\mathbf{W}$, Γ, π, *and* Ψ *be defined above. Suppose also that* $\mathbf{X}$ *is locally convex and that* Γ *is convex-valued on* $\mathbf{W}$. *Let* $\varphi(x, w)$ *be defined by (3) where* μ *is continuous on* $\mathbf{X} \times \mathbf{W}$ *and strictly quasi-concave in* x *for each fixed* w, *and* σ *is continuous on* $\mathbf{W}$. *Then* Ψ *is nonempty, continuous and convex-valued on* $\mathbf{W}$.

Proof. I repeat here the proof of Robinson and Day. The composite function φ must be quasi-concave in x for fixed w, Ψ is obviously convex-valued. It is upper semicontinuous on $\mathbf{W}$ by the Maximum Theorem; hence we need only show it is lower semicontinuous there. Let $w_0 \in \mathbf{W}$. If $\Psi(w_0)$ is a singleton, then the upper semicontinuity easily implies continuity at w_0, and there is nothing more to prove. Therefore, assume that $\Psi(w_0)$ contains at least two points. Let $Q \subset \mathbf{X}$ be any open set such that $Q \cap \Psi(w_0) \neq \emptyset$. We shall construct an open neighborhood $U(w_0)$ such that for each $w \in U$, we have $Q \cap \Psi(w) \neq \emptyset$. First, note that for each point $z \in \Psi(w_0)$, we have $\varphi(z, w_0) = \sigma(w_0)$; if this were not true, then the continuity and strict quasi-concavity of μ could be used to show that $\Psi(w_0)$ would have to be a singleton, contrary to our assumption. Let $p_0 \in Q \cap \Psi(w_0)$; since Q is open, $\mathbf{X}$ is locally convex, $\Psi(w_0)$ contains more than one point, and we can find some $p_1 \neq p_0$ such that $[p_0, p_1]$ lies in $Q \cap \Psi(w_0)$. Let $\bar{p}$ be the midpoint of the segment $[p_0, p_1]$; since $\theta(p_0, w_0) = \theta(p_1, w_0) = \sigma(w_0)$, we have $\mu(p_0, w_0) \geq \sigma(w_0) \leq \mu(p_1, w_0)$ and, hence, by strict quasi-concavity, $\mu(\bar{p}, w_0) > \sigma(w_0)$. Using the continuity of μ and σ, we can find open neighborhoods $U_1(w_0)$ and $V(\bar{p}) \subset Q$ such that for $w \in U_1$ and $x \in V$, we have $\mu(x, w) > \sigma(w)$. But since Γ is continuous at w_0, there is an open neighborhood $U_2(w_0)$ such that $w \in U_2$ implies $\Gamma(w) \cap V \neq \emptyset$. Let $U := U_1 \cap U_2$; choose any $w \in U$. Let $p^* \in \Gamma(w) \cap V$. Then $\mu(p^*, w) = \sigma(w)$ so $\varphi(p^*, w) = \sigma(w)$; thus p^* must be in $\Psi(w)$. But also $p^* \in V \subset Q$, so $Q \cap \Psi(w) \neq \emptyset$. This completes the proof.

Corollary. *Satisficing choices are continuous with respect to the datum w.*

Proof. Note that $\Psi(w)$ is a singleton if for $x^* \in \Psi(w)$, $\mu(x^*, w) \leq \sigma(w)$ but it is multi-valued when $\mu(x^*, w) > \sigma(w)$, i.e., when the satisficing level is surpassed. In the latter event, $M(w) = \{x \mid \varphi(x, w) \geq \sigma(w)\}$ so $\Psi(w) = \Gamma(w) \cap \{x \mid (x, w) \geq \sigma(w)\}$.

Lexicographic Choice

Let N be an index set which is either a finite set $\{1, \ldots, n\}$ or the set of positive integers $\mathbb{N}^+$. Let $\{\varphi_i : \mathbf{X} \to \mathbb{R}, i \in N\}$ be a family of utility or preference functions arranged in a *priority order* given by the index i and consider the lexicographic sequence of choice problems

$$\pi_i(w) := \max_{x \in \psi_{i-1}(w)} \varphi_i(x, w), \quad i \in N \tag{5}$$

where

$$\psi_i(w) := \psi_{i-1}(w) \cap \{x \mid \varphi_i(x, w) = \pi_i(w)\}, \quad i \in N \tag{6}$$

and where, for convenience, we define $\Psi_0 \equiv \Gamma$. The *lexicographic choice* correspondence $\Psi_l : \mathbf{W} \to 2^{\mathbf{X}}$ is defined by

$$\Psi_l(w) := \bigcap_{i \in N} \Psi_i(w), \quad w \in \mathbf{W} \tag{7}$$

For a given index i the decision maker is indifferent among all choices in Ψ_{i-1}, according to the criteria $1 \ldots, i-1$, but prefers a choice y to another choice x in Ψ_{i-1} whose utility is greater, according to the i th criterion. The decision maker is indifferent among all those in Ψ_i because they are actually good, according to criteria i. Among these he prefers those that have higher values, according to the criterion $i + 1$, and so on. Clearly, $\Psi_i(w)$ $\subset \Psi_{i-1}(w)$ for all $w \in \mathbf{W}$. This is a reflection of the "narrowing down" aspect of making choices recursively, according to a priority order.

For this narrowing down to be nontrivial, that is, for the lower order choice criteria to matter, there must be room at least in the choice correspondence Ψ_1 for further choice, according to the second criterion φ_2.

Encarnación defined such a class by adopting the hypothesis of satisficing in priority order using a family of satisficing functions $\{\sigma_i: \mathbf{W} \to \mathbb{R}, i \in N\}$ and a family of utility functions $\{\mu_i: \mathbf{X} \times \mathbf{W} \to \mathbb{R}, i \in N\}$. His L^* family of utility functions is

$$\varphi_i(x, w) := \min \{\mu_i(x, w), \sigma_i(w)\}, \; x \in \mathbf{X}, \; w \in \mathbf{W}, \; i \in N \quad (8)$$

If the utility functions of the lexicographic choice sequence (5)–(6) constitute an L^* family, then Ψ_i is called an L^* *choice correspondence*. A decision maker described by (5)–(8) will be called an L^* *agent*. A choice $x^* \in \Phi_i(w)$ will be called an L^* decision.[3]

Existence, Convexity and Continuity of L^*-Choices

Obviously, for any given problem i in the sequence (6) to have a solution and hence for each correspondence (7) to be nonempty, the preceding problem in the sequence must have

---

[3]For an example of this concept in an interesting applied case, see the paper by Day, Wang and Zou.

had a solution and, given the Maximum Theorem, each operator Ψ_i, $i = 1, \ldots, n-1$ must be continuous.

Theorem 2. Continuity of L^* Choices. *Assume the following:*

i)   **W** *is a topological space and* **X** *is a locally convex, linear topological space;*

ii) $\Gamma: \mathbf{W} \to 2^{\mathbf{X}}$ *is a nonempty, continuous, convex-valued correspondence;*

iii) $\mu_i: \mathbf{X} \times \mathbf{W} \to \mathbb{R}$ *is continuous on* $\mathbf{X} \times \mathbf{W}$, *strictly quasi-concave in x for each* $w \in \mathbf{W}$, $i \in N$;

iv) $\sigma_i: \mathbf{W} \to \mathbb{R}$ *is continuous on* **W**, $i \in N$

then $\Psi_i: \mathbf{W} \to 2^{\mathbf{X}}$ *defined by (7) is a single valued, continuous function.*

Proof. The proof proceeds by induction. $\Psi_0(w) = \Gamma(w)$ is a continuous, nonempty, convex valued correspondence by hypothesis. By the Maximum Theorem and Remark 1, Ψ_1 is nonempty, continuous, and convex valued. Proceeding recursively, assume the proposition is true for i, then again it is true for $i+1$ for all $i = 1, 2, 3, \ldots$. Obviously, each set $\Psi_{i+1}(w) \subset \Psi_i(w)$ and, as it is compact, we have by the finite intersection axiom (Berge 1963: 69, Theorem 6) that $\Psi_i(w) \neq \varnothing$.

Theorem 3. *Assume that N is finite, that is, $N := \{1, \ldots, n < \infty\}$. Assume (i)-(iv) of Theorem 2. Let*

v) $\varphi_{n+1}: \mathbf{X} \times \mathbf{W} \to \mathbb{R}$ *be a utility function continuous on* $\mathbf{X} \times \mathbf{W}$ *and for each w quasi-concave.*

then $\Psi_i: \mathbf{W} \to 2^{\mathbf{X}}$ *is nonempty, upper semicontinuous and convex-valued.*

Proof. By the argument of Theorem 1, Ψ_{n-1} is continuous and convex-valued. The result follows from the Maximum Theorem and Remark 1.

For subsequent reference, we shall call L^* choice problems satisfying the assumptions of Theorem 2, *strong L^* choice* *problems;* L^* choice problems satisfying the assumptions of Theorem 3, we shall call *weak L^* choice problems.*

Remark 2. Given the Corollary, there must exist an l^*, $1 \leq l^* \leq n$, such that $\varphi_i(x, w) = \sigma_i(w)$, $1 \leq i < l^*$ and $\varphi_{l^*}(x, w) \leq \sigma_{l^*}(w)$. I shall call l^* *the last criterion governing choice.*

Remark 3. The continuity of L^* decisions suggests that L^* behavior can be rationalized by a single ordering. Indeed, a trivial ordering exists if the decision space is given a norm. Analogous to the approach of Arrow and Hahn (1970: 83) for the standard case, a single utility function representing Ψ_l is just the map which associates with each pair (x, w) the distance (with reverse sign) from x to $\Phi_l(w)$. For each w, this (negative) distance is single valued and continuous by virtue of the fact that $\varphi_l(w)$ is convex. Of course, this is just a rationalization. In general, it is not possible to find a single, continuous utility function independent of w.

Opportunity Cost of High-Order Satisficing

At each stage in the lexicographic choice sequence, choices are constrained, not only to be feasible, but also by the requirement that they satisfice all higher order utility indexes. Consequently, the more criteria are satisfied, the more constrained the choice. This implies that high order satisficing bears an opportunity cost in terms of the first nonsatisficed criterion. This yields interesting insights in various applications.

To formalize this idea, let us introduce a family of *constraint functions* $\beta_i : \mathbf{X} \times \mathbf{W} \rightarrow \mathbb{R}$, $i = 1, ..., m$, and a family of *limitation functions* $\gamma_i : \mathbf{W} \rightarrow \mathbb{R}$, and assume that $\mathbf{X}$ is a vector space with the feasibility correspondence $\Gamma(w)$ defined by

$$\psi_0(w) \equiv \Gamma(w) := \{x \mid \beta_i(x, w) \leq \gamma_i(w), i = 1, ..., m\} \qquad (9)$$

Now, given Remark 3 and given a fixed value $\bar{w} \in \mathbf{W}$, the choice correspondence Ψ_l is the solution set of the constrained optimization problem

$$\text{maximize } \varphi_{l*}(x, \bar{w}) \tag{10}$$

subject to

$$\beta_i(x, \bar{w}) \leq \gamma_i(\bar{w}), \quad i = 1, \ldots, m \tag{11}$$

and subject to

$$\varphi_j(x, \bar{w}) \geq \sigma_j(\bar{w}), \quad j = 1, \ldots, l*-1 \tag{12}$$

and to the non-negativity restriction $x \geq 0$. This problem is equivalent to the Kuhn-Tucker problem:

$$\pi_{l*}(\overline{w}) = \max_{x \geq 0} \min_{y \geq 0} \{\varphi_{l*}(x, \overline{w}) + \tag{13}$$

$$\sum_1^m [\gamma_i(\overline{w}) - \beta_i(x, \overline{w})] y_i + \sum_{m+1}^{m+l*-1} y_i [\varphi_i(x, \overline{w}) - \sigma_i(\overline{w})]\}$$

Let (x^l, y^l) be a solution of this dual problem, then where the partial derivatives with respect to the constants $\bar{\gamma}_i := \gamma_i(\bar{w})$ and $\bar{\sigma}_j = \sigma_j(\bar{w})$ are taken independently of their dependence on w. The expression on the left has the usual interpretation: it is the marginal payoff in terms of the criterion $l*$ of a marginal increase in the limitation coefficient (resource) c_i. The expression on the right is analogous; it is the marginal increase in payoff in terms of the criterion $l*$ of a marginal decrease in the satisficing level. It is a decrease because the satisficing level places a lower bound on choice so that decreasing it expands the region of choices that are both feasible and $l*-1$ satisficing.

Let us summarize:

Theorem 4. *Corresponding to every L* decision x* is a dual imputation vector y* defined by (14) which gives the marginal opportunity cost of each resource and each satisficing coefficient in terms of the last criterion governing choice.*

Competitive Equilibrium With L^* Agents

Could an economy of lexicographic agents possess a competitive equilibrium? The simple example discussed in Section 2 shows that supply and demand functions and, therefore, excess demand functions will be more complicated than is usually represented in texts, but the continuity of choice with respect to parameter perturbations suggests that the answer is affirmative anyway. To explore this possibility, let us consider the Arrow-Debreu economy in its original form. To translate the general L^* model into the specific Arrow-Debreu framework would require considerable notational details. To save space, I shall merely sketch the association and relevant analytical considerations for the pure exchange economy.

For consumers, the choice variable x is a consumption vector of commodities in a consumption space $\mathbf{X}$, the datum is a price vector $w \equiv p$, which appears in the consumer k's budget set, say $\Gamma_k(w) \equiv B_k(p) := \{x \in \mathbf{X} \mid p(x - \xi_k) \leq 0\}$ where ξ_k is the vector of (positive) initial commodity endowments, but which does not influence the preference orderings (that is, agents' preferences are independent of their environments).

Now suppose each consumer has an L^* family as defined above, $\{\mu_j^{\,k}(x) := \min\{\mu_j^{\,k}(x), \sigma_j^{\,k}\}, j = 1, ...\}$ where the σ_k are satisficing constants and where the utility functions μ_j and satisficing constants do not depend on prices. Assume that each $\mu_j^{\,k}(\cdot)$ is strictly quasi-concave and assume the nonsatiation requirement: that for each $x^k \in \mathbf{X}^k$ there exists a $j \geq 1$ (depending on k) and a consumption vector $y^k \in \mathbf{X}^k$ such that

$$\varphi_j^{\,k}(y^k) > \varphi_j^{\,k}(x^k) \tag{15}$$

By Remark 1, this implies that $\varphi_i^{\,k}(x^k) = \sigma_i^{\,k} = \varphi_i^{\,k}(y^k)$, $i = 1, ..., j-1$. If the L^* family is strong, this implies that each criterion can be satisficed but that the consumer never exhausts his/her list of needs and wants. If we assume a weak L^* preference ordering, it means that the last $(n + 1)$st criterion is nonsatiable and cannot be satisficed.

The excess demand correspondence is $z(p) = \Sigma_k \Psi_i{}^k(p)$. Assume p belongs to the unit simplex. Then a competitive pure exchange equilibrium is a vector p^* and a set of vectors x^{k^*}, such that for each k

$$x^{k^*} = \Psi_i{}^k(p^*)$$

$$z(p^*) \le 0$$

$$p^* z(p^*) = 0$$

Each consumer's demand correspondence defined by $\Psi_i{}^k(p^*)$ is an upper semicontinuous correspondence by virtue of Theorem 2 or 3. Given this, the conditions of existence are met. The argument can be extended to the case of a production economy where the firms have the single criterion of maximizing profits. Without going into details, we can assert

Theorem 5. *Consider an economic system whose firms and households are described by Assumptions I of Arrow-Debreu, and II and IV of Arrow-Debreu, respectively. And where households are L* agents who satisfy the nonsatiation requirement (15) and the assumptions of either Theorem 1 or 2 above. This economic system possesses a competitive equilibrium.*

Remark 4. A competitive equilibrium depends on all the parameters of preference and technology, in particular on both the order and satisficing coefficients of the several utility functions. Any change in priorities or satisficing levels will change the equilibrium solutions.

Characterization of an Abstract Adaptive Society with *L** Agents

I now want to consider the implications of *L** preferences when agents adapt out of equilibrium in response to experience and to changes in the environment. For this purpose, I will formulate an abstract adaptive society as an extension of Debreu's concept of an abstract economy.[4] The abstract adaptive society is made up of interacting agents with *L** preferences and a co-evolving environment. The agents take action based on plans which are in turn based on information obtained by observing the state of the environment. The emerging environmental state depends on its previous value and on the various agents' actions. For simplicity, I shall model this interactive process in discrete time.

The Abstract Adaptive Society

Begin with an environmental state, z_t. Agents observe this state and derive information, w_t, from it. On the basis of this information, plans, x_t, are formed. Actions, a_t, are not in general the same thing as plans but generally involve a more or less conscious attempt to control behavior according to plan, but which are also contingent on the current state of the environment and on information not taken explicitly into account in the plan. The dependence of actions on states can cause deviation from plans despite the controlling function.

In formal terms, let

  A be the action space,
  X be the plans space,
  W be the information space,
  Z be the state space.

Define

  $\delta : \mathbf{A} \times \mathbf{Z} \to \mathbf{W},$ the information function
  $\psi : \mathbf{W} \to \mathbf{X},$ the planning correspondence

---

[4]The basic idea I am using here was developed first in Day (1975).

$\zeta : \mathbf{A} \times \mathbf{X} \times \mathbf{W} \times \mathbf{Z} \to \mathbf{A},$ the control function
$\omega : \mathbf{A} \times \mathbf{X} \to \mathbf{Z},$ state transition operator.

Begin with a state $z_t \in \mathbf{Z}$. This leads to an information $\delta(a_t, z_t) = w_{t+1} \in \mathbf{W}$. On the basis of this information, a plan is formulated $x_{t+1} = \psi(w_{t+1})$. Given this plan, given the available information, and given the state, an action emerges $a_{t+1} = a_t + \zeta(x_{t+1}, w_{t+1}, z_t)$, which we consider to be a modification or departure of the previous action a_t. This is just a discrete counterpart of the concept of action as a continuous trajectory in an action space. In the meantime, a new state unfolds $z_{t+1} = \omega(a_t, z_t)$.

An action *operator* $\alpha: \mathbf{A} \times \mathbf{Z} \to \mathbf{A}$ can now be derived by the composition

$$\alpha(a, z) := a + \zeta(\psi(\delta(a, z), z), \delta(a, z), z).$$

The co-evolution of agent and environment is then given by the discrete time dynamic system

$$a_{t+1} = \alpha(a_t, z_t) \tag{16}$$

$$z_{t+1} = \omega(a_t, z_t).$$

It will be convenient below to define

$$u := (a, z) \in \mathbf{U} := \mathbf{A} \times \mathbf{Z} \text{ and } \theta(u) := (\alpha(u), \omega(u)).$$

Then (16) can be re-expressed as

$$u_{t+1} = \theta(u_t). \tag{17}$$

To accommodate many agents interacting and co-evolving within a common environment, index the information plan and action operators and spaces with a superscript i so that for each agent $i \in K = \{1, ..., k\}$, the triplet of operators $(\delta^i, \psi^i, \zeta^i)$ governs behavior of the ith agent. The action operator can then be defined as a map $\alpha^i(a, z) := a^i + \zeta^i(\psi^i(\delta^i(a, z), w^i, z)$. Defining $\alpha(a, z) := (\alpha^1(a, z), ..., \alpha^k(a,z))$ gives the co-evolving system (16). In this formulation, each agent's action is a departure from his/her previous action and depends in general on what other agents have done—but not simultaneously on what other agents are doing.

Viability

For trajectories to exist for all t beginning at some initial condition $u_0 = (a_0, z_0)$, actions must be viable. To capture the latter idea, each agent has a feasible region defined by a viability correspondence

$$\Omega^i : \mathbf{A} \times \mathbf{Z} \to 2^{\mathbf{A}i}$$

which describes the set of possible actions for agent i, $\Omega^i(a_t, z_t)$, given the current behavior of the society and the state z. The product map $\Omega(a, z) := (\Omega^1(a, z), ..., \Omega^k(a, z))$ defines the condition for viability for the society that begins at some initial condition (a_0, z_0). This condition is

$$a_{t+1} = \alpha(a_t, z_t) \in \Omega(a_t, z_t) \neq \varnothing, \quad t = 0, ... \qquad (18)$$

Assume there exists a set $U \subset \mathbf{U}$ such that

$$\Omega(u) \neq \varnothing \text{ for all } u \in U.$$

Then a sufficient condition for the abstract adaptive society to be viable is that

$$\Omega(u) \in U, \text{ all } u \in U. \qquad (19)$$

The set U is called the *viability domain*.

The condition (18) does not imply (19). For (19) to hold, there must be a further requirement that agent's actions are compatible. To formalize this notion, let $\mathcal{A}: u \to 2^{\mathbf{A}}$ be a compatibility correspondence defined by

$$\mathcal{A}(z) := \{a \,|\, (a, \omega(a, z)) \in U\}.$$

Given a state z, the pair (a, z) will be *compatible* if (19) holds. With this we can state the following:

Theorem 6 . *If there exists a set U such that*

(i) $\alpha(u) \in \Omega(u)$ *for all* $u \in U$ *(agents are viable);*

(ii) $\alpha(u) \in A(\omega(u)) \neq \emptyset$ *(agents are compatible).*

Then trajectories exist for all initial conditions $u \in U$.

Proof. Suppose $u_0 \in U$. Then $\alpha(u_0) \in \Omega(u_0) \neq \emptyset$ because agents are viable. Moreover, $\alpha(u) \in A(\omega(u)) \neq \emptyset$ because agents are compatible. This implies that $(a_1, z_1) = (\alpha(u_0), \omega(a_0, z_0)) \in U$. Define the iterated maps $\theta^0(u) \equiv u$, $\theta^1(u) = \theta^0(u)$, $\theta^{t+1}(u) = \theta^t(u)$. Then by recursion, $\theta^t(u) \in U$ for all $u = u_0 \in U$.

L* agents in an Abstract Adaptive Society

Now consider an economy made up of agents whose plans are determined by state dependent *L** preferences. Denote the *i*th agent's choice correspondence by $\Psi_I{}^i$. And assume the regularity conditions of Theorem 2 or 3. The choice set $\Psi_I{}^i(w)$ need not be a singleton. Assume that there exists a plan function ψ that selects a plan among those that is best according to the *L** criterion, i.e., there exists a ψ such that

$$\psi(w) \in \Psi_I(w) \tag{20}$$

then we can proceed as before.

Viability and Multiple Phase Dynamics in L* Preferences

Viability

L* agents are rational in that their plans optimize an *L** preference ordering. In the present context, the feasibility correspondence $\Gamma(w)$ is an estimate of the viability correspondence $\Omega(a, z)$. That is, what the individual considers to be feasible may be distinct from what is actually the set of viable actions. It is essential that the control function make up for this possibility and that together the information, planning and control functions are practical in the sense that

$$a + \zeta(\psi(\delta(a, z), w, z) \in \Omega(a, z) \tag{21}$$

at each stage of the process as it evolves through time. The mere requirement that $\psi(w) \in \Psi_f(w) \subset \Gamma(w)$ does not guarantee this. The existence statement of Theorem 6 needs to be modified slightly.

Theorem 7. *If there exists a U such that*

(*i*) $\Gamma(\delta(u)) \neq \emptyset$ *for all* $u \in U$ *(agents think they have feasible plans)*;

(*ii*) $\psi(\delta(u)) \in \Gamma(\delta(u))$ *(agents select a feasible plan)*;

(*iii*) $\alpha(u) = \zeta(\psi(\delta(u)), \delta(u), z) \in \Omega(u)$ *(agents' control functions are practical)*;

(*iv*) $\alpha(u) \in \mathcal{A}(\omega(u)) \neq \emptyset$ *(agents' actions are compatible)*.

Then trajectories exist for all initial conditions $u = u_0 \in U$.

Proof. The proof differs from Theorem 6 only in taking account explicitly of the need for rational agents to have feasible plans (otherwise they could not arrive at a decision).

Multiple Phase Dynamics

Now take into account the structure of perceived constraints that underlie the feasibility operator defined in (9). It was noted in (9)–(13) that a choice $x \in \Psi_f(w)$ could be characterized by a programming problem. This implies that the choice function ψ satisfies a dual system of equated constraints associated with that solution. If the information on which plans are based changes from period to period, then this system of equated constraints will change also and the characterization of ψ in terms of this system will change correspondingly. There are a finite number of possible dual systems. Let us index these sets by a subscript $i \in \{1, ..., p\}$. Then associated with each w there is at least one system of equated constraints, e.g., the $i(w)$th, a single-valued map $\psi_{i(w)}$ (**W** → **X**) which I shall call a *planning rule* and an *information zone* **W**$_i \subset$ **W** such that for each $w \in \mathbf{W}_i$, $\psi_{i(w)}(w) \in \Psi_i(w)$

As $w = \delta(a, z)$, each action/state pair will lead to an information in one or the other of these information zones. This induces a partition on $U \subset \mathbf{A} \times \mathbf{Z}$, $U_p, \ldots, U_k$ with $\cup\, U_i = U$ such that for each $u \in U$ there exists an i such that

$$\delta(u) \in W_i$$

Now define the *p action rules*

$$\alpha^i(u) := \zeta(\psi_i(\delta(u)), \delta(u), u), \quad i \in U_i$$

and let $\theta_i(u) := (\alpha_i(u), w(u))$. Then we arrive at the multiple phase dynamical system

$$u_{t+1} = \theta(u_t) := \theta_i(u_t), \quad u_t \in U_i$$

As the system evolves, from time to time u_t may cross the boundary from one phase zone U_i to another implying that the system of equated constraints will have changed. The phase structure switches endogenously. The implication is that different constraints (associated with different resources, for example) may be binding or—and this is the point in the present context—a different set of needs and wants may be satisfied. The particular preferences governing choice at any time and the values imputed to the various constraining factors will therefore change. The map $\psi(w)$ may not be continuous even if the assumptions of Theorem 3 are satisfied. This means that trajectories can exhibit discrete jumps from time to time even when change may have been very gradual in between times.

Reordering Priorities

In reality, people change their minds about priorities which are reordered from time to time. To account for this phenomenon within the adaptive abstract economy framework, assume that not only the criterion and satisficing functions depend on states, but their order does also. Let $N(w) := \{i_1(w), i_2(w), \ldots\} \subset N := \{1, 2, \ldots\} \subset \mathbb{N}^+$. We can then refer to the *j*th element in $N(w)$, $i_j(w)$ by the index *j*. Now consider the L^* family defined in (8) except replace *N* by *N(w)*. For any information datum *w*, the L^* decision operator is well defined and can be characterized by Kuhn-Tucker dual optimization problem (10)–(13) with the change that now the criterion *l* is the l^*th element in *N(w)*.

Given this interpretation, the number *and* order of criteria satisficed evolve. Extended to all agents in an adaptive abstract society, this implies an endogenous evolution in the distribution of satisficed wants and needs; a possible convergence—or divergence—of social values, a development of social accord or discord. These social developments could have an important feedback effect on action and on the potential viability of a given system.

References

Ardrey, R. (1970) *The Social Contract*. New York: Dell.

Arrow, K. and G. Debreu (1954) "Existence of an Equilibrium for a Competitive Economy," *Econometrica* 22: 265–290.

Arrow, K. and F. Hahn (1971) *General Competitive Analysis*. San Francisco: Holden-Day.

Berge, C. (1963) *Topological Spaces*. New York: Macmillan.

Chipman, J.S. (1960) "The Foundations of Utility," *Econometrica* 28: 193–224.

Cyert, R. and J. March, et al. (1963) *A Behavioral Theory of the Firm*. Englewood Cliffs, NJ: Prentice-Hall.

Day, R. H. (1971) "Rational Choice and Economic Behavior," *Theory and Decision* 1: 229–251.

_____. (1975) "Adaptive Processes and Economic Theory," in R.H. Day and T. Groves (eds.). *Adaptive Economic Models*. New York: Academic Press.

_____. (1979) "Cautious Suboptimizing," Chapter 7 in J. Roumasset, J. M. Boussard, and I. Singh (eds.). *Risk Uncertainty and Agricultural Development*. New York: Agricultural Development Council.

Day, R. H. and S.M. Robinson (1973) "Economic Decisions with L^{**} Utility," in J.L. Cochrane and M. Zeleny (eds.). *Multiple Criteria Decision Making*. Columbia: The University of South Carolina Press.

Debreu, G. (1952) "A Social Equilibrium Existence Theorem," *Proceedings of the National Academy of Sciences* 38: 886–893.

_____. (1954) "Representation of a Preference Ordering by a Numerical Function," in R.M. Thrall, C.H. Coombs, and R.L. Davis. *Decision Processes*. New York: Wiley.

_____. (1969) "Neighboring Economic Agents," in 'La Décision,' *Editions du Centre National de la Recherche Scientifique*. Paris: 85–90.

Encarnación, J. (1964) "A Note on Lexicographical Preferences," *Econometrica* 32: 215–217.

_____. (1964) "Constraints and the Firm's Utility Function," *Review of Economic Studies* 31: 113–119.

_____. (1964) "Optimal Saving and Social Choice Function," *Oxford Economic Papers* 16: 213–220.

_____. (1970) "On the Specification of Social Welfare Functions," *SSRI Workshop Paper* No. 7023. University of Wisconsin, Madison.

Ferguson, C.E. .(1965) "The Theory of Multidimensional Utility Analysis in Relation to Multiple Goal Business Behavior: A Synthesis," *Southern Economic Journal* 32: 169–175.

Georgescu-Roegen, N. (1954) "Choice, Expectations, and Measurability," *Quarterly Journal of Economics* 68: 503–504.

Hildenbrand, W. (1970) "On Economies With Many Agents," *Journal of Economic Theory* 2: 161–188.

Maslow, A.H. (1954) *Motivation and Personality*. New York: Harper and Row.

Richter, M. (1966) "Revealed Preference Theory," *Econometrica* 34: 635–645.

Robinson, S.M. and R.H. Day (1974) "A Sufficient Condition for Continuity of Optimal Sets in Mathematical Programming," *Journal of Mathematical Analysis and Applications* 45: 506–511.

Schultze, C.L., E.R. Fried, A.M. Rivlin and N.H. Teeters (1972) *Setting National Priorities: The 1973 Budget.* Washington, D.C.: Brookings Institute.

Simon, H. (1957) *Administrative Behavior*, 2nd edition. New York: Free Press.

Rational Addicts and Peasants: Reflections on Lexicographic Ordering

James Roumasset[*]

Introduction

Professor José Encarnación, Jr. has been the world's most enthusiastic and consistent advocate of the lexicographic ordering approach to modeling decision-making. I can think of no more fitting tribute to him, therefore, than to add my own reflections, inadequate as they may be, on this technique.

Dean Encarnación made two important contributions to my own work on peasant decision-making (Roumasset 1976). First, his theory of lexicographic decision-making under uncertainty provided the foundations for the models that I used to capture low-income farmers' concern to secure at least a subsistence level of living. Second, it was Dean Encarnación, the theorist, who gave me invaluable advice on empirical methods for soliciting risk preferences. He counseled me to eschew the "lottery" approach and to discover instead how the subsistence requirement and coping strategies available to the farm household combine to determine the critical threshold for farm income. The

[*]Professor of Economics, University of Hawaii at Manoa

theme of the discussion below is that these two contributions (theoretical and empirical methodology) are closely related. Indeed the primary advantage of lexicographic modeling may be not so much the innate superiority of lexicographic ordering over the expected utility approach, but the way it helps the researcher to frame empirical investigation.

In particular, I consider the use of lexicographic ordering for modeling the rational decision of drug addicts as well as peasant farmers. Despite the apparent dissimilarity of these two groups, there are marked similarities in the way they have been treated in the economics literature.

Before Theodore Schultz's (1964) celebrated discussion of the prototypical "rational-but-poor" peasant, small-farm cultivators in developing economies were often assumed (especially by observers from developed economies) to be tradition-bound, ignorant and possibly lazy, and therefore indescribable within the rationality paradigm. Even after Schultz's thesis became widely accepted, economists still hypothesized that, when subsistence is at risk, farmer behavior under uncertainty is fundamentally different than what is describable by commonly accepted models of utility maximization.

Similarly, the process of becoming addicted to drugs, and the choices of addicts generally, have been thought until recently to be outside of the rationality paradigm. However, Becker and Murphy (1988) have established that even the process of addiction can be illuminated within the maximum-utility framework. Economists and others may still be suspicious, however, regarding the applicability of the commonly-used utility functions to preferences of consumers who have already become addicted.

In the present paper, I maintain that lexicographic ordering is an ideal framework for modeling the behavior of peasants, addicts, and other economic agents whose preferences are thought to be "threshold-dependent." Moreover, while real-valued utility functions can be found that approximate threshold-dependent preferences, empirical research oriented to the identification of lexicographic preferences is likely to be more revealing than that designed to estimate real-valued utility functions.

Rational Peasants

Some Lexicographic Models

Peasant farmers are said to be particularly risk-averse due to their alleged over-riding concern to achieve at least their subsistence levels of living. Expected utility theory, as usually applied, is poorly suited to the task. Utility functions commonly used to express risk aversion can usually be at least roughly approximated by variance aversion. But if farmers are concerned about the probability of falling below a critical threshold income level, they may be variance-averse or variance-preferring, depending on the relationship between expected income and the threshold level. If the threshold level is above expected income, then a higher distribution with a higher variance will tend to have a higher probability of success.

One alternative to expected utility is to posit that farmers maximize expected accounting profits subject to a "change constraint" that requires that the probability of income falling below the threshold level not exceed a specified maximum level. The primary disadvantage of this approach is that it only provides a partial ordering of alternative farming techniques. In particular, if all techniques fail to satisfy the constraint, the method cannot select a best technique.

Lexicographic ordering solves this dilemma. One possible model may be represented as follows. First let "security" be defined as:

$$S(x) = 1 - \max [\alpha, F_x(d)]$$

where x is a vector of choice variables, α is the acceptable risk of failure, F_x is the corresponding frequency distribution of accounting profits, and $F_x(d)$ is the probability that profits fall below the "disaster" threshold, d. Now associate each choice, x, with the vector:

$$W(x) \equiv [S(x), E(x)]$$

where the first element is security and the second is expected accounting profits. The suggested model posits that the decision-maker's preferences are described by a lexicographic ordering of the Ws. Heuristically, the model calls for maximizing expected accounting profits when the probability of failure is less than or equal to α and minimizing the probability of failure otherwise.

Several variations on this "safety-first" theme are also possible. Instead of minimizing the probability of failure, a lexicographic model can be constructed that maximizes the disaster level that is attainable at the probability, α, when the target threshold is unattainable at that security level.[1] Other variations include ruling out overinvesting relative to the risk-neutral optimum in order to increase the probability of success.[2]

Applications

Proponents of the expected utility theory tend to favor lottery methods of preference revelation. In one such method, farmers are asked to determine their certainty equivalents for various gambles. Alternatively, farmers can be asked, e.g. in gambling games, to choose among a menu of stochastic payoffs in such a way as to reveal gambles towards which a farmer is indifferent.

The trouble with these experiments is that the context of these games is not closely related to the farmer's experiences. Even when farmers are gambling for real, (e.g. as described in

---

[1]This is the "safety-fixed" variant.

[2]See Roumasset (1976) for further details.

Binswanger (1980)), the framework of the experiment appears to be hypothetical. Given the pervasive inconsistencies that have been reported in numerous experiments (see e.g. Machina (1989)) framing of experimental questions is bound to be critical. For example, subjects respond very differently to gambles stated in terms of possible losses and the same gambles when the outcomes are reported in terms of income totals after adding non-stochastic income.

In contrast, researchers estimating lexicographic preferences are less likely to resort to indirect and artificial frameworks. In order to estimate preferences in the lexicographic models discussed above, it is natural to design direct methods for estimating the critical income threshold. This requires two steps. First, one estimates "necessary" household expenditures. Second, the analyst investigates the strategies by which the household copes with low income in providing necessities.

Coping strategies include dissaving, borrowing, seeking off-farm income, and selling durable assets. If interest rates are too high on durable assets sold at too great a loss, however, overusing coping strategies may drastically reduce security in future periods. In Roumasset (1976), this was handled by rejecting coping strategies where the equivalent of borrowing was greater than 100% interest per-annum. This rule-of-thumb permits the construction of a "risk sensitivity index." The index measures necessities and often unavoidable liabilities that must be met before the next harvest, minus off-farm income and other allowable coping strategies that can meet the necessary expenditures. This residual is the critical threshold level of farm income.

The risk sensitivity index and the confidence level, $1-\alpha$, are the two parameters needed to implement the lexicographic ordering rules. They play the same role as measures of risk aversion in expected utility theory. Their advantage is that they utilize a framework that directly analyzes the decision-maker's situation. The analyst is called to explore the consequences of loss and gain with the decision-maker instead of asking hypothetical lottery-type questions that call for greater consistency than subjects reveal.

An Indirect Utility Alternative?

A natural question to arise at this point is whether a direct empirical method could be developed for use in conjunction with utility theory that would also be based on the coping strategies and the consequences of gain and loss. In particular, one may ask whether utility of current period farm income can be estimated as an indirect function of the asset and liability structure facing the farm household.

Such an approach does exist, though it requires some fairly severe restrictions on the utility function. The central presumption is that risk aversion regarding current income is the result of transaction costs that create asymmetries in the consequences of loss and gain. For low-income farmers in developing countries, such asymmetries are especially severe. High transportation and other marketing costs lead to large wedges between buying and selling prices. As a consequence farm households suffer more in bad years (when they face high buying prices) than they gain in locally good years (when they must dispose of their market surplus at low prices). Similarly, effective savings rates are typically very much lower than borrowing rates, with the same consequences for good and bad years.

These asymmetries create substantial risk aversion toward variations in current income even if the farmer is risk-neutral towards variations in lifetime income. Indeed for the mild risk-aversion towards variations in lifetime incomes that plausibly exists, transaction-cost-induced risk-aversion swamps the former source and renders it relatively unimportant.

Nonetheless, given a lifetime utility function over consumption, a utility function in current-period income has been shown not to necessarily exist, unless some restrictive assumptions are made (Spence and Zeckhauser 1972). One set of assumptions sufficient for existence has been provided by Masson (1972). If only current period income is random and if that income is realized before the decision-maker chooses current consumption, then each value of current-period income leads to a specific and calculable lifetime utility. Alternatively, even if income in future periods is also unknown, utility of current-period income can be determined so long as the lifetime utility function is separable by time periods.

Another approach would be to show formally that risk-neutrality towards lifetime consumption provides a good approximation for the derivation of current-period utility functions. This would be done by showing that the error caused by the risk-neutrality assumption becomes arbitrarily small as the number of decision periods is increased. One can also demonstrate through simulation, for plausible values of lifetime risk-aversion, length of life, and other parameters, that risk-neutrality-induced error is small relative to other sources of error. This provides practical ground for the assumption that farm households maximize expected accounting profits and clears the way for empirical application of that model.

To my knowledge, however, none of these methods has been used. Perhaps the implementation of these approaches is thought to be cumbersome and tedious. Whatever the reason, expected-utility practitioners continue to ignore the Spence-Zeckhauser (1972) non-existence result, assume without any justification whatsoever that utility functions are concave throughout, and utilize experimental procedures without proper regard for the framing problem.

I am left to conclude that, while utility theory could be adapted to deal with thresholds, discontinuities, and wedges between buying and selling prices, in practice analysts do not make such adaptations and use instead models that are inappropriate for peasant farmers. Lexicographic ordering continues to provide a plausible alternative and a theoretical framework likely to motivate empirical work that is grounded in real-world difficulties faced by peasant households.

Rational Addicts

One reason that addicts are thought to be irrational is their apparently self-destructive behavior. But the fact that addicts may act contrary to their own long-run satisfaction does not imply irrationality in the economic sense. Economic rationality requires only that choices are made in accordance with a consistent set of preferences.

Another alleged source of irrationality is the notion that addicts will go to extraordinary lengths to "get their fix" and have a completely inelastic demand curve for their drug of choice. This allegation contains fallacies. First, thresholds and discontinuities in preferences do not imply irrationality. Second, drug consumption by addicts is not well described by a single, minimum threshold. At the very least, a maximum threshold (overdose) must also be recognized. Third, the price elasticity may be dominated by the effect of drug prices on real income and be correspondingly elastic.

The contention of this section is that preferences of heroin addicts can be characterized by three thresholds. The first threshold is the amount of real income (including labor endowments) needed to afford subsistence consumption (including necessary leisure). Discretionary income can be correspondingly defined as real income minus the value of subsistence consumption, thus leaving only the second and third thresholds, both of which can be described in terms of discretionary income. The second threshold is the amount of heroin that an addict needs to "take the sick off", i.e., to function without withdrawal symptoms. In the Becker et al. (1991) model of rational addiction, this minimum threshold of heroin consumption is the amount below which the addict's stock of "addictive capital" declines such that, eventually, he is no longer addicted. In the short-run, however, the minimum threshold plays no role, i.e., the addict spends all of his discretionary income on heroin, both below and immediately above the minimum threshold consumption level.

What is important rather for the heroin consumption decision is the third threshold, i.e., the level beyond which the benefits of heroin cease and overdose symptoms occur. In the following model, I assume accordingly that the rational addict spends all of his discretionary income on heroin, up to the maximum threshold.

Note that in this model, the addict has inelastic demand only with respect to the maximum threshold, which is beyond the expected daily income of most addicts. Before the maximum threshold, the addicts' demand curve is unitary elastic, not inelastic as is usually assumed. For a fixed discretionary income, the addict will hold expenditure constant, not quantity. It is only for rich addicts, who can consistently finance the maximum heroin dose, that the demand curve will be inelastic.

The preferences just described can be represented by the following lexicographic ordering model. First, define

$$V = \min [H, H_{max}]$$

where H is actual heroin consumption, and H_{max} is the maximum desirable heroin consumption. Next, define,

$$W = [V, Y_D - P_H H]$$

where Y_D is real discretionary income (after minimum leisure, food, and other necessities), and P_H is the price of heroin. Note that the addict's preferences are described by a lexicographic ordering of the *W*s. In other words, the addict spends all discretionary income on heroin until the maximum threshold is reached.

Note that the income elasticity of demand is infinity at real income levels higher than that necessary for subsistence and lower than that needed for the maximum heroin level. The price elasticity is negative one over the same range. At higher income levels, both elasticities are zero.

This behavioral model is suggestive of a very different empirical approach than either an elaborate econometric estimation of a system of equations, or an experimental approach designed to provide choices that illuminate demand through revealed preferences. Rather, the entire focus of the relevant empirical method is directed at estimating the threshold levels. For example, interviews with addicts in East Oakland, California, were used to identify both the second and third threshold levels. For "successful" and mature addicts, i.e., those that have been relatively unconstrained by income limitations for periods of six months or more, and have thus maximized the stock of addictive capital, the range from minimum to maximum heroin consumption goes from one to ten bags. The commensurate range for an immature addict may range from ½ to 5 bags (cf. Roumasset and Hadreas (1975) for further discussion).

The threshold perspective also has rather dramatic effects on the assessment of policy options. The traditional view has resulted in a drug policy that focuses on supply interdiction as a means to reduce the availability of illicit drugs. In the threshold model, we see immediately that demand-management may be a more effective policy instrument. If an addict's discretionary income is pushed below the minimum threshold, then she will be motivated to seek treatment (e.g., methadone maintenance). For addicts in the intermediate range, between the minimum and maximum thresholds, a reduction in discretionary income will result in a corresponding reduction in consumption. Both cases result in a reduction in the consumption externality associated with drug use.

Heroin addicts typically derive most of their discretionary income from illegal sources, especially property crime, and there are several unexploited or underexploited instruments for reducing illegal income. For example, heroin addicts in East Oakland typically derive most of their discretionary income from stealing household goods. The most common institution for fencing these consumer durables is pawn brokers, and yet enforcement against fencing by pawn brokers is almost nil (Roumasset and Hadreas 1974).

Concluding Remarks

Advocates of lexicographic ordering may have expected that, by now, their favored approach to representing preferences would have made more inroads as a substitute for real-valued utility functions. After all, lexicographic orderings, or vector-valued utility functions have a number of advantages. While real-valued utility theory begs the question of decision-making process and must fall back on the renown "as-if" rationalization, lexicographic ordering is constructed according to the process of decision-making by priorities. In addition, some decisions may not lend themselves to the calculus of tradeoffs at the margin. Finally, standard utility analysis is a special case of lexicographic ordering, since a scalar is a special case of a vector.

The apparent theoretical advantages have not, however, compelled economists to abandon real-valued utility functions in favor of lexicographic ordering. Indeed there is no reason to abandon standard utility theory at all. Real and vector-valued utility functions can co-exist in the economist's tool kit.

Lexicographic ordering is particularly valuable for modeling threshold-dependent behavior as exemplified by peasant households and rational addicts. Real-valued utility functions could, in principle, be used for these cases, but in practice they are not. This may be because empirical methods have not been developed for estimating real-valued utility functions for threshold-dependent behavior. On the other hand lexicographic methods focus the analyst's attention on the centrality of identifying the thresholds in question.

Lexicographic ordering may also make promising reforms more transparent. Using lexicographic ordering to extend the rationality paradigm to drug-use facilitates the derivation of optimal drug policy as an application of the standard principles of public economics. Drug-use generates consumption externalities. Drug-use impacts the welfare of those who care about the welfare of drug-users, or who are impacted by the behavior of drug-users. The corrective policy for consumption externalities is a Pigouvian tax. Thus "sin-taxes" need not be defended on moral grounds but have an efficiency rationale. Moreover, since prohibition is equivalent to a prohibitive consumption tax, it is a special case of Pigouvian taxation and cannot therefore be superior. Finally, the consumption externality model affords a perspective for calculating the amount of the tax.

References

Becker, G. and K. Murphy. (1988) "A Theory of Rational Addiction," *Journal of Political Economy* 96(4): 675–700.

Binswanger, H.P. (1980) "Attitudes Toward Risk: Experimental Measurement in Rural India," *American Journal of Agricultural Economics*: 395–407.

Machina, M. (1989) "Dynamic Consistency and Non-Expected Utility Models of Choice Under Uncertainty," *Journal of Economic Literature*: 1622–1668.

Masson, R.T. (1972) "The Creation of Risk-Aversion by Imperfect Capital Markets," *American Economic Review* 62: 77–86.

Roumasset, J. (1976) *Rice and Risk: Decision-making Among Low-income Peasants.* Amsterdam: North Holland.

———— and J. Hadreas (1974) "Addicts, Fences, and the Market for Stolen Goods," *Public Finance Quarterly* 5(2):247–272.

Schultz, T. (1964) *Transforming Traditional Agriculture.* New Haven, Conn.: Yale University Press.

Spence, M. and R. Zeckhauser (1972) "The Effect of the Timing of Consumption Decisions and the Resolution of Lotteries on the Choice of Lotteries," *Econometrica* 40: 401–403.

Empirical Methods in Computable-General-Equilibrium Modelling

*John S. Chipman**

Introduction

The 1950s were the great years in the development of econometric methods applicable to general-equilibrium models, on the part of Tjalling Koopmans (1950) and his collaborators and followers at the Cowles Commission in Chicago. This development was in turn largely inspired by the pioneering work of Haavelmo (1944), who persuaded the profession to abandon the *ad hoc* regression and correlation methods that had been the stock-in-trade of most applied economists up to that time, in favor of models that were formulated stochastically so that one could confront them with data using the principles of statistical inference.

*Professor of Economics, University of Minnesota. My connection with José Encarnación, Jr. dates back to our mutual interest in lexicographic ordering in utility theory in the 1950s, and indirectly with my brief acquaintance in Konstanz with his associate Emmanuel de Dios one summer. But both our interests have spread out, and in particular Professor Encarnación has made many contributions to econometric modelling; see, e.g., the many papers he co-authored in the *Philippine Economic Journal*, Vol. 11, No. 2, Second Semester 1972. It is thus with great pleasure that I contribute this paper for his *Festschrift*.

Since that time, a new methodology has gradually evolved in the development and application of "computable-general-equilibrium" (CGE) models growing out of the pioneering work of Scarf (1983). This approach, which has come to be known by the name of "calibration," assigns numerical magnitudes to parameters on the basis of data at a single point in time, but without relying on an explicit philosophy of empirical inference. To many econometricians, this has seemed like a reversion to the pre-Haavelmo type of methodology; and yet, calibrationism has continued to thrive and even to gain new adherents.

The aim of this paper is to try to build a bridge between the two camps, and in particular, to find an interpretation of calibrationism in terms of probability and statistical inference. The paper originated as a discussion of a stimulating address given by John Whalley at a workshop on CGE-modelling held at the University of Konstanz in the summer of 1991; unfortunately this address was not written up, and the reader can only infer its contents from my discussion. But I believe and hope that I have not distorted its meaning.

In Section 1, I discuss the defeatist proposition that the number of parameters in typical CGE models is so huge that estimation of them by traditional econometric methods is not possible given our lack of sufficiently long time series. I show that this proposition is based on an erroneous calculation of the degrees of freedom in a simultaneous-equations model, and that this can therefore not be used as a valid excuse to eschew econometric methods.

In Section 2, I take up the simplest possible case of a calibration procedure, that used by Leontief in determining input-output coefficients, and ask whether there is a way to interpret the procedure in terms of statistical inference. I come to the conclusion that calibration can be given a valid statistical (Bayesian) interpretation provided one makes the *a priori* assumption that prior variances of the input-output coefficients are small. I go on to argue that under this interpretation there is no reason to limit oneself to observations from a single sample period (the "benchmark" year) when observations are available for more than one period.

In Section 3, I outline the history of the calibration procedure in CGE modelling, which evolved gradually before the term "calibration" came to be adopted as a description of the process, and has become even more explicit as a method. I observe that a parallel development has been taking place in the macroeconomic literature, and that the macroeconomists and CGE modelers have apparently been unaware of their mutual activities. In the macroeconomic field there has also been a tension between calibration and conventional statistical inference, as well as a recent attempt to merge the two.

In Section 4, I challenge the point of view that existence of equilibrium is of no policy interest, particularly if the true state of the economy is one of growth and/or cyclical fluctuation. Finally, in Section 5, I offer some suggestions for improvements over existing procedures, and in particular stress the need for *post hoc* verification of policy prognoses based on CGE models.

Are Traditional Methods of Statistical Inference Applicable?

Whalley (1991) has told us that since CGE models typically contain up to 10,000 parameters, one would need over 10,000 observations to estimate them statistically. If one has quarterly observations, this means that one would have to have a time series of over 10,000/4 = 2,500 years. If the last year is 1990, the first would have to be before 510 B.C.—the time of the Pharaohs.[1] And one could not assume that over that time period there was no structural change. Ergo, statistical estimation in CGE models is impossible. Let us consider this argument.

---

[1]The last of the Egyptian kings was Psamtik III, who was defeated in 525 B.C. in the battle of Pelusium by Cambyses, King of the Persians.

Suppose for simplicity one takes a Taylor approximation of the CGE model around the initial equilibrium point. Then the CGE model could be represented as a classical simultaneous-equations model of the form

$$Y\Gamma = X B + U \tag{1}$$

where Y is an $n \times m$ matrix of n observations on m endogenous variables, X is an $n \times k$ matrix of n observations on k exogenous variables, Γ and B are $m \times m$ and $k \times m$ matrices of unknown parameters to be estimated, and U is an $n \times m$ matrix of random errors with zero means $Eu_{tj} = 0$ and covariances $Eu_{si}u_{tj} = \tau_{st}\sigma_{ij}$ where $R = [\tau_{st}]$ is a matrix of serial correlations and $\Sigma = [\sigma_{ij}] = [Eu_{ti}u_{tj}]$ is the simultaneous covariance matrix. It is known from standard simultaneous-equations theory that the parameter matrix $[\Gamma', B']$ is identifiable if each of its $m \times (m + k)$ rows is subject to $m - 1$ homogeneous linear restrictions and if $n > k$. Let us look at the so-called "reduced form" of (1). This may be written as

$$Y = X \Pi + V \tag{2}$$

where $\Pi = B\Gamma^{-1}$ and V is a matrix of random error terms v_{tj} with zero means and covariances $Ev_{si}v_{tj} = r_{stu}\omega_{ij}$, where $\Omega = [\omega_{st}]$ is related to Σ by $\Gamma^{-1}\Sigma\Gamma^{-1}$. Denoting

$$Y = [y^1, \ldots, y^m] \quad \Pi = [\pi^1, \ldots, \pi^m]$$

where

$$y^j = \begin{bmatrix} y_{1j} \\ y_{2j} \\ \vdots \\ y_{nj} \end{bmatrix} \quad \text{and } \pi^j = \begin{bmatrix} \pi_{1j} \\ \pi_{2j} \\ \vdots \\ \pi_{kj} \end{bmatrix}$$

for $j = 1, 2, \ldots, m$, we may write the reduced form (2) as a set of m equations.

$$y^j = X \pi^j + v^j \quad (j = 1, 2, \ldots, m) \tag{3}$$

Now stacking these on top of one another we get

$$
\begin{bmatrix} y^1 \\ y^2 \\ \vdots \\ y^m \end{bmatrix} = \begin{bmatrix} X & 0 & \dots & 0 \\ 0 & X & \dots & 0 \\ & & \ddots & \\ 0 & 0 & \dots & X \end{bmatrix} \begin{bmatrix} \pi^1 \\ \pi^2 \\ \vdots \\ \pi^m \end{bmatrix} + \begin{bmatrix} v^1 \\ v^2 \\ \vdots \\ v^m \end{bmatrix} \tag{4}
$$

or in more compact notation

$$\text{col } Y = (I \otimes X) \text{ col } \Pi + \text{col } V.$$

This shows that the correct number of observations is not the number of time periods, n, but this number times the number of endogenous variables m. The number of parameters is km. Thus, the correct measure of the degrees of freedom is not

$$n - km$$

but rather

$$nm - km = (n - k)m$$

If for example we take $k = m = 100$ then we have $m^2 = 10{,}000$ parameters to be estimated, and the required number of years of quarterly observations is not $10{,}000/4 = 2{,}500$ but rather $100/4 = 25$. Therefore we need not go back as far as 510 B.C. but only as far as 1966 A.D.

This assumes that there are no *a priori* linear restrictions imposed on the π_{ij}s.[2] However, there are many examples in which such linear restrictions are indeed imposed. Take the case, for example, of a system of consumer demand functions when the structural form is that of the linear expenditure system. It there are demands for m commodities as functions of

---

[2] Such linear restrictions on the columns of Π will result from so-called overidentifying restrictions on the structural parameters, i.e., restrictions in excess of the $m - 1$ homogeneous linear restrictions on the corresponding rows of $[\Gamma', B]$ needed for identifiability of the parameters in that row.

m prices and income, then from homogeneity there are in general m independent parameters for each equation, or m^2 parameters altogether. But in terms of the linear expenditure system the demand functions have the form

$$q_{ti} = \frac{Y_t \alpha_i}{p_{ti}} + \frac{1}{p_{ti}} \sum_{j=1}^{m} p_{tj} \gamma_j (\alpha_i - \delta_{ij}) + e_{ti} \quad (i = 1, \ldots, m) \quad (5)$$

where q_{ti} is the quantity of commodity i demanded at time t, p_{tj} is the price of commodity j at time t, and Y_t is disposable income at time t (δ_{ij} denotes the Kronecker delta). It will be noted that there are $m \, \alpha_i$s and $m \gamma_i$s in (5) hence a total of $2m$ rather than m^2 parameters to be estimated. The number of degrees of freedom is then

$$nm - km = nm - 2m = (n - 2)m,$$

hence for the sample size to exceed the number of parameters to be estimated we need have only more than two quarters. For the estimates to be approximately normally distributed we need $n - 2 \geq 30$ hence $32/4 = 8$ years of quarterly observations. One need only go back to 1983—hardly the times of the Pharaohs!

A Statistical Interpretation of Calibration

The practice, though not the terminology, of calibration goes back at least to Leontief's input-output models (cf. Leontief 1951). For each industry, j, the ratio in a particular time period of the input from industry i to the output of industry j is used as an estimate of the corresponding input-output coefficient a_{ij}. Since for each input-output coefficient there is one observation and one parameter to be estimated, there are zero degrees of freedom. Leontief assumed the input-output coefficients to be fixed.

In practice, Leontief used values of inputs and values of outputs. As was pointed out by Klein (1953:205–206),[3] the form of production function for which these ratios of input values to output values are constant is the Cobb-Douglas, and the ratios are precisely the exponents of the inputs in the production function. It was suggested by Klein (1953:193) that one could use geometric means of observed input shares over a sample period to estimate these exponents. Can one justify the practice of estimating these exponents from a single observation?

We may formulate the problem as follows. Let w_{tij} denote the share of the ith input in the cost of production of the jth commodity at time t. In a deterministic model, this should be exactly equal to the exponent β_{ij} of the ith input in the Cobb-Douglas production function for the jth commodity. Allowing for error, however, we could postulate that in a sample of size n,

$$\omega_{tij} = \beta_{ij}\,\varepsilon_{tij} \quad (t = 1, 2, \ldots, n)$$

or

$$\log \omega_{tij} = \log \beta_{ij} + \log \varepsilon_{tij} \quad (t = 1, 2, \ldots, n),$$

where $\log \varepsilon_{tij}$ is assumed to have mean 0 and variance σ^2_{ij}. The least-squares estimate of $\log \beta_{ij}$ being the sample mean

$$\log \hat{\beta}_{ij} = \left(\sum_{t=1}^{n} \log \omega_{tij} \right) \Big/ n$$

the corresponding estimate of β_{ij} is the geometric mean

$$\hat{\beta}_{ij} = \left(\prod_{t=1}^{n} w_{tij} \right)^{1/n}$$

$$(6)$$

---

[3] See also Klein (1952-53) for a more detailed development, in particular one allowing for joint production.

The variance of the estimator log $\hat{\beta}_{ij}$ is

$$\text{Varlog } \hat{\beta}_{ij} = (\sigma^2_{ij})/n \qquad (7)$$

and since the best quadratic unbiased estimator of σ^2_{ij} is

$$\frac{1}{n-1}\left\{\left(\sum_{t=1}^{n}\log \omega_{tij} - \frac{1}{n}\sum_{t'=1}^{n}\log \omega_{t'ij}\right)^2\right\}$$

our estimate of the variance of the estimator log $\hat{\beta}_{ij}$ is

$$\frac{1}{n(n-1)}\left\{\sum_{t=1}^{n}\left(\log \omega_{tij} - \frac{1}{n}\sum_{t'=1}^{n}\log \omega_{t'ij}\right)^2\right\}$$

$$(8)$$

In a sample of size 1, the estimator (6) reduces to

$$\hat{\beta}_{ij} = \omega_{1ij}$$

which is the estimator used by Leontief. However, since (8) is now undefined, there is no way to assess its reliability. It may be inferred from some of Leontief's writings, however (cf., e.g., Leontief 1954), that he makes the implicit assumption that the variance, σ^2_{ij}, is small, e.g.,

$$\sigma^2_{ij} \leq \delta,$$

where δ is a small positive number. In that case from (7) we obtain for the variance of the logarithm of $\hat{\beta}_{ij}$ the estimate

$$\text{Varlog } \hat{\beta}_{ij} \leq \frac{\delta}{n}$$

so that for $n = 1$ this variance does not exceed δ.

An alternative way to formulate the problem is as follows. Let y_{tij} denote the contribution at time t of the input of commodity i to the cost of production of the output x_{tj} of commodity j (i.e., y_{tij}/x_{tj} corresponds to ω_{tij} in the previous formulation), and let us assume a regression of the form

$$y_{tij} = x_{tj}\beta_{ij} + \varepsilon_{tij} \qquad E\,\varepsilon_{tij} = 0 \quad E\,\varepsilon_{tij}\varepsilon_{t'ij} = \delta_{tt'}\,\sigma^2_{tij} \qquad (9)$$

Ordinarily one assumes $\sigma^2_{tij} = \sigma^2_{ij}$ for all t. The least-squares estimator from a sample of size n is

$$b_{ij} = \frac{\sum_{t=1}^{n} x_{tj} y_{tij}}{\sum_{t=1}^{n} x_{tj}^2} \qquad (10)$$

which is unbiased with variance $\sigma^2_{ij}/\sum_{t=1}^{n} x^2_{tj}$. The best quadratic unbiased estimator of σ^2_{ij} is then

$$s^2_{tj} = \frac{\sum_{t=1}^{n}\left(y_{tij} - x_{tj}b_{ij}\right)^2}{n-1} \qquad (11)$$

hence the corresponding estimator of the variance of b_{ij} is

$$\text{Est Var } b_{ij} = \frac{1}{n-1}\;\frac{\sum_{t=1}^{n}\left(y_{tij} - x_{tj}b_{ij}\right)^2}{.\sum_{t=1}^{n} x_{tj}^2}$$

the estimator (2.5) reduces to

$$b_{ij} = \frac{x_{1j}y_{1ij}}{x^2_{1j}} = \frac{y_{1ij}}{x_{1j}} \qquad (12)$$

which of course is the estimate used by the "calibration" procedure. It is unbiased, with variance σ^2_{ij}/x^2_{1j}, but there is now no way to estimate σ^2_{ij} and thus to assess the significance of one's estimate.

Suppose, however, that in (9) one replaces the assumption $\sigma^2_{tij} = \sigma^2_{ij}$ by the assumption

$$\sigma_{tij} \leq \rho x_{tj} \quad (\rho > 0) \tag{13}$$

where ρ is assumed to be known. If $\rho = 0.1$, say, this means that one "knows" that the standard deviation of the error term in (9) is not more than 10 percent of the value of output. Under this assumption the variance of b_{ij} is at most ρ^2 which is assumed known. This may be seen as follows. If we replace (13) by an equality, then the best linear unbiased estimator of β_{ij} is readily seen to be

$$\tilde{\beta}_{ij} = \frac{\sum\limits_{t=1}^{n} \dfrac{y_{tij}}{x_{tj}}}{n} \tag{14}$$

whose variance is ρ^2/n. Using this approach one would estimate the input-output coefficients (in value terms) as the arithmetic means rather than the geometric means of the observed input-output ratios. In the case $n = 1$ the estimator (14) reduces to the same formula as (12). Reverting to the inequality (13), we may conclude that

$$\text{Var } \frac{y_{1ij}}{x_{1j}} \leq \rho^2$$

It may be quite justifiable to make the assumption (13). If so, this provides a justification or at least a rationalization for the "calibration" process in terms of statistical theory.

Historical Development of the Calibration Concept

In the published CGEM literature, the term "calibration" apparently first appeared in Whalley (1982:350), but only in the title of a section. The section described the method used to adjust the parameters of the model to the empirical data, a method which had already been explained in considerable detail in Brown and Whalley (1980). Both the terminology and the general formulation of the methodology became much more explicit in St. Hilaire and Whalley (1983) which contains the following succinct summary:

> The motivation for data assembly is the current widely used practice of calibrating "empirical" general equilibrium models so as to exactly reproduce a base year data observation as an equilibrium model solution. The procedure enables empirically based models to evaluate counterfactual equilibria in a way which corresponds to comparative static analysis in theoretical literature. Under· this approach parameters for underlying demand and production functions which characterize the model are determined directly from the model equilibrium conditions. The model is initially solved for the equation parameters from the assumed equilibrium observation. The parameters are then used to solve the model in the opposite direction for a counterfactual equilibrium typically involving a proposed policy change. Policy evaluation then proceeds by comparing the counterfactual and historical (or benchmark) equilibria. The origins of this approach can be found in Harberger (1962) ....

Thus, Harberger (1962) may be regarded as the father of the calibration procedure in CGE models. The grandfather, however, as already suggested, was Leontief (1951). And as Jorgenson (1984) has stressed, the method was also pioneered by Johansen (1960).

The calibration procedure was described and applied in Piggot and Whalley (1985), and a very systematic discussion, constituting what appears to be the most explicit account to date, was presented in Mansur and Whalley (1984). These methods have been applied and extended by Kimbell and Harrison (1984) and Harrison (1986). Jorgenson (1984) has shown how econometric methods can be used in place of calibration.

Parallel developments have taken place in macroeconomics, but apparently in complete isolation from those in the CGEM field. Kydland and Prescott (1982) introduced a method of "calibration" for a macroeconomic model (though it is, and is described as, a general-equilibrium model, in the dynamic sense); Altug (1989) showed how econometric methods could be used to estimate this same model, with different results. And recently, Gregory and Smith (1990) have studied the Kydland-Prescott calibration procedure, considered as a method of estimation, and compared it with the generalized method-of-moments estimation procedure introduced by Hansen (1982).

It is to be hoped that in the future there will be greater communication between "calibrationists" and econometricians, as well as between macroeconomists and CGE modelers, so that empirical methods may evolve that are both practicable and soundly based on principles of statistical inference.

The Question of Existence of Equilibrium

The most startling statement made by Whalley (1991) is that "existence of equilibrium is of no policy interest." How can one explain or justify the great efforts undertaken to compute a general equilibrium if no such equilibrium exists?

My colleague Hans Weinberger of the University of Minnesota Mathematics Department once remarked to me that he could not understand economists' obsession with equilibrium. In physics, a theory is modelled in dynamic terms to begin with, leading to a system of total or partial differential equations. One possible property of such a system is that it has a singular point, or "equilibrium"; but this is a very special case. Many other types of solutions are possible, such as limit cycles; and no equilibrium need exist. Nevertheless the system is perfectly determinate.

There are many examples one could cite in economics as well. Arrow (1951) provided an example in which no competitive equilibrium exists. Scarf (1960) and Gale (1963) provided examples of situations in which the only competitive equilibria were dynamically unstable. Such examples are not necessarily unrealistic, as argued in Chipman (1965). The problem with them is that they are incomplete; one needs to posit a dynamic process of adjustment in order to find out what the actual solution of the system would be—most likely a limit cycle. Goodwin (1951) showed that a simple macroeconomic model without technological change had one unstable equilibrium and a stable limit cycle, and that a model with technological change had a stable limit cycle but no equilibrium. Goodwin (1951: 15–16) adjusted his models to data using a calibration method. In the 1960s, business-cycle analysis fell out of fashion, and many economists were heard to say that the business cycle was obsolete, or dead; few people would say that today.

If the true state of the economy is an oscillatory one, one could get very different results in CGE modelling depending upon whether the "benchmark year" was chosen to be the peak or the trough of a cycle.

Another observation made by Whalley (1991) struck me as curious: that numerical calculations in economics were pioneered by Graham (1948). In fact, by theorizing in terms of numerical examples Graham was continuing a tradition begun by Ricardo and followed by Mill, Mangoldt, Marx, Taussig, and many others. Certainly, Graham brought this process to the status of a high art, and his examples had a much greater air of realism than those of his predecessors. It was one of the singular accomplishments of one of Graham's students, McKenzie (1954), to demonstrate the existence of equilibrium in Graham's model, as well as to develop topological methods for computing efficient patterns of specialization in this model. Of course, McKenzie's method was nonconstructive, and Scarf's (1973) contribution was of major importance in providing a constructive method, i.e., providing a method of establishing existence of equilibrium under given assumptions by providing an algorithm for computing it. It is true that an author who reasons in terms of numerical examples is likely to keep potential real-world applications in the forefront, whereas there is always the danger that abstract analysis of economic models will take on a life of its own and eventually lose sight of their *raison d'etre*. There is an opposite danger, too: those who come up with numbers, however obtained, are more likely to be believed than those who make less precise prognostications, if only because they easily intimidate those who are unacquainted with the fine points of their methods.

Concluding Remarks

The scope and sweep of the CGE work carried out by Whalley and his colleagues are extremely impressive. To apply general-equilibrium models to real data for purposes of policy prognosis is one of the most important things economists can do; no doubt the most important. On this point I have no argument. It should also be possible to agree that it should be done right. To do it right requires the diverse skills and talents of a wide spectrum of theorists, econometricians, and applied workers. For this, I think the most important requirement is communication. The calibration methods used need to be further formalized so that they can be better understood by econometricians. Then it should be possible to progress towards methods that use to advantage the *a priori* assumptions implicit in the calibration procedures, and which are soundly based on principles of statistical and logical inference.

The use of extraneous estimators gleaned from literature searches, while perhaps better than guesswork, is quite questionable in many cases. More often than not, elasticity estimates found in the literature are based on partial-equilibrium and ill-specified models. At least, allowance should be made for error—in particular, possible bias—in these estimates.

Work on CGE modelling should not be allowed to ossify. Movement is needed towards dynamic models that allow for oscillations and growth; and better integration of calibration with state-of-the-art econometric methods should be an important objective.

Finally, there is the need for verification. A policy prognosis made before adoption of a policy is not of much use unless there is a way to verify its correctness after the policy has been adopted. Of course, this is very difficult to do, since other variables have changed. But the exercise is hard to justify unless verification is possible. Whalley (1991) has referred to projections made before the U.S.-Canada free trade agreement that suggested a substantial welfare gain for Canada. Has anybody tried to verify the correctness of these projections after the fact? I am reminded of an experience I had when spending a summer with an advisory group in the Brazilian Ministry of Planning. One day, a member of the Brazilian staff made a presentation in which he set out projections of value added in the ten industrial subdivisions of the Brazilian economy for the next ten years. After the talk, I asked a naive question: could he please provide the corresponding data for the past ten years? Of course not, he replied; such data are not available. He was presumably confident that ten years hence such data would still be unavailable, so there would never be a danger that his projections would be falsified. When the future is known better than the past, my suspicions are aroused.

References

Altug, S. (1989) "Time-to-Build and Aggregate Fluctuations: Some New Evidence," *International Economic Review* 40 (November): 889–920.

Arrow, K. J. (1951) "An Extension of the Basic Theorems of Classical Welfare Economics," in *Proceedings of the Second Berkeley Symposium on Mathematical Statistics and Probability.* Berkeley: University of California Press: 507–532.

Brown, F. and J. Whalley (1980) "General Equilibrium Evaluations of Tariff-Cutting Proposals in the Tokyo Round and Comparisons with more Extensive Liberalization of World Trade," *Economic Journal* 90 (December): 838–1866.

Chipman, J. S. (1965) "A Survey of the Theory of International Trade: Part 2, The Neo-Classical Theory," *Econometrica* 33 (October): 685–760.

_____, F. Schneider, and B. Genser (1991) "The Pay-off of Investment in CGE Modelling," Universität Konstanz, Sonderforschungsbereich 178, "Internationalisierung der Wirtschaft," *Diskussionsbeiträge*, Serie II, Nr. 156, October.

Gale, D. (1963) "A Note on Global Instability of Competitive Equilibrium," *Naval Research Logistics Quarterly* 10 (March): 81–87.

Goodwin, R. M. (1951) "The Nonlinear Accelerator and the Persistence of Business Cycles," *Econometrica* 19 (January): 1–17.

Graham, F. D. (1948) *The Theory of International Values.* Princeton, N.J.: Princeton University Press.

Gregory, A. W. and G. W. Smith (1990) "Calibration as Estimation," *Econometric Reviews* 9 (No. 1): 57–89.

Haavelmo, T. (1994) "The Probability Approach in Econometrics," *Econometrica* 12 (July), Supplement: 1–115.

Hansen, L. P. (1982) "Large Sample Properties of Generalized Methods of Moments Estimators," *Econometrica* 50 (July): 1029–1054.

Harberger, A. C. (1962) "The Incidence of the Corporation Income Tax," *Journal of Political Economy* 70 (June): 215–240.

Harrison, G. W. (1986) "A General Equilibrium Analysis of Tariff Reductions," in T.N. Srinivasan and John Whalley, (eds.). *General Equilibrium Trade Policy Modeling.* Cambridge, Mass.: The MIT Press, 101–123.

Johansen, L. (1960) *A Multi-Sectoral Study of Economic Growth.* Amsterdam: North-Holland Publishing Co.

Jorgenson, D. W. (1984) "Econometric Methods for Applied General Equilibrium Analysis," in Herbert E. Scarf and John B. Shoven (eds.). *Applied General Equilibrium Analysis.* Cambridge: Cambridge University Press, 139–203.

Kimbell, L. J. and G. W. Harrison (1984) "General Equilibrium Analysis of Regional Fiscal Incidence," in Herbert E. Scarf and John B. Shoven (eds.). *Applied General Equilibrium Analysis.* Cambridge: Cambridge University Press, 275–313.

Klein, L. R. (1953) *A Textbook of Econometrics.* Evanston, Ill.: Row, Peterson and Company.

Koopmans, T. C., H. Rubin, and R. B. Leipnik (1950) "Measuring the Equation Systems of Dynamic Economics," in Tjalling C. Koopmans (ed.). *Statistical Inference in Dynamic Economic Models.* New York: John Wiley and Sons, Inc., 53–237.

Kydland, F. E. and E. C. Prescott (1982) "Time to Build and Aggregate Fluctuations," *Econometrica* 50 (November): 1345–1370.

Leontief, W. W. (1951) *The Structure of American Economy 1919–1939,* 2nd edition. New York: Oxford University Press.

_____. (1954) "Mathematics in Economics," *Bulletin of the American Mathematical Society* 60 (May): 215–233. Reprinted in Wassily W. Leontief, *Essays in Economics: Theories and Theorizing.* New York: Oxford University Press, 1966: 22–44.

Mansur, A. and J. Whalley (1984) "Numerical Specification of Applied General Equilibrium Models: Estimation, Calibration, and Data," in Herbert E. Scarf and John B. Shoven (eds.). *Applied General Equilibrium Analysis.* Cambridge: Cambridge University Press, 69–127.

McKenzie, L. W. (1954) "On Equilibrium in Graham's Model of World Trade and Other Competitive Systems," *Econometrica* 22 (April): 147–161.

Piggott, J. and J. Whalley (1985) *UK Tax Policy and Applied General Equilibrium Analysis.* Cambridge: Cambridge University Press.

Scarf, H. (1960) "Some Examples of Global Instability of the Competitive Equilibrium," *International Economic Review* 1 (September): 157–172.

_____. (1973) *The Computation of Economic Equilibria.* New Haven: Yale University Press.

St. Hilaire, F. and J. Whalley (1983) "A Microconsistent Equilibrium Data Set for Canada for Use in Tax Policy Analysis," *Review of Income and Wealth* 29 (June): 175–204.

Whalley, J. (1982) "An Evaluation of the Tokyo Round Trade Agreement Using General Equilibrium Computational Methods," *Journal of Policy Modeling* 4 (November): 341–361.

_____. (1991) "General Equilibrium Economics: Computation and Application," Opening Address, Workshop on *Issues in International Economics: Questions to and Answers from Computable General Equilibrium Analysis.* University of Konstanz, 8 July.

Development and Entrepreneurship, Productivity or Rent-Seeking

*William J. Baumol**

Entrepreneurship and Vitality of the Economy: Preliminary

Schumpeter is, of course, the prime sponsor of the theoretical analyses in which the entrepreneur is assigned the double role

*The author is director of the C. V. Starr Center for Applied Economics, New York University, and Professor Emeritus, Princeton University. He is extremely grateful to the Alfred P. Sloan Foundation and the C. V. Starr Center for Applied Economics, New York University, for their support of this work.

There is no more effective way for a teacher to be honored than by the outstanding performance of a former student. All of us who were on the economics faculty at Princeton when José Encarnación attended that institution recognized his outstanding capabilities and the impressive quality of his mind. We were then proud to have him working with us, and he has done us proud in his subsequent career. It is indeed a welcome opportunity to have the chance to contribute to his *festschrift*. Happily, the occasion arises when I have just been thinking of issues pertinent to economic development and, hence, relevant for the well being of the economy in which Dr. Encarnación resides, as it is for many other lands. It is to a subject, the role of the entrepreneur, growing out of my recent work in this arena that this paper is devoted.

of guide and driver of development. It is he who introduces the new ideas, the practical person who knows how to adapt those ideas and make them remarkable, the individual with the drive and initiative requisite for raising the necessary capital and to carry out the necessary production and marketing. Without his efforts the economy is apt to be mired in tradition and condemned to poverty.

This view of the matter, interpreted naively, suggests that there must be a tight correlation between the number of active entrepreneurs in an economy and the speed with which an economy grows. Thus, when an economy slows, either absolutely or relatively, as the United Kingdom did toward the end of the nineteenth century, or as many of the industrial economies did after the middle of the 1970s, one is apt to hear the conjecture that in those places the spirit of entrepreneurship has diminished and the number of entrepreneurs is in marked decline. Why the sources of entrepreneurship have suddenly dried up seems rarely to be explained, but the implied reasons seem to range from governmental interference that undermines the opportunities for profitable business initiative to a withering of some ill defined entrepreneurial spirit—a decline in national drive for achievement grounded in the processes of history and social psychology.

Two critical premises implicitly underlie this way of thinking. First, it assumes that entrepreneurial activity is a binary variable—like an electrical switch, it is either on or off. Second, it holds, virtually by definition, that entrepreneurial acts must be acts that contribute to production and its growth. Of course, one cannot reject a definition, but one can conclude that it is not helpful and that it impedes understanding instead of facilitating it. Rather than simply equating entrepreneurship with virtue, I will suggest, it is more illuminating to try to characterize the type of activity that is implied in discussions of the subject, leaving until later deductions about the extent to which it contributes, if it contributes at all, to economic output.

The entrepreneur is generally taken to be driven by more than the profit motive, but the pursuit of wealth is assumed to be one of his main objectives, with power and prestige as coordinate or ancillary goals. The term "entrepreneur" usually is accorded one of two meanings: first, it is often taken to refer to any founder and organizer of a business firm—even a small retail establishment or a new farm, who may be doing what has been done by others a thousand times before. Alternatively, the entrepreneur is often defined as the innovator, as the disturber of the current arrangements, whose alertness to profit opportunities leads him to upset equilibria by the injection of new products, new productive processes, new marketing techniques or new forms of organization into the circular flow, but who is just as effective in recognizing disequilibria and bringing them to an end by innovative steps that take advantage of the arbitrage opportunities each disequilibrium provides. Both types of entrepreneur, clearly, can make a contribution to the economy. However, in the Schumpeterian tradition, here I will focus on the latter, the substantially more romantic and swashbuckling character of the two, the one that economic theory seems rarely able to capture and incorporate into its models.[1] To see what this set of attributes, ascribed to entrepreneurship, implies about its role in growth a few preliminary words on the nature of the market are required.

Remarks on the Workings of the Market Mechanism

As has recently become widely recognized, indeed adopted almost as an article of faith, there is nothing that approaches

---

[1]The reasons theoretical writings usually fail to deal with entrepreneurs in this category, despite their acknowledged importance for economic growth is discussed in my forthcoming book [1993], where the opportunities for formal analysis of his role are also explored and illustrated.

the capitalistic market mechanism as an instrument capable of providing abundance of output, and growth in that abundance, to a degree unparalleled in human history. Marx was well aware of this contribution of capitalism and was not reticent about proclaiming it in poetic terms. As early as the *Communist Manifesto* (1848) he remarked "The bourgeoisie ...has accomplished wonders far surpassing Egyptian pyramids, Roman aqueducts, and Gothic cathedrals ...during its rule of scarce one hundred years, has created more massive and more colossal productive forces than have all preceding generations together." And little could he have known what was to come. Since then, per capita output in the United States has probably risen tenfold and, because the number of hours worked per year has fallen almost in half, labor productivity can be estimated to have risen almost twice as much. Despite that, the U.S. lead is being threatened by France, Holland and Belgium, with Germany and Japan not very far behind. All of those countries, then, have surely achieved growth records at least equal to that of the U.S.

But achievement of such wonders by the market is not automatic. The method by which it is driven to produce such accomplishments is what may be described as "channeled greed." There are kinder terms such as "the profit motive" that are used to put the matter in a more favorable light, but such words can be treated as evasions of the fact that the market operates through unalloyed pursuit of self interest—through naked greed. Indeed, it punishes the businesspersons sufficiently weak to permit charitable and public welfare considerations to divert them from their purpose. If they are moved voluntarily to spend substantial amounts on control of pollutant emissions, the training of unskilled workers or other forms of good works, they make themselves vulnerable to the competition of less scrupulous rivals who can undercut their costs and prices and drive them from the market.

Yet, the wonder of the competitive market is its ability to *channel* that greed, to force it to work in only one direction, the aggressive enhancement of output. It is this illuminating observation that is, arguably, Adam Smith's most brilliant contribution. That is what the "invisible hand" passage is really about: "As every individual ...endeavours as much as he can ...to employ his capital ...that its produce may be of the greatest value; every individual necessarily labours to render the annual revenue of the society as great as he can. He generally, indeed, neither intends to promote the public interest, nor knows how much he is promoting it ...by directing that industry in such a manner as its produce may be of the greatest value, he intends only his own gain, and he is in this, as in many other cases, led by an invisible hand to promote an end which was no part of his intention. Nor is it always the worse for society that it was no part of it. By pursuing his own interest he frequently promotes that of the society more effectually than when he really intends to promote it" (Book IV, Chapter II).

The market mechanism is a harsh and relentless taskmaster. It shows no mercy in imposing financial disaster upon those who fail to meet its standards. But it balances this off by the rewards beyond dreams of avarice that it provides to those who are successful in their economic performance.

In a competitive market, as Smith pointed out, that performance consists in contribution to economic output. By producing more or more cheaply, or by providing products that better satisfy the desires of consumers, the businesspersons join the economic elect, those entitled to the shower of wealth that is their object in this exercise. But productive contribution is the hard way to obtain the market's rewards. And so entrepreneurs are driven constantly to seek alternative and easier paths to their goal. To do this they must attempt to free themselves from the painful constraints of the competitive mechanism, and there's the rub, the source of the difficulty with which this paper is concerned.[2]

On Entrepreneurial Rent Seeking

The basic premise of the analysis here is that *technical* innovation, the introduction into the market of a new product or a new process, is to most entrepreneurs only a means to the ends they really seek. As already postulated, that goal is a compound of wealth, power and prestige. The means by which that objective is attained is to them, at least to a degree, an irrelevancy. It is true that for a particular entrepreneur who has chosen to pursue some definite avenue for the purpose, the value of experience and of other past investment forecloses choice among means to pursue the target. But the body of entrepreneurs is constantly fed by a stream of new recruits that replace those who retire, die, or are ejected from the group by incompetence or fortuitous failure. These novice entrepreneurs do have a choice of instruments, and that choice is frequently made on the basis of promise for attainment of the goal, rather than the relative social or productive contribution of the different available activities among which a selection is to be made, not as concrete processes such as computer manufacturing or pharmaceutical production, but as abstract variants among the class of instruments whose end product is wealth, power and prestige, and which do yield computers or medicines as incidental by-products of little direct interest.

This is undoubtedly an exaggeration of the real state of affairs. Entrepreneurs, like lawyers, doctors and professors, are a heterogeneous group, some with profound personal commitment to the general welfare, others driven by

---

[2]Smith was well aware of the problem, and repeatedly called it to the reader's attention. Thus: "People of the same trade seldom meet together, even for merriment and diversion, but that the conversation ends in a conspiracy against the public, or in some contrivance to raise prices" (Book I, Chapter XI, Part II).

overpowering greed, with the bulk of each group composed of persons who fall somewhere between these two extremes. Still, the view of the matter taken in the preçeding paragraph, while it undoubtedly oversimplifies reality, does represent an important side of it, and it does permit clearer evaluation of the consequences than any model which attempts to incorporate all the complexities of human motivation. In essence, it' is an extension to the analysis of entrepreneurship of the standard assumption of economic theory that the sole object of the business firm, to the exclusion of all other considerations, is maximization of profit. For that premise, too, has clearly contributed to the analytic power of economic theory, even though that assumption, in its extreme form, is also clearly wrong.

The point of all this is that the entrepreneurs *do* have considerable choice among the means they adopt to pursue their goals, and not all of those means contribute equally to productivity growth. Indeed, as I have argued elsewhere (1993, Chapter 2), some of the avenues available for the purpose add little or nothing to production, and in some cases actually impede it. Yet all of these activities are strictly entrepreneurial in the sense of the definition adopted here. Success in the undertakings can require innovation, boldness and organizing ability. They can entail substantial disturbance of the current state of affairs, whether that state is one of equilibrium or disequilibrium.

The extreme example of destructive entrepreneurship, pertinent throughout the world in an earlier age, and still all too relevant in less-developed countries, is the activity of the warlord. Whether driven by naked pursuit of booty and self-aggrandizement or acting as a self proclaimed liberator, the warlord's realm is entrepreneurship with all rules of good conduct abandoned. Success in the undertaking requires or at least benefits greatly from innovative strategy and tactics. Alertness to opportunities is one of the warlord's prime talents.

Boldness, and the ability to accumulate and organize the resources required for his activities are his stock in trade. Yet entrepreneurial though the activity undoubtedly is, it surely cannot be suspected of contributing to the economy's production. History is full of pitiful depictions of the miserable life led by a population whose existence is colored by the constant incursions of warlords.

Yet, it is arguable that an impediment to production comparable in its power is constituted by the activities of a type of entrepreneur who is more widely respected or at least accepted in his society. This is the rent-seeking entrepreneur. Gordon Tullock, who first explored the concept and coined the term (see, e.g., Tullock (1980)), has suggested that the notion is not well defined. However, one can interpret it to cover all socially-accepted and, hence, legitimate activities whose objective is to *redistribute* wealth or income to the benefit of the individual that undertakes it, and who contributes little or nothing to the economy's output in the process. In an absolute monarchy, competitive efforts by courtiers to acquire the king's favor in order to secure the grant of some monopoly is a clear example. In a modern industrial economy one readily encounters comparable efforts to secure monopoly licenses to supply electricity or cable television to some community. In less-developed countries, rent seeking most characteristically takes the form of the activity from which the concept derives its name. That is, entrepreneurial activity often seeks to gain its objectives through land ownership and rent collection, rather than through farming or manufacturing activity.

It may not be obvious that rent seeking is seriously detrimental to productivity. After all, the main object of the game is the *transfer* of wealth, and economics often takes the position that from the point of view of value of the nation's output a mere transfer is neutral—what one individual loses another gains, and so the result is zero. However, that overlooks two important considerations. First, the source of the redistributive gain is apt to be costly to society. This is most obvious in the case of a grant of a monopoly power. However, capable entrepreneurs are not so passive. They do not, characteristically, wait for opportunities to be provided by happenstance. A good entrepreneur can be counted upon to seek to create such opportunities. It is not by accident that a king was led to offer a salt monopoly—it was undoubtedly at the suggestion of someone who stood to profit from it. In an industrial economy such a goal is pursued with the help of an army of "lobbyists," paid professionals whose occupation entails the exercise of influence over legislative bodies. Thus, many times, the efforts of the lobbyists are devoted to getting the legislature to restrict entry into some economic field, and to permit operation in the field only upon acquisition of a government license, in effect, the grant of a monopoly or a quasi monopoly.

That is by no means the end of the story. The social costs of rent seeking are usually far higher than just the costs of monopoly. Indeed, much of rent-seeking activity employs little or no monopoly power. The second and, perhaps, far greater cost of rent seeking is suggested by a hypothesis first proposed by Posner (1975). Though his ostensible theorem, about to be described, has been discredited as a generality by extended critical discussion, enough truth remains to the idea to suggest the order of magnitude of the second source of cost to society. That second cost is the opportunity cost of the resources wasted in the rent-seeking process, not the least among these, the time and talents of the entrepreneurs themselves that, from the viewpoint of society, might far better have been devoted to productive activities.

The quasi theorem is easily described intuitively by means of an example. Consider a monopoly license that can be expected to permit its possessor to earn rents whose discounted present value is X dollars. While *use* of the license does entail the exercise of monopoly power, that is not necessarily true of the struggle to *acquire* the license in the first place. Entry into the business of license-acquisition can be entirely free and it can therefore be highly competitive. Anyone with the funds can hire lobbyists or offer bribes or invest in any other of the means used to battle for that license, and innovative approaches to license acquisition are clearly possible. If this struggle is a process that is a reasonable approximation to perfect competition, Posner observed, we can be sure of the equilibrium expenditure that those seeking the license will end up incurring. For in perfect competition, as we know, expected equilibrium profits are always zero, so that one can expect those who compete with one another in pursuit of the monopoly license to end up, in aggregate, spending exactly the X-dollar return that the license promises. If they have spent less than this, the competitive battle for the license cannot have attained an equilibrium, for it must still promise more than a competitive return on the investment, and other bidders will find it attractive to enter the fray.

The implication is that rent seeking exacts a substantial social cost in the form of forgone productive opportunities, and that the order of magnitude of those wasted resources is approximately that of the rents that the activities promise to bring. This can, indeed, be a heavy burden for an economy, particularly one whose objective is to embark on a course of substantial economic growth, but in which a large proportion of the available entrepreneurial talent devotes itself to rent seeking rather than to productive activities.

We conclude that entrepreneurial activity is not always and necessarily productive, and that the nature of the activities selected by an economy's entrepreneurs can make a great deal of difference for its productivity and rate of growth.

The Economy's Payoff Structure and the Allocation of Entrepreneurship

The immediate question, then, is what determines the directions in which an economy's entrepreneurs tend to expend their efforts? A moment's thought will indicate that there is no simple answer. There are many influences, including tradition, religion, and many other obvious or subtle determinants, many of which lie well outside the economist's province. However, there is one key influence that clearly *is* an economic matter. That is what is often referred to as the rules of the game that determine earnings—the structure of the payoffs to different activities. At different times and in different places the relative payoffs to rent-seeking activities and those to productive entrepreneurship differ markedly. Those payoffs can change because of developments that from viewpoint of the economy can be considered accidental and exogenous. For example, the emergence of a strong central political authority can cause the profits available to the entrepreneurial warlord to dry up, as happened in Europe at the end of the Middle Ages, or in China after the Second World War.

Often such a change is the consequence of a deliberate economic act adopted for the purpose or for other reasons. For example, in the United States after 1980, when regulation of railroad freight transportation was eased and transformed into a more rational regime, there was apparently a sharp drop in rent-seeking litigative activity before the regulatory agency, an activity that had previously sought to protect the parties from effective competition. Because under the new regime that sort of regulatory interference was severely reduced if not eliminated altogether; there was a substantial decrease in the payoffs promised by large expenditure of funds on lawyers and others required by such litigation. The railroad firms began to rely less for their earnings on the activities of their lawyers and more on those of the companies' executives. Casual observation indicates that one of the results was a considerable upgrading in the quality of the railroads' management personnel.

Another example is provided by Japan that has reduced the waste caused by rent-seeking litigation in at least two ways. It has adopted rules severely restricting the number of lawyers who can be trained and graduated each year. It has also adopted rules making it extremely difficult for a firm to sue another in the courts. The result is that entrepreneurs, finding themselves severely restrained in the opportunity to pursue their goals through litigation, are driven, perhaps even reluctantly, to seek other means to attain their objectives, among them the production of automobiles or television sets, as well as innovation in those productive processes.

Two conclusions follow from the preceding discussion. First, the allocation of an economy's entrepreneurial resources can be influenced heavily by the relative payoffs promised by those activities. Second, it follows that the structure of those payoffs does change, sometimes by happenstance, but in other cases by deliberate policy.

That, in turn, offers two other observations. First, it sheds some light on an issue with which we began—does the cadre of entrepreneurs available to an economy often vanish suddenly or suddenly expand out of nowhere? One cannot exclude that possibility. But a much more plausible explanation for sudden expansion or contraction of productive entrepreneurial activity is that there has been a change in the structure of payoffs that elicited a reallocation of entrepreneurial talent between productive and unproductive activities.

Second, the argument suggests that if an LDC seeks to facilitate a takeoff of its economy it may be good strategy to look for opportunities to cut down the rewards to unproductive entrepreneurship or to facilitate entrepreneurial earning of rewards in productive activities. If productive entrepreneurship is determined exclusively by history, tradition or social psychological circumstances, the designer of policy is powerless to do much about it. However, if the structure of payoffs does play an important role, then the way is open for the formulation of an effective policy for the encouragement of productive entrepreneurship.

Preliminary Remarks on a Pertinent Dynamic Model

Let me now illustrate how the preceding discussion can begin to be incorporated into a formal analysis, and how the resulting model can be used to offer some insights on matters of public policy. All of the postulated relationships and premises that follow are purely hypothetical and are not intended to correspond to reality in any particular economy.

Let us assume that entrepreneurs can engage in their innovative activity in two arenas, which one can think of, for concreteness, as manufacturing and landholding, with innovation in the latter consisting in the design of novel tenure arrangements and the introduction of new methods for extraction of rents. Let us assume that one pertinent policy instrument is available, to which we can refer as a "Henry George tax," a tax upon pure economic rents. Since such a tax cannot be shifted, it must reduce the income available to entrepreneurs if they devote themselves to enterprising rent seeking.

For simplicity, let us assume that the time path of the economy's income is determined by a first-order difference equation

$$y_{t+1} = a(\pi_t)f(y_t) \quad a' > 0 \tag{1}$$

where we use the notation

y_t = national income in period t

π_t = time spent by entrepreneurs in productive activities

r_t = time spent by entrepreneurs in rent seeking

b = the Henry George tax rate on economic rent

and π and r satisfy the relationships

$$\pi_t = g(r_t) \quad g' < 0 \tag{2}$$

and

$$r_t = G(h) \quad G' < 0 \tag{3}$$

Here, relationship (2) merely describes the competition between productive activity and rent seeking for the available time of the economy's body of entrepreneurs, while (3) depicts the disincentive effect of the tax upon the amount of entrepreneurial time devoted to rent seeking. By successive substitution of (3) into (2) into (1) we readily obtain

$$y_{t+1} = \alpha(h)f(y_t) \tag{4}$$

where $\alpha' = a'g'G' > 0$

Now, let us assume for illustration that the graph of (4) is as shown by curve FF' in the phase diagram Figure 1, in which the ray depicted is the 45 degree line. We see that there are two equilibrium points (points at which $y_{t+1} = y_t$), i.e., points A and B. The former is, clearly, a stable equilibrium point. Thus, if the economy starts off from any initial point between A and B as, for example, point y_0 in the figure, there will follow a time path, *rstuv*... which moves the economy directly toward low-income equilibrium point A, where it will stagnate. Even if the economy starts off to the left of A, while it is true that income will rise, going asymptotically toward that at A, stagnation will again be the ultimate target of the time path. Only if the economy can execute a major leap that takes it to the right of B, say to y_0', will a takeoff (path *hjk*...) ensue.

One can postulate that the initial point itself will be a function of h. That is, if h is replaced by a higher land tax, h^*, the value of y in the next period may be shifted rightward by the exogenous disturbance that moves talent and resources from rent seeking to productive activities. However, this effect may well prove transitory. If it is insufficient to move y all the way to the right of B, the fated sort of time path—one that

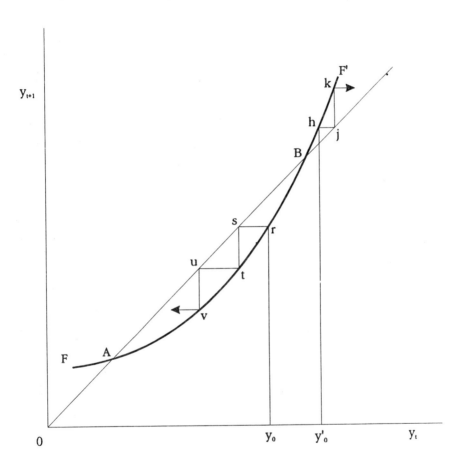

Figure 1

Stagnant and Growth Equilibria

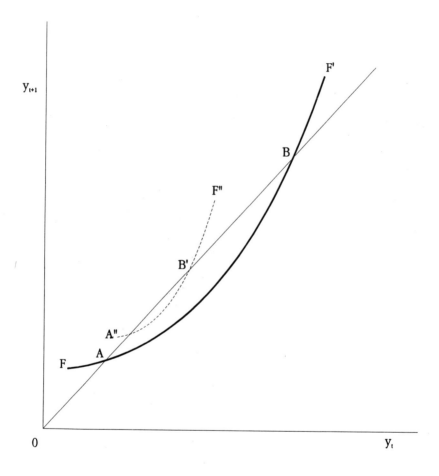

Figure 2
A More Attainable Growth Equilibrium

moves the economy, apparently inexorably, back downward toward A—will be resumed.

However, we see from (4) that the once-and-for all rise in the value of h also has an enduring consequence. It causes a "permanent" change in the value of $\alpha(h)$ in (4). The result is an upward shift in the graph of the difference equation (Figure 2), moving it, perhaps from AF' to A"F". That brings the unstable equilibrium point B to B', moving it closer to A. The result is that a much smaller once-and-for-all enhancement in the "initial" value of y is required to launch the economy upon a takeoff.

None of this is intended to be more than suggestive. It is a cliché to note that greater realism and complexity will have to be injected into the model before it can be taken seriously as a guide for policy. But a cliché is not necessarily a distortion. The ideas suggested in this paper, and the approach suggested for their formalization and systematic analysis seem to me to hold considerable substance. The discussion represents a modest contribution to the analysis of development policy, but, I believe, some contribution, nevertheless.

References

Baumol, W.J. (1993) *Entrepreneurship, Management and the Structure of Payoffs.* Cambridge, Mass.: MIT Press.

Posner, R.A. (1975) "The Social Costs of Monopoly and Regulation," *Journal of Political Economy* 83 (August): 807–27.

Tullock, G. (1980) "Efficient Rent Seeking," in Buchanan, J.M., Tullinson, J. R., and Tullock, G. *Toward a Theory of The Rent Seeking Society.* College Station: Texas A & M Press.

Convergence and Divergence: Human Capital Deepening, Inequality, Demographic Events Along the Asian Rim

*Jeffrey G. Williamson**

Sources of Growth Along the Asian Pacific Rim

In the mid-1970s, Edward Denison and William Chung (1976) used sources of growth accounting to show us *How Japan's Economy Grew So Fast*. The limitations to this kind of analysis are well known, but one of their chapters might be particularly useful to help organize our thinking about the sources of economic dynamism along the Asian Pacific Rim. Denison and Chung (1976, Ch. 12) pose this question: Could Japan's growth rate up to 1973/74 be sustained in the long run? They searched

*Professor of Economics, Harvard University. Among his varied interests, Pépe Encarnación worked at the interface between development and demography, and thus this paper seems especially appropriate for his *festschrift*. Pepe's integrity, professionalism and patriotic commitment (at some personal cost) has always been a brilliant beacon to me in an academic sea of contrary signals. I present this paper to him with affection and respect. It is a revised and augmented version of the author's "Human Capital Deepening, Inequality, and Demographic Events Along the Asia-Pacific Rim," in N. Ogawa, G. Jones and J. G. Williamson (eds.), *Human Resources in Development Along the Asia-Pacific Rim* (Singapore: Oxford University Press, 1993).

Table 1

Sustainable and Transitional Components of Japan's Growth
According to Denison and Chung (percent per annum)

Rate of Growth	Total	Contribution in percentage points 1967–71 Sustainable	Transitional	Year Transitional Contribution Expires
	(1)	(2)	(3)	(4)
Output	9.56	3.24	6.32	
Labor	1.78	0.68	1.10	
Employment	1.09	0.33	0.76	1973
Hours	0.11	-0.15	0.26	1974
Age-sex composition	0.19	0.11	0.08	1977
Education	0.35	0.35	0.00	
Unallocated	0.04	0.04	0.00	
Capital	2.57	0.86	1.71	
Inventories	0.86	0.21	0.65	1976
Nonresidential structure and equipment	1.44	0.38	1.06	1976
Dwellings	0.27	0.27	0.00	
International assets	0.00	0.00	0.00	
Land	0.00	0.00	0.00	
Advances in knowledge	2.43	1.28	1.15	2002
Contraction of agricultural inputs	0.62	0.00	0.62	1982
Reduction in trade barriers	0.01	0.00	0.01	2002
Economies of scale measured in US prices	1.14	0.42	0.72	
Income elasticities	0.82	0.00	0.82	1995

Source: Denison and Chung (1976:115, Table 12-1).

for the answer by decomposing the fast growth of the 1960s
into that part of the performance which was sustainable in the
long run and that part which was only transitional. The
transitional part was attributed to her latecomer status, to
special transitory demographic features, and to economic
inefficiencies which had been mostly eliminated by the early
1970s. The result is reproduced in Table 1 while Figure 1 uses
that information to trace out Denison and Chung's projections

into the future. Figure 1 also plots Japan's actual growth performances since 1971, and, apart from the macroeconomic shocks around 1973–74, those projections were remarkably close to the mark. Both show a retardation across the 1970s, as

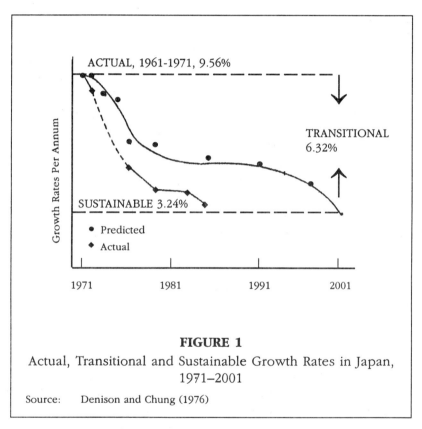

FIGURE 1

Actual, Transitional and Sustainable Growth Rates in Japan, 1971–2001

Source: Denison and Chung (1976)

Japan's economy approached the long-run sustainable growth path, and both show that much of the transition to the sustainable growth path was completed by the late 1970s. Furthermore, the slowdown also confirms a prediction made by Kazushi Ohkawa and Henry Rosovsky even before *How Japan's Economy Grew So Fast* appeared (Ohkawa and Rosovsky 1973: 232–250).

Not all of the Denison-Chung projected growth retardation into the 21st century can be attributed to demographic, labor market, and human capital accumulation factors, but a good share of it can. Of the 6.32 percentage point decline in the growth rate, they attributed 1.10 percentage points to labor force effects, 0.81 percentage points to the exhaustion of inefficiencies associated with the demise of self-employment and the farm sector, and 1.71 percentage points to the slowdown in conventional accumulation. Based on the recent research of J. Bradford DeLong and Lawrence Summers (1991, 1993), we now know that the impact of the slowdown in conventional accumulation is likely to be greatly understated. It is likely to be far bigger if properly measured as equipment investment. We shall have more to say about this below.

If the decline in (DeLong's and Summers' adjusted) conventional accumulation can be shown to be related largely to demographic and labor force events, then these three sources are likely to account for more than half of Japan's growth slowdown. That is certainly a big enough share to warrant the theme of this paper, and it seems to be consistent with the hypothesis that a good share of the differences in growth performance along the Asian Pacific Rim, or between it and Latin América, can also be explained by human capital and demographic forces, and investment choices.

There is another way to motivate this focus on human capital, namely, the recent theories of endogenous economic growth (e.g., Becker and Murphy 1988; Lucas 1988; Barro 1991; Mankiw, Romer and Weil 1992; Barro and Salai-Martin 1992). These theories imply that if human to physical capital ratios are initially high, a country's subsequent economic performance will feature high rates of physical capital investment and rapid per capita income growth. Indeed, when Robert Barro applies these theories to cross-national data spanning the period between 1960 and 1985, he shows that growth is positively correlated with schooling levels in 1960, and the correlation is very strong. This is especially true of countries like Korea and

Japan (Barro 1991), whose growth rates were raised by as much as 1.5 percent per annum due to above average schooling commitments in 1960. My guess is that Barro's findings might be even stronger if his aggregate investment variable was replaced by equipment investment, as argued by DeLong and Summers.

Denison and Chung, Ohkawa and Rosovsky, and endogenous growth thinking have together thrown down a challenge. What attributes of earlier economic and social history explain the above average commitment to human resource development, like schooling, in some countries and the below average commitment in others? What would we learn if this kind of analysis were applied in a comparative way to all of the economies—fast growers and slow growers, rich and poor—along the Asian Pacific Rim? Oddly enough, very little comparative work of this sort has yet been applied systematically to the recent economic history of the Asian Pacific Rim. The time certainly seems ripe to do so since a fairly well-documented post-World War II history now stretches over almost four decades.

Not only is there great value in doing a comparative assessment of the sources of growth along the Asian Pacific Rim over the past quarter century, but we also need to understand far more about the underlying mechanisms which account for these sources. I believe one of the most important of these is the human capital-deepening, inequality, and demographic connection.

Age Distributions, Dependency Rates and Accumulation Responses

The implications of recent fertility and mortality trends for age distribution patterns and dependency rates are well known. What may not be quite so familiar is the enormous variance in those rates across the Asian Pacific Rim, and their projected

Table 2

Past, Present and Future Dependency Rates Along the Asian Pacific Rim

Country	Year	Age 0–14	Age 65+	Total	Ages 0–14 and 65+	
					Country j Minus Japan	Year 2010 Minus 1980
China	1950	35.4	4.9	40.3		
	1980	23.6	9.0	32.6	0.0	
	2010	17.4	19.5	36.9		+4.3
Japan	1950	33.5	4.5	38.0		
	1980	35.5	4.7	40.2	+7.6	
	2010	21.1	8.1	29.2		-11.0
Hong Kong	1950	30.3	2.6	32.9		
	1980	25.5	6.4	31.9	-0.7	
	2010	17.5	11.4	28.9		-3.0
South Korea	1950	41.7	3.1	44.8		
	1980	36.0	3.7	39.7	+7.1	
	2010	23.6	7.2	30.8		-8.6
Indonesia	1950	39.2	4.0	43.2		
	1980	41.0	3.3	44.3	-11.7	
	2010	25.2	6.3	31.5		-12.8
Malaysia	1950	40.9	5.1	45.5		
	1980	39.3	3.7	43.0	+10.4	
	2010	25.4	5.7	31.1		-11.9
Philippines	1950	43.6	3.6	47.2		
	1980	42.0	3.4	45.4	+12.8	
	2010	31.1	4.4	35.5		-9.9
Singapore	1950	40.5	2.3	42.8		
	1980	27.1	4.7	31.8	-0.8	
	2010	18.2	9.3	27.5		-4.3
Thailand	1950	42.5	3.0	45.5		
	1980	39.9	3.5	43.4	+10.8	
	2010	24.6	6.2	30.8		-12.6

Source: UN (1989:130–346), "medium variant".

trends over the next three decades. They may have very important economic implications for the region so it might be useful to review the evidence once more.

Table 2 reports past, present and future dependency rates. There we summarize United Nations data for the share of populations aged 14 years or less, aged 65 years or more, and the two combined. The data was readily available for nine countries along the Rim.

Although the table does not show it, some of these countries have undergone important declines in their dependency rates over the past three decades, but in such cases all of the decline appears to have been concentrated in the 1970s. Even so, the differences between Japan and the other eight nations are still enormous in 1980. Four of these are especially notable: the Philippines (whose dependency rate was 12.8 percent higher than Japan), Thailand (10.8 percent higher), Malaysia (10.4 percent higher), and Indonesia (11.7 percent higher). These differences are very large even compared with the spectacular historical fall in Japan's dependency rate since 1950. China and Korea also have higher dependency rates, though the differentials relative to Japan are not quite so high, 7.6 and 7.1 percent, respectively. The rich city states of Hong Kong and Singapore are much more like Japan.

Equally striking are the projected trends to the year 2010, and the correlation between those trends and the size of the 1980 Japan differential appears to be almost perfect. That is, dependency rates will have converged sharply along the Asian Pacific Rim over the three decades following 1980. Indeed, every single country will have dependency rates below Japan in 2010, a striking reversal in demographic features along the Rim. However, Japan will still have the lowest youth dependency rates since all of the projected rise in her dependency rate will be attributable to the impressive increase in those 65 and over. The distinction may matter not only to savings behavior, but also to human capital accumulation. As Allen Kelley (1988b:38) has recently pointed out, "in some countries we are beginning to see a decline in real per student expenditures on education at the same time that we observe an increase in real per capita spending on the aged [suggesting] a tension between generations in the allocation of the public purse."

What are the economic implications of these demographic trends along the Rim? The crudest cut at this problem is reported in Table 3. Here we first calculate GNP per worker by applying the 1980 labor participation rate (percent aged 15–64) to the 1981 GNP per capita estimates. Next we calculate GNP per capita in the year 2010 given the projected labor participation rate for that year, and assuming for the moment that GNP per worker remains unchanged. Finally, we report the implications of the drift in the labor participation rate over the three decades on per capita GNP growth rates. Note, first, the correlation between level of development and the growth rate impact. Poor countries along the Asian Pacific Rim gain the most, while Japan, in fact, loses. As it turns out, these demographic forces will also serve to help the slower growers[1] (Indonesia, the Philippines, Thailand, and Malaysia: Table 6), and in some cases they will help a lot.

The calculation in Table 3 is, of course, much too simple. It ignores the possibility that the decline in dependency rates everywhere along the Asian Pacific Rim, with the important exception of Japan, might quicken the rate of growth in labor productivity. The latter would take place if capital deepening was stimulated by the decline in the dependency rate.

Is there any reason to expect that the decline in the dependency rate will stimulate accumulation and capital deepening everywhere along the Asian Pacific Rim, outside Japan? Around 1970, the answer would have been an unambiguous affirmative. At that time, the views of Ansley

---

[1]The "slower" growers are identified by long-run performance over the 1960s and 1970s. Many of these countries have done very well, of course, in the 1980s and 1990s.

Table 3
Exploring the Dependency-Labor Participation Rate Impact on Growth Along the Asian Pacific Rim

Country	1981 GNP per Capita Index		1981 GNP per Worker Index Using 1980 Labor Participation Rate		2010 GNP per Capita Using 1981 GNP per Worker Index and 2010 Labor Participation Rate		Contribution to Growth Rate per Annum (%)
Japan	10,080	(1,000)	14,995	(1,000)	9,437	(1,000)	-0.23
Singapore	5,240	(520)	7,683	(514)	5,570	(590)	0.21
Hong Kong	5,100	(506)	7,489	(501)	5,325	(564)	0.15
Malaysia	1,840	(183)	3,228	(216)	2,224	(236)	0.66
Korea	1,700	(169)	2,819	(188)	1,951	(207)	0.48
Philippines	790	(78)	1,447	(97)	933	(99)	0.58
Thailand	770	(76)	1,360	(91)	941	(100)	0.69
Indonesia	530	(53)	952	(64)	652	(69)	0.72
China	300	(30)	502	(34)	355	(38)	0.58

Source: World Bank (1983), World Development Report. The 1981 GNP per capita figures are from the World Bank (1983: 148–9), World Development Report. The labor participation rates are shares aged 15–64, from Table 4.2.

Coale and Edgar Hoover (1958) dominated. Coale and Hoover focused their attention on the impact of fertility decline, rather than population growth itself. A decline in fertility, they argued, lowers the number of young dependents (augmenting savings rates), and raises female labor participation rates, thus fostering economic growth. Coale (1986) repeated the point more recently by showing that while population and per capita income growth may be poorly correlated, total fertility rates and per capita income growth are negatively correlated.

Nathanial Leff's (1969) pioneering empirical study confirmed the impact of dependency rate effects on conventional saving, ignoring potential human capital responses. Two decades or so late, the profession is far less certain, but Coale, Hoover and Leff would have suggested we proceed with the analysis which follows.

There have been a number of econometric studies which have estimated the impact of dependency rates on savings, and the estimated elasticity varies considerably from a high of -1.49 (Leff 1969), to a low of -0.13 (Singh 1975). Recent estimates for Asia alone appear to fall somewhere in the middle (Fry and Mason 1982; Fry 1984; both reported in Mason 1987, Table 4: 530). What would the implications of such estimates be for the Asian Pacific Rim? Table 4 offers some answers. There I pose two counterfactuals. First, what would each country's savings rate have been like had they had the advantage of Japan's lower dependency rate? Second, what will each country's future savings rate be like given the projected decline in dependency rates everywhere along the Rim (with the exception of Japan)? The results can be summarized most conveniently if we view the "middle" elasticity as most likely.

The implications emerging from Table 4 are striking. The slower growers would have enjoyed the most pronounced savings rate increases had they had Japan's more favorable dependency rates: Malaysia, a gain of 5.0 percentage points in her savings rate; the Philippines, a gain of 5.6; Thailand, a gain of 4.6; and Indonesia, a gain of 4.9. If these countries were

Table 4
Exploring the Dependency Rate-Savings Rate Connection along the Asia Pacific Rim

Country	Actual 1981 Gross Domestic Savings Rate (%)	Elasticity	Counterfactual Gross Domestic Savings Rate (%) Calculated at:	
			Japan's (1980) Dependency Rates	Projected 2010 Dependency Rates
China	28	High	35.9	39.4
		Middle	32.2	34.1
		Low	28.7	29.0
Japan	32	High	n.a.	5.7
		Middle	n.a.	28.6
		Low	n.a.	31.5
Hong Kong	24	High	23.2	27.4
		Middle	23.6	25.8
		Low	23.9	24.3
South Korea	22	High	27.9	29.3
		Middle	25.1	25.9
		Low	22.5	22.6
Indonesia	23	High	32.1	32.9
		Middle	27.9	28.3
		Low	23.8	23.9
Malaysia	26	High	35.4	36.7
		Middle	31.0	31.8
		Low	26.8	26.9
Philippines	25	High	35.5	33.1
		Middle	30.6	29.4
		Low	25.9	25.7
Singapore	33	High	31.8	39.6
		Middle	32.3	26.7
		Low	32.9	33.6
Thailand	23	High	31.5	32.9
		Middle	27.6	28.3
		Low	23.7	23.9

Source: The 1981 actual gross domestic savings rates are taken from World Bank (1983:156–7, Table 5), World Development Report. The counter factuals use the dependency rates (ages 0–14 and 65+) in Table 2, and the elasticity of savings rates with respect to dependency rates are: "high" (-1.49) (Leff 1969); "middle" (-0.80) (Adams 1971); and "low" (-0.13) (Singh 1975)—all reported in Hammer (1985:13).

n.a. = not available

really savings-constrained, then the calculation implies that the slower growers along the Asian Pacific Rim suffered significantly from high dependency rates. Assuming an incremental capital-output ratio (ICOR) of 4:1, it implies that Malaysia has a lower growth rate of 1.25 percent because of it (5.0 × .25 = 1.25). Had she not had that disadvantage, she would have closed a good share of the growth gap in 1960–1981 between herself and Japan (4.3 + 1.25 = 5.55 versus 6.3 for Japan: see Table 6). According to UN projections, that disadvantage will have disappeared by the year 2000. If the dependency rate-savings rate connection holds, the implications are for big future increases in savings rates among the poorer nations on the Asian Pacific Rim. In contrast, Japan's savings rate will decline by 3.4 percentage points. Again assuming an ICOR of 4:1, Table 4 implies that due to the dependency rate effect alone, growth rates in the poor, slower growing countries will converge on Japan: that is, Japan's 1961–1980 growth rate would drop to about 5.5 percent per annum by 2010, while that of the four slower growers would rise to something like 5.3 percent per annum.

These illustrative calculations certainly suggest that the dependency rate-savings rate connection has great potential for the Asian Pacific Rim. However, few development economists now believe that this Coale-Hoover-Leff argument holds.

The life-cycle model underlying the calculations came under attack in the early 1980s (Hammer 1985), especially for developing countries where the assumptions of the life-cycle model were more likely to be violated. Furthermore, post-Leff econometric studies taking a crude cut at the data concluded, prematurely it appears, that the dependency rate effect was generally weak (Kelley 1988a). Andrew Mason was one of the first to breathe new life into the thesis by more careful attention to the underlying economic argument (Mason 1986, 1988; and Collins 1989), and Matthew Higgins (1992) has brought to the debate the most comprehensive econometric analysis so far. Higgins has shown unambiguously that age structure matters: high dependency rates tend to lower savings rates (especially government savings rates), raise investment rates, *and* increase dependency on foreign capital. The latter result has been confirmed with late 19th century data during a period of massive international capital flows and when dependency rates were very high in the capital-importing New World (Taylor and Williamson 1991). These correlations between demographic dependence and foreign capital dependence are also revealed by Korea's switch from capital import to capital export in the late 1970s (Kang 1990). Finally, it seems relevant to point out Mason's finding (Mason 1986, 1988) that falling dependency rates raise savings primarily in fast-growing countries. Since so many of the East Asian countries have been fast growers in the post-World War II period, the argument developed here has even more to recommend it.

In any case, even that part of the literature which rejects the Coale-Hoover-Leff argument has failed to appreciate the implications of the result. If savings and investment rates will be unaffected by a fall in the dependency rate expected over the next three decades along the Asian Pacific Rim, then the rate of accumulation will also be unaffected, allowing the rate of capital deepening to accelerate if labor force growth rates eventually decline following the decline in dependency rates. That the effect of the dependency rate on savings is weak does not necessarily imply that the impact on the rate of capital deepening is weak, and it is the latter that matters.

Far more research needs to be done on the dependency rate-savings rate connection along the Asian Pacific Rim. If such research were forthcoming, one of the first tasks would be to determine whether in fact these economies are savings-constrained. If they are not, then the dependency rate effect would simply translate into changes in net foreign capital flows, not growth. But for many countries, like South Korea in the 1970s (Williamson 1979a), a reduction in external capital dependence has been an additional policy target, so even if these economies can be shown to be investment-driven, the dependency rate-savings rate connection still matters. Indeed, given the magnitude of the projected future changes in dependency rates along the Rim, it implies equally big changes in the patterns of external capital flows. We shall have more to say about this important inference in the next section.

The literature on the dependency rate-savings rate connection has also been much too narrow in the sense that it has ignored human capital responses, like schooling. Low dependency rates among the young imply sparsely populated cohorts among those of schooling age, placing weak demands on the schooling sector. The schooling sector is likely to respond by increasing the resources available per student, either crowding in some potential students who otherwise might not have attended, or raising the quality of the schooling of those who attend. Of course, low dependency rates among the young may also make it easier for parents to send their children to school. On the other hand, falling dependency rates in the future among the young are likely to coincide with rising dependency rates among the old, and, as Allen Kelley has pointed out, this may serve to deflect public resources from educating the young to supporting the old, especially among the more advanced countries in East Asia who have moved into more mature demographic stages. We need to learn more about the dependency rate-human capital connection, and later in this paper I will offer some evidence which suggests that it matters a great deal.

Further Speculations: Dependency Burdens, Equipment Prices and Policy

Policy debates along the Rim about the choice between inward-looking import substitution policies and outward-looking export oriented policies have been intense since the late 1950s. Thus, it is useful to remember one of the important insights of trade theory, the factor-price-equalization theorem (or what Heckscher in 1919 and Ohlin in 1924 called factor-price-convergence: see O'Rourke and Williamson 1992). That is, the relative wage of unskilled labor in poor countries should be raised by trade (since they export labor-intensive products), while the relative wage of skilled labor and capital should be lowered. The corollary of the theorem is that inward-looking policies should have the opposite effect in poor countries, augmenting capital scarcity and raising the skill premium (since they are used intensively in the protected import-competing sectors), while lowering the wages of the unskilled. These trade-induced factor price convergence predictions have not been explored systematically along the Rim, and they should be.

In addition, the same inward-looking policies should serve to raise the cost of importable capital equipment and machines. DeLong and Summers (1991, 1993) have shown for both developed and developing countries that where the relative price of machines is high, (deflated) investment in equipment is low and growth suffers.

To the extent that countries along the Rim with rapid rates of population growth and high dependency rates have also selected inward-looking policies, their recent history should be characterized by high skill premia and low equipment investment rates. Is there reason to expect this correlation between high dependency burdens and inward-looking policies along the Rim? Certainly Higgins' (1992) work cited earlier suggests so. Recall that Higgins found that high dependency rates in the post-World War II period have tended to foster external capital dependence and, presumably, pressure on the balance of payments. Historically, such pressure has been central in contributing to the adoption of inward-looking policies. Thus, there is reason to believe that high dependency rate regimes foster inward-looking policies, high equipment prices and slow accumulation.

These potential connection between dependency burdens, equipment prices, accumulation and inequality certainly seem plausible. What we need is explicit evidence from the Rim to test them.

The Inequality Connection

The classical economists developed their models of growth and development during the British industrial revolution when economic life was relatively simple. They could talk about three inputs—labor, land, and physical capital, and about three social classes—laborers, landlords, and capitalists. When dealing with the sources of growth, they could discuss physical capital accumulation, while ignoring human capital accumulation. When dealing with inequality, they could reduce the problem to the functional share trilogy—wages, rents, and profits, while ignoring the distribution of human capital. And when dealing with the Smithian trade-off, they could restrict their focus to the impact of redistribution on conventional savings, ignoring investment in schooling, health, housing, nutrition and migration. Late twentieth century economic life is more complex. Human capital matters to a far greater extent. This simple point is central to the trade-off debate and deserves amplification.

Support for the growth and equality trade-off has always rested on the belief that redistribution from the poor to the rich augments the supply of private saving and thus raises the rate of accumulation.[2] Not only was this belief central to 19th century models of growth and distribution developed by British economists to explain their industrial revolution, but it is also central to W. Arthur Lewis' (1954) labor surplus model and to recent debates over productivity slowdown in the advanced countries. In such models, the trade-off through marginal propensities to save (MPS). Any force redistributing income may raise aggregate savings and accumulation if those

---

[2]The next four paragraphs draw heavily on Lindert and Williamson (1985:342–359).

benefiting have higher mps's than the rest of society. Since higher income classes were always thought to have higher mps's, it would seem natural to conclude that any redistribution toward the rich would raise savings and capital accumulation. This argument should apply equally to 18th or 19th century redistributions through market forces and to 20th century redistributions through government action.

While intuitively plausible and a staple in political economy since Adam Smith, redistribution has had little quantitative impact, in fact, on the aggregate savings rate. True, even in Asia, distribution variables help explain aggregate savings rates (Williamson 1968). But when more sophisticated tools are applied, the trade-off seems modest. So say studies on aggregate United States data (Husby 1971; Blinder 1975), on Latin American data (Cline 1972), and on international cross-sections (Della Valle and Ogushi 1976; Musgrove 1980). Rough calculations for 19th century America (Williamson 1979b) and 19th century Britain (Williamson 1985) say the same. (See the summary in Williamson 1991, Lecture 3.)

With the spread of national independence, literacy and suffrage in the Third World, rejection of the Smithian trade-off gained momentum under the leadership of Robert McNamara and some World Bank economists (Chenery et al., 1974; Ahluwalia 1976, 1980). Their competing view was that the Third World overlooked a vast range of policy options that would enhance growth by raising the value of the poor's assets: investment in public health, mass education, and rural infrastructure.

Indeed, these are exactly the prescriptions which appear to be backed by so much of 20th century Asian experience. That is, the economic history of the Asian Pacific Rim appears to offer evidence which not only rejects the trade-off, but appears to offer some tentative support for the view that equality may foster growth. Consider the kind of evidence which encourages this revisionist position.

Table 5 augments Montek Ahluwalia's data (Ahluwalia 1976) with more recent country estimates from the World Bank, cross-sectional information which Ahluwalia used to explore the Kuznets Curve. Simon Kuznets (1955) hypothesized that inequality should rise with early development, falling as countries pass from NIC to advanced development stages. However, the upswing of the hypothesized Kuznets Curve has generated the most active debate. After all, the variance around any estimated Kuznets Curve is always greatest from low to middle levels of development. Thus inequality does not rise systematically across a pooled cross-section of early Industrial Revolutions. Even if many countries undergo increasing inequality during early modern economic growth, such correlations are bound to be poor since history has given less developed countries very different starting points.

Let me expand on this point a bit. Production in traditional agrarian economies tends to be driven by two inputs, land and unskilled labor. In some traditional agrarian economies, like the European Old World and the Latin American New World, the holdings of the asset which matters, land, was highly concentrated, much more highly concentrated than was human or physical capital in urban sectors (Griffin 1976; Hirashima 1978). The forces of inequality driven by industrialization must push hard to increase aggregate inequality in such economies as the sector where assets and incomes are most unequally distributed declines in relative importance. Such economies will have higher inequality in early stages of development, but they may exhibit less steep upswing on the Kuznets Curve. In contrast, other traditional agrarian economies, like East Asia, Africa, and the American North, had less concentrated land holdings and more equal agrarian income distributions. Such economies are likely to exhibit lower inequality in early stages of development, but they may exhibit more steep upswings on the Kuznets Curve, *ceteris paribus*. The *ceteris paribus* is important, since initial Latin inequality may have created a path dependent inegalitarian policy regime throughout the East

Table 5
The Kuznets Curve and the Virtuous Asians

Variable	Dependent Variable							
	Share of Bottom 20%				Share of Top 20%			
	[1]	[2]	[3]	[4]	[5]	[6]	[7]	[8]
Constant	26.16	23.81	26.90	28.78	-51.66	-39.67	-54.64	-62.26
	(4.32)	(4.30)	(4.62)	(4.95)	(1.84)	(1.47)	(2.00)	(2.23)
ln (GNP/POP)	-6.95	-6.35	-7.26	-7.67	36.96	33.92	38.22	40.55
	(3.60)	(3.39)	(3.91)	(4.21)	(4.14)	(3.96)	(4.39)	(4.89)
[ln (GNP/POP)]^2	0.54	0.50	0.57	0.60	-3.13	-2.93	-3.24	-3.41
	(3.61)	(3.46)	(3.93)	(4.22)	(4.52)	(4.43)	(4.79)	(5.30)
Dummy: ASIA		1.15				-5.90		
		(2.33)				(2.60)		
Dummy: PACIFIC RIM			1.29				-5.17	
			(2.35)				(2.02)	
Dummy: BIG 3				2.54				-12.27
				(2.95)				(3.24)
adjusted R^2	0.17	0.23	0.23	0.27	0.39	0.45	0.43	0.49
F-stat	6.52	6.52	6.56	7.88	18.80	16.15	14.65	18.28

Sources: Ahluwalia (1976:340–1); World Bank (1987: 252–3); *World Development Report*.

Notes: Figures in parentheses are t-statistics. The underlying data are taken from Ahluwalia (1976), excluding the socialist countries and augmented by Hong Kong and Indonesia in the *World Development Report*, World Bank. BIG 3 = Japan, Taiwan and Korea; PACIFIC RIM = BIG 3 plus Thailand, the Philippines, Malaysia, Hong Kong and Indonesia; ASIA = PACIFIC RIM plus Pakistan, Sri Lanka and India. The total sample includes 56 countries.

Asian industrial revolution. These issues of initial conditions and path dependence are important, and I will return to them later in this paper. They suggest that economic history is important to understanding contemporary events along the Asian Pacific Rim.

More to the point, however, Table 5 shows unambiguously that, after controlling for level of development, the Asian nations tend to have more egalitarian distributions. Thus, the coefficient on the dummy variable ASIA indicates that the eleven Asian countries in the sample (Hong Kong, Indonesia, Pakistan, Sri Lanka, India, Thailand, the Philippines, Korea, Taiwan, Malaysia and Japan) are significantly more egalitarian than the rest, and the differences are big. More or less the same results are forthcoming when only the Asian Pacific Rim countries are included (dummy variable PACIFIC RIM). When only Japan, Taiwan, and Korea are included (dummy variable BIG 3), the results are even more striking: on average, the top 20 percent claimed 12 percent less of total income compared with other countries at comparable stages of development.

These differences warrant explanations. We also need to know more about what contribution, if any, the more egalitarian distributions have made to impressive growth along the Asian Pacific Rim.

Not only are Asian nations more egalitarian, but the more egalitarian among them seem to have grown fastest during the post-World War II decades. Table 6 offers some World Bank data for sixteen nations, eight Asian along the Pacific Rim and eight Latin American. While the correlation between growth and equality is hardly perfect, the evidence not only rejects the Smithian trade-off postulate but suggests that equality may contribute to fast growth. That is, the four fast growers in East Asia had half the inequality than did the four slow growers in East Asia, and all eight of these East Asian countries had less than half the inequality than did the eight much slower growing Latin American countries.

	Table 6			
	Inequality and Growth: Which Drives Which?			
Country	GNP per capita growth, per annum (1960–81)	Income Share of Bottom 20%	Top 20%	Ratio Top to Bottom
VIRTUOUS ASIANS				
Fast growers:				
Korea (1976)	6.9	5.7	45.3	7.95
Hong Kong (1980)	6.9	5.4	47.0	8.70
Japan (1979)	6.3	8.7	37.5	4.31
Taiwan (1976)	6.6	9.5	35.0	3.68
Unweighted Average	6.7	7.3	41.2	5.64
Slower growers:				
Indonesia (1976)	4.1	6.6	49.4	7.48
The Philippines (1985)	2.8	5.2	52.5	10.10
Thailand (1975–76)	4.6	5.6	49.8	8.89
Malaysia (1973)	4.3	3.5	56.1	16.03
Unweighted Average	4.0	5.2	52.0	10.00
BAD LATINS				
El Salvador (1976–77)	1.5	5.5	47.3	8.60
Peru (1972)	1.0	1.9	61.0	32.11
Costa Rica (1971)	3.0	3.3	54.8	16.61
Brazil (1972)	5.1	2.0	66.6	33.30
Mexico (1977)	3.8	2.9	57.7	19.90
Panama (1973)	3.1	2.0	61.8	30.90
Argentina (1970)	1.9	4.4	50.3	11.43
Venezuela (1970)	2.4	3.0	54.0	18.00
Unweighted Average	2.7	3.1	56.7	18.29

Source: Inequality: World Bank (1987: 252–3, Table 26), *World Development Report*, and for Taiwan (Myers 1986: 24). Growth rates: World Bank (1983: 148–9, Table 1), *World Development Report*, and for Taiwan (1960–1978), World Bank (1980: 111, Table 1), *World Development Report*.

What might account for this pattern? There are four connections well worth pursuing, since they may have important implications for understanding dynamic growth along the Asian Pacific Rim. First, more egalitarian societies may find it easier to pursue pro-growth government policies. Second, more egalitarian societies may find it easier to accumulate human capital. Third, demographic forces—a glut in the young age groups—may have·contributed both to slow growth (via dependency rate effects and slow savings) and inequality (Paglin 1975; Kuznets 1976; Morley 1981). Fourth, there is the role of inward-looking versus outward-looking policies which, as argued above, may be related to demographic events, policies which are likely to have an impact on both accumulation and inequality. Not only do outward-looking policies encourage a labor-intensive growth path (with egalitarian implications), but they also contribute to high domestic investment rates by keeping the relative price of machines low.

Jeffrey Sachs (1987) recently reminded me of the potential inequality-growth connections which have been cited in the East Asian literature, and I think it might be useful to repeat these arguments.[3] Sachs and others have argued that by historical accident, Japan, Korea, and Taiwan were all forced to introduce fundamental land reforms in the late 1940s and early 1950s.[4] The conditions making the land reforms possible were, of course, unique, but in all three cases land reform virtually eliminated farm tenancy. In fact, it could be argued that these land reforms were among the greatest in modern history (Fei et al. (1979); Mason et al. (1980); Oshima (1988: S111); P. Kuznets (1988: S15)). Not only was land redistributed, raising incomes of the poor at the bottom of the distribution, but those with middle incomes did not have to pay much for the redistribution (through taxes) since the value of government bonds used to

---

[3]I have drawn liberally on Professor Sachs's paper for the remainder of this paragraph (Sachs, 1987:12–15).

[4]Sachs overdraws the case in three ways. First, he ignores the fact that Japan underwent important land reforms early in the Meiji Restoration. Second, he ignores the fact that the poor in all three countries had relatively high levels of literacy and access to public health long before the late 1940s. Third, he ignores the fact that, compared with Latin America, land was also more equally distributed in much of South East Asia (the Philippines being an obvious exception).

compensate the landlords at the top of the distribution were eroded away by rapid inflation. There was another force at work to redistribute wealth and income in these three economies—the destruction of wealth by war and inflation. Between 1935 and 1955, the wealth-income ratio in Japan declined precipitously from 4.15 to 2.20 (Egan 1985: 63). This massive decline in the wealth-income ratio had two effects: (i) it tended to equalize incomes, since the rich held most of the physical and financial assets destroyed; and (ii) it must have contributed to the impressive rise in the savings rate which was characteristic of Japan's dynamic postwar development, as individuals tried to restore the prewar wealth-income ratio. While I do not have similar evidence for Taiwan and Korea, some observers feel that the same forces may well have been at work there too, at least in Korea (Koo 1984; Oshima 1988: S16). This may offer one explanation for the rapid growth in Korea, Taiwan, and Japan relative to other nations along the Asian Pacific Rim.

These land reform explanations make much of historical accident in accounting for equality in Korea, Taiwan, and Japan (and China, of course; Perkins and Yusuf 1984: 105–130). What about the other eight countries underlying the ASIA dummy in Table 5? Here it might be helpful to stress comparative advantage and agricultural technologies. Rice culture is small scale, encouraging family farms, labor-intensive technology, and more egalitarian ownership. Sugar cane, coffee, and other export crops typical of 19th and 20th century in Latin America are large scale, encouraging commercial farms, inegalitarian ownership, and what Marx and British economic historians call a proletarianized agricultural labor market. This early specialization in different agricultural technologies is likely to have launched East Asia and Latin America on two quite different development paths.

So it is that Sachs and others argue that his inequality experience may have had important effects on postwar growth experience in these three dynamic economies. First, by replacing a tiny class of contentious landlords with a large class of contented peasants, the resulting political stability meant that government policy could focus attention on growth rather than rent-seeking. Second, the egalitarian revolution served to contribute to a minimum of labor unrest in the cities. Third, a dynamic agriculture was supported by protection and investment in rural infrastructure. As a result, a nationwide egalitarian distribution was reinforced by an egalitarian agriculture, and by small and declining income gaps between rural and urban areas. The agricultural sector is now, of course, very small in Japan, Korea, and Taiwan, but it is still very large in the developing countries in the South of the Asian Pacific Rim. We can add another item to Sachs's list. To repeat, a more egalitarian distribution may have served to foster a rapid rate of human capital accumulation as the liquidity-constrained poor— facing imperfect capital markets—were better able to finance such investments from their own resources. Surely these facts of history made it easier for the poor in Asia to invest in human capital than was true of their counterparts in Latin America or even in 18th century Britain. And surely these facts of history were translated into more interventionist government policies which favored mass education in East Asia (Oshima 1988: S109; 1987: 301–313) while suppressing it in Latin America and 18th century Britain.

It seems to me that we need far more research on this inequality connection. How much of the economic dynamism along the Asian Pacific Rim can be attributable to egalitarian distributions? If so, what were the strongest links? The pro-growth policy path outlined by Sachs? Human capital accumulation responses at the household level as the bottom income classes were better able to finance improved nutrition, education, migration and other forms of human capital creation? Human capital responses accommodated by an interventionist government heavily committed to mass education, sensitive to strong peasant lobbying interests? A contented and stable labor force which encouraged firms to invest in firm-specific training? And how much of the inequality in the slower growing nations can be attributed to demographic forces? This list of questions is much too ambitious to attempt an answer here, but I will try to shed some flickering light on one important part of the list—the schooling-inequality connection.

A Brief Glance at Some Historical Experience with Schooling

That there has been a revolutionary increase in human-capital deepening over the past century or so is well known, at least as it is reflected in formal schooling. We see it in enrollment rates (an investment flow per capita) and we see it in schooling achievement (a stock per capita). T. Paul Schultz (1987) recently documented the revolutionary magnitude of this schooling experience between 1960 and 1980, and I reproduce it here in Table 7.

The rise in the schooling indicators there has been truly spectacular. Even more striking is the fact that the percentage gains in schooling were greatest among the poor countries who had lower educational levels in 1960. The gap between rich and poor countries in what Schultz calls the "expected years of schooling" collapsed dramatically over those two decades. While such evidence might suggest to some that this catching up by the poor countries is a recent phenomenon, Richard Easterlin (1981) has shown that it has a much longer history. The sharp rise in enrollment rates in much of the Third World can be dated back at least to 1920, and in a few cases even in the late 19th century. Furthermore, Figure 2 suggests that these Third World countries were also closing the gap with America and the European leaders long before 1960. The only event that made the 1960–1980 period truly unique is how many more poor countries had joined the catching up club.

While there is evidence that the poor countries have been catching up to the rich in schooling investment rates, there is

Table 7

Growth in Educational Enrollment by School Level and Countries by Income Class, 1960–1981

World Bank Country Class (number)	Primary Education (6–11)		Secondary Education (12–17)		Higher Education (20–24)		Expected Years of Schooling		Percentage Increase in Enrollment Ratios (1960–81)			
									Primary	Secondary	Higher	Expected
	1960 (1)	1981 (2)	1960 (3)	1981 (4)	1960 (5)	1981 (6)	1960 (7)	1981 (8)	(9)	(10)	(11)	(12)
Low income (34)	0.80	0.94	0.18	0.34	0.02	0.04	5.98	7.88	18	89	100	32
Excluding China and India	0.38	0.72	0.07	0.19	0.01	0.02	2.75	5.56	89	171	100	102
Middle income (38)												
Oil exporters	0.64	1.06	0.09	0.37	0.02	0.08	4.48	8.98	66	311	300	100
Oil importers	0.84	0.99	0.18	0.44	0.04	0.13	6.32	9.23	18	144	225	46
Upper-middle income (22)	0.88	1.04	0.20	0.51	0.04	0.14	6.68	10.00	18	155	250	50
High-income Oil exporters (5)	0.29	0.83	0.05	0.43	0.01	0.08	2.09	7.96	186	760	700	281
Industrial market (18)	1.14	1.01	0.64	0.90	0.16	0.37	11.50	13.30	-11	41	131	16
East European non-market (8)	1.01	1.05	0.45	0.88	0.11	0.20	9.31	12.60	4	96	82	35

Source:　Schultz (1987: 417, Table 1).

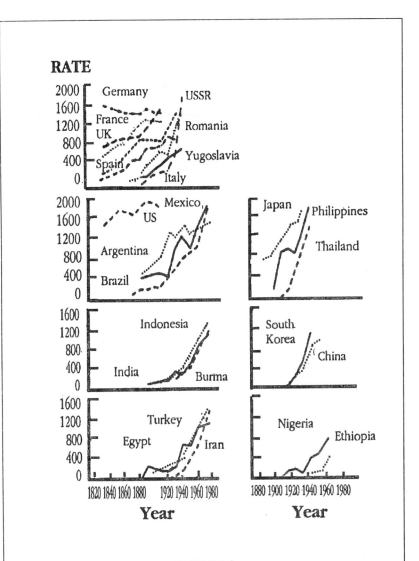

FIGURE 2

Primary School Enrollment Rates, 1830–1975
(per 10,000 population)

Source: Easterlin (1981: 8, Fig. 1)

considerable variance in performance nonetheless. In the 19th century, America and Germany had far higher educational commitments than did France and the United Kingdom, suggesting quite different education accumulation regimes. Furthermore, conditions along the Asian Pacific Rim over the past century look different. In 1900, the primary school enrollment rates were higher in Japan than they were in 1840 everywhere among the European industrial leaders (with the exception of Germany), and all of these countries were at comparable stages in their industrial revolutions. In addition, Figure 2 shows that Japan, the Philippines, Thailand, Korea and China all underwent far steeper increases in their commitment to educational investment after 1900 than did all the 19th century industrializers and almost all of the precocious developers in the 20th century Third World. The latter suggests that whatever the source of the heavy commitment to human capital accumulation along the Rim, it has its roots well back in history.

We can do a little better than the evidence presented in Figure 2. After all, the East Asian countries may have been able to raise their commitment to educational investment more rapidly from the late 19th century onwards simply because they may have enjoyed more rapid income growth for other reasons. Table 8 controls for that fact and also expands the sample of countries (to 85 in the 1970s). However, the dependent variable is limited to the secondary school enrollment ratio, since that will be our focus in the next section. Equations 8 and 9 include the full 20th century sample, including all countries as far back in times as the data made possible. Once again, considerable variety in country experience is documented—the Latin American countries always having invested less in secondary education, the East Asian countries always having invested more, and Korea, Japan, and Taiwan always having invested far more. Furthermore, these regional differences were more pronounced the farther back in history we look. That is, the East Asian dummy has its highest

Table 8

Has East Asia Always Invested More in Schooling?
Twentieth-century Secondary School Enrollment Ratio
(Dependent Variable = Log of Secondary Enrollment Ratio)

Equation	Time Period (Sample Size)	R^2	Constant	Log GNP or GDP Per Capita	Latin America Dummy	East Asia Dummy	S. Korea/ Japan/ Taiwan Dummy	Other East Asia Dummy
(1)	Pre-1950 (315)	0.739	-2.517 (76.240)	0.904 (15.327)	-0.746 (8.997)	1.966 (19.338)	—	—
(2)	1950–59 (482)	0.486	-2.005 (44.205)	0.879 (18.629)	-0.474 (6.091)	1.254 (9.963)	—	—
(3)	1950–59 (482)	0.495	-2.006 (44.573)	0.873 (18.610)	-0.475 (6.148)	—	1.539 (9.662)	0.887 (4.974)
(4)	1960–69 (732)	0.574	-1.801 (56.872)	0.860 (29.164)	-0.134 (2.193)	1.039 (11.220)	—	—
(5)	1960–69 (732)	0.577	-1.802 (57.029)	0.891 (30.790)	-0.134 (2.191)	—	1.220 (9.739)	0.845 (6.528)
(6)	1970–79 (449)	0.561	-1.568 (46.338)	0.685 (22.247)	0.037 (0.540)	0.675 (6.477)	—	—
(7)	1970–79 (449)	0.565	-1.569 (46.538)	0.654 (22.171)	0.038 (0.558)	—	0.884 (6.169)	0.496 (3.286)
(8)	Total 20th Century (1,978)	0.486	-1.916 (90.755)	0.816 (39.207)	-0.280 (6.847)	1.135 (18.383)	—	—
(9)	Total 20th Century (1,978)	0.490	-1.916 (91.120)	0.814 (39.211)	-0.280 (6.870)	—	1.319 (17.109)	0.849 (8.958)

Notes: For the pre-1950 period in equation (1), the East Asian sample is limited to Japan. The dependent variable is the log ratio of those in secondary school to secondary school age population.

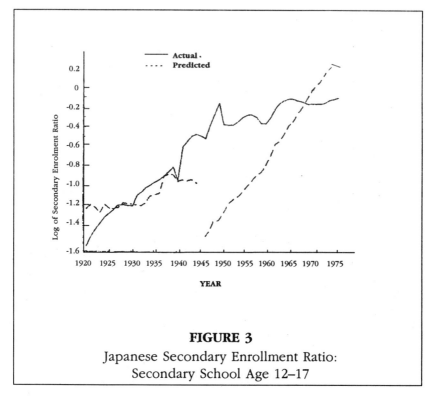

FIGURE 3
Japanese Secondary Enrollment Ratio:
Secondary School Age 12–17

coefficient for the pre-1950 period, falling somewhat in the 1950s, falling again in the 1960s, and falling still more in the 1970s. The same trend is apparent for Korea, Japan, and Taiwan. Furthermore, Figure 3 shows that while Japan has had, since 1930, higher secondary enrollment rates than would be predicted from Table 8 (equation [1]), the biggest gap between actual and predicted occurred in the 1940s and 1950s, a gap that disappeared by the 1970s. Thus, while East Asia has always invested more in secondary schooling compared with other nations at comparable stages of development, that edge has diminished over time. Whatever are the forces which have produced the heavy commitment to educational investment along the Asian Pacific Rim, they are rooted deeply in the past,

but they have weakened over time. The same has been true of
Latin America. While Latin America has always underinvested
in secondary education, the historical forces that account for
that result appear to have weakened over time as the negative
coefficient on the Latin American dummy declines systematically
from the pre-1950 period to the 1970s.

Why does history show so much variance between countries
in the commitment to schooling? Why is it that East Asia seems
to have made the bigger commitment and Latin America the
smaller commitment, patterns that clearly emerge in the
residuals from Schultz's model (1987:447)? Why have these regional differences diminished over time?

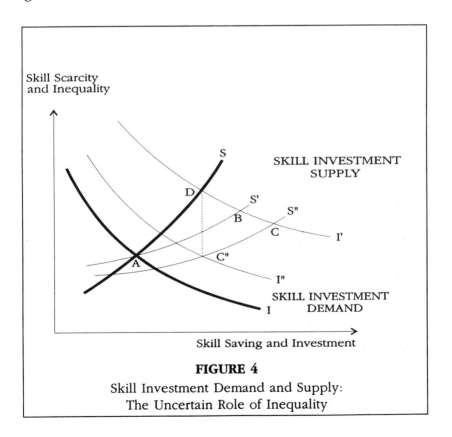

FIGURE 4

Skill Investment Demand and Supply:
The Uncertain Role of Inequality

Schooling, Inequality, Dependency Rates and Culture

If the argument emerging is plausible, then I should see a negative correlation between inequality and the commitment to education investment. That is, I should be able to find historical evidence that rejects the Smithian trade-off even more soundly when investment is augmented to include human capital. Unfortunately, history tends to be unkind to simple mono-causal theories like this one. Figure 4 tells us why. While changes in income and earnings inequality are highly correlated—a proposition which has been confirmed at least by the economic histories of Britain and America (Williamson 1991, Lecture 1), levels of earnings and income inequality need not be. Thus, while we can put both skill scarcity and earnings inequality on the vertical axis, we must remember that different economies with the same earnings inequality may have different income inequality due to the initial distribution of land and other factors like those listed above for East Asia. Along the horizontal axis we have what might be called skill saving and investment, like school enrollment rates. Let some industrial revolutionary event create a boom in skill investment demand, written here as a shift to I'. Left solely to private sector responses, one economy with more inequality and lower incomes for the poor might exhibit an inelastic response to the skill scarcity starting at A and ending at D. Another more egalitarian economy is likely to find its poor better able to respond to skill scarcity ending up at B. This more egalitarian economy is also likely to set in motion political forces to increase the commitment to public education, perhaps shifting the skill investment supply function to the right, generating a new equilibrium at C. Were that all there was to the story, we would have the historical correlation we are looking for, equality associated with high investment in skills and a rejection of the trade-off. However, there is no reason to expect that all countries will be faced with the same demand forces. Suppose the more egalitarian economy pursues a more unskilled-labor intensive growth regime (perhaps associated with outward-looking policy as discussed above) so that the boom in skill investment demand is muted, say to I". The new equilibrium for the more egalitarian economy is now at C". What will history now reveal? No correlation at all between inequality and investment in skills since D and C" imply the same commitment to human capital accumulation.

Can we unravel the influence of growth regime from skill supply response when assessing the trade-off? Which has dominated in the past? Nineteenth century Britain clearly looks like the inequality-regime scenario which moves along the path from A to D (Williamson 1985, Ch. 7), much like contemporary Brazil, while East Asia looks more like the egalitarian-regime scenario which moves along the path from A to C or C". But we need more evidence, and for this I turn once more to Schultz's 1987 paper.

Using a price dual of the production of school services and an aggregate demand for school services, Schultz estimated a reduced-form equation for school expenditures per child and enrollment rates, based on a large world cross-section countries. While Schultz includes a wide range of explanatory variables, three account for the vast majority of the variance: income, or GNP per adult; the relative price of teachers, or teacher cost relative to GNP per adult; and relative cohort size, or share of population school aged. What is missing from the model, however, is an explicit statement of the market forces generating different investment demand for education, or of the income distributional forces influencing educational supply responses. I have been able to add the latter to his model, but, alas, not the former.

Table 9 presents the results for a somewhat smaller sample than Schultz's, since income distributional evidence is available for fewer countries (but the sample does include the following along the Rim: Japan, Korea, Hong Kong, Malaysia, the Philippines, and Thailand). Only two dependent variables (all

Table 9

Estimates of Secondary School Expenditures and Components
with the Price of Teachers Exogenous:

(35 Countries, 1960–1980)

Explanatory Variable	Enrollment Ratio*	Total Expenditure per Secondary School Age Child*
GNP per adult in 1970 (log)	0.313	1.330
	(2.379)	(10.931)
Relative price of teachers (log)	-0.457	0.629
	(5.272)	(7.839)
Proportion of population urban	0.346	0.644
	(0.608)	(1.222)
Proportion of population of secondary school age	-1.860	-6.261
	(0.809)	(2.944)
National household income distribution (bottom 40%/top 20%)	0.796	0.956
	(1.234)	(1.603)
Intercept	-3.045	-5.638
	(4.410)	(8.820)
R^2	0.831	0.956

Notes: * in logarithms; relative price of teachers is treated as exogenous and estimated with ordinary least squares. Absolute values of t-ratio are reported in parentheses beneath regeression coefficient.

in logs) are reported in the table: the enrollment ratio and expenditure per school-aged child. Furthermore, the analysis is limited to secondary education where the variance across countries is greatest. The explanatory variables include four of Schultz's—income, the relative price of teachers, percent urban, and the share of the population of secondary school age, plus our added distributional variable. To repeat, our expectations here are: Given GNP per adult, the country with the more equal income distribution is likely to have the stronger schooling demands, and thus the higher enrollment rates. I am motivated by the suspicion that this is why Schultz finds positive residuals for East Asia where, as we have seen, incomes have been far more equally distributed in the postwar period. Any extension of Schultz's analysis to the Asian Pacific Rim should pursue this connection between inequality and schooling. While we are all aware of the impressive schooling commitment along the Asian Pacific Rim, we need to know why. Can it be explained in part by income inequality patterns, or is the explanation wholly cultural?

The estimated parameters on Schultz's variables more or less reproduce his results. Let's take each in turn.

First, educational commitment rises with income (GNP per adult), and the elasticity on total expenditures is high enough, about 1.3, so that the schooling investment share rises with development.

Second, urbanization has no significant impact on educational commitment.

Third, there is strong evidence supporting the Coale and Hoover dependency-rate effect. Cohort size effects are, of course, tied closely to the dependency rate effects discussed at length in section II. Any increase in the relative size of the school-aged population will put pressure on the educational system, the latter accommodating the pressure by spreading resources more thinly across the school population and lowering schooling quality. That is, and according to Table 9, a Malthusian glut of school-aged children tends only weakly to crowd children out of the schools (the t-statistic on the enrollment ratio is small), but it has a very powerful negative effect on expenditures per school-aged child. The elasticity here is very high, -6.261, and, given the weak impact on the number of children in school, it implies that the expenditure commitment per enrolled child declines as human capital-widening diverts resources from human capital-deepening. In short, the quality of education in the secondary schools must be very sensitive to the size of the school-aged cohort. One can only conclude that the high dependency rates in 1980 among the poorer countries to the South along the Rim has inhibited their human capital accumulation and contributed to their slower growth compared with those to the North where the Malthusian forces have been far less pronounced. One must also conclude that the enormous projected decline in the dependency rates up to 2010 along the Rim (see Table 2) will have a big positive impact on growth potential if the quality of schooling matters as we think it does.

Fourth, the relative price of teachers matters, a result that is symmetric to the DeLong and Summers (1991, 1993) finding that the relative price of equipment matters. Expenditures on teachers are by far the biggest component of direct schooling costs, and the relative price of teachers serves to tell us how well the schooling sector is doing in keeping up with the growth in demand. When teacher prices rise, schooling costs per child rise, and the quantity of schooling may be choked off as a consequence. If the demand for schooling is price inelastic, total expenditures on schooling may, of course, rise, but enrollment rates—the critical proxy for human capital deepening—will decline. In short, where the relative price of teachers is high (that is, where schooling-capital goods are expensive), fewer children are educated (the enrollment rates are low). This is exactly what we find in Table 9. And the demand for schooling is price inelastic (about -0.5), so that expenditure rates are swollen where the relative price of teachers is high. This is an important finding which deserves stress. Given the quality of education, it's the quantity of schooling (enrollment rates) that matters to future economy-wide productivity growth, not the expenditures committed to schooling. If we are looking for evidence of human-capital deepening, we need to look at (quality-adjusted) enrollment rates and levels of educational attainment, not the dollars committed to schooling. Furthermore, and to restate the obvious, the finding that the relative price of teachers matters suggests that current schooling performance will be conditioned by previous commitments to schooling. The heavy commitments to schooling along the Rim in the 1960s and 1970s would have been much harder to achieve without the heavy commitments to schooling in the 1940s and 1950s.

Finally, income distribution has the predicted effect: more egalitarian societies (where the bottom 40% have high income shares relative to the top 20%) make a greater commitment to education—they have higher enrollment rates, and they commit more resources to each child enrolled. However, the t-statistics are lower than we conventionally accept. There is no evidence here which supports the Smithian trade-off, but there is also only weak evidence which confirms the contrary view. I suspect the reason for those small t-statistics on the income distribution variable in Table 9 can be found in Figure 4: societies with high inequality also pursue growth regimes that generate big booms in skill investment demand like that at I', while the opposite is true of more egalitarian societies. I have not been able to prove that assertion unambiguously, and it seems to me to have high research priority. And any such project should simultaneously explore the connections suggested by Higgins (1992) and DeLong and Summers (1991, 1993).

What about the role of culture? In Harry Oshima's words, "besides asserting the importance of the rise of Protestant ethics in the emergence of capitalism in the West, ...Max Weber thought that Confucianism and Mahayana Buddhism of the East Asians were more favorable to the development of a capitalist society (Oshima 1988: S108)" than was Catholicism. Can we find evidence in support of this proposition in attitudes towards schooling in the 1970s? Schultz found some evidence to support that view in his secondary education regressions (Schultz 1987:449, Table 14), but his negative residuals for Latin America were far larger than his positive residuals for East Asia. But since income inequality is so highly correlated with region—low in East Asia and high in Latin America, we cannot include inequality and the regional dummies in the same regression. Therefore, we still don't know whether and how "culture" mattered.

A Concluding Remark

There is certainly no shortage of research tasks still left undone regarding the contribution of human capital deepening to economic dynamism along the Asian Pacific Rim. I am convinced that a systematic comparative assessment of the recent economic histories along the Rim will teach us a great deal about that contribution. The enterprise, however, will have to draw on more than one corner of the discipline. Rather, it will have to integrate Coale and Hoover's insights into dependency rate burdens, the theorems of trade theory and the new growth theory.

References

Adam, N. (1971) "Dependency Rates and Savings Rates: Comment," *American Economic Review* June: 472–475.

Ahluwalia, M. (1976) "Inequality, Poverty and Development," *Journal of Development Economics* 3: 307–342.

_____. (1980) "Growth and Poverty in Developing Countries," in H. Chenery (ed.). *Structural Change and Development Policy.* New York: Oxford: 45–95.

Barro, R.J. (1991) "Economic Growth in a Cross Section of Countries," *Quarterly Journal of Economics* 106, 2; May: 407–43.

_____ and X. Sala-i-Martin (1992) "Convergence," *Journal of Political Economy* 100, 2; April: 223–51.

Becker, G.S. and K.M. Murphy (1988) "Economic Growth, Human Capital, and Population Growth," mimeo. University of Chicago, June.

Blinder, A.S. (1975) "Distribution Effects and the Aggregate Consumption Function," *Journal of Political Economy* 83: 447–475.

Chenery, H. et al. (ed.) (1974) *Redistribution with Growth.* London: Oxford.

Cline, W.R. (1972) *Potential Effects of Income Redistribution on Economic Growth: Latin American Cases.* New York: Praeger.

Coale, A.J. (1986) "Population Trends and Economic Development," in J. Menken (ed.). *World Population and US Policy: The Choice Ahead.* New York: Norton.

_____ and E. Hoover (1958) *Population Growth and Economic Development in Low-Income Economies.* Princeton, N.J.: Princeton.

Collins, S. (1989) "Savings Behavior in Ten Developing Countries," paper given at the NBER Conference on Savings, (Maui, Hawaii, January 6–7).

DeLong, J.B. and L.H. Summers (1991) "Equipment Investment and Economic Growth," *Quarterly Journal of Economics* 106; May: 445–502.

_____. (1993) "How Strongly Do Developing Economies Benefit from Equipment Investment?" Department of Economics, Harvard University. March.

Della Valle, P.A. and N. Ogushi (1976) "Distribution, the Aggregate Consumption Function and the Level of Development: Some Cross-Country Results," *Journal of Political Economy* 84: 1325–1334.

Denison E.F. and W.K. Chung (1976) *How Japan's Economy Grew So Fast.* Washington, D.C.: Brookings.

Easterlin, R.A. (1981) "Why Isn't the Whole World Developed?," *Journal of Economic History* 41; March: 1–19.

Egan, E.L. (1993) *The Effects of World War II Wealth Destruction on the Savings Rate in Postwar Japan,* Seniors Honors Thesis, Harvard University. March.

Fei, J.C.H., G. Ranis and S.W.Y. Kuo (1979) *Growth with Equity: The Taiwan Case.* New York: Oxford University Press.

Fry, M.J. (1984) "Terms of Trade and National Savings Rates in Asia," mimeo. University of California-Irvine.

_____ and A. Mason (1982) "The Variable Rate of Growth Effect in the Life-Cycle Saving Model," *Economic Inquiry.* 426–442.

Griffin, K. (1976) *Land Concentration and Rural Poverty.* London: Macmillan.

Hammer, J.S. (1985) "Population Growth and Savings in Developing Countries," World Bank Staff Working Paper No. 687. Washington, D.C.: World Bank.

Higgins, M. (1992) "The Demographic Determinants of Savings, Investment and International Capital Flows." Department of Economics, Harvard University, Fall.

Hirashima, S. (1978) *The Structure of Disparity in Developing Agriculture.* Tokyo: Institute of Developing Economies.

Husby, R.D. (1971) "A Nonlinear Consumption Function Estimated from Time-Series and Cross-Section Data," *Review of Economics and Statistics* 53: 76–79.

Kang, K.H. (1990) "Korean Savings and a Life Cycle Model." Department of Economics, Harvard University.

Kelley, A.C. (1986) "The Demise of the Age-Dependency Argument: Lessons and Puzzles from Africa," revised 1987 version of paper presented to the IUSSP Seminar on the Consequences of Population Trends in Africa, (Nairobi, December 8–10).

_____. (1988a) "Economic Consequences of Population Change in the Third World," *Journal of Economic Literature* 26; December: 1685–1728.

_____. (1988b) "Australia: The Coming of Age," *Research Paper No. 194.* Department of Economics, The University of Melbourne. April.

Koo, H. (1984) "The Political Economy of Income Distribution in South Korea: The Impact of the State's Industrialization Policies," *World Development* 12; October.

Kuznets, P.W. (1988) "An East Asian Model of Economic Development: Japan, Taiwan, and South Korea," *Economic Development and Cultural Change* 36, 3 Supplement; April: S11–S43.

Kuznets, S. (1955) "Economic Growth and Income Inequality," *American Economic Review* 45: 1–28.

_____. (1976) "Demographic Aspects of the Size Distribution of Income: An Exploratory Essay," *Economic Development and Cultural Change* 25: 1–94.

Leff, N. (1969) "Dependency Rates and Savings Rates," *American Economic Review* 59: 886–896.

Lewis, W.A. (1954) "Economic Development with Unlimited Supplies of Labor," *Manchester School of Economic and Social Studies* 22: 139–191.

Lindert, P.H. and J.G. Williamson (1985) "Growth, Equality and History," *Explorations in Economic History* 22; October: 341–377.

Lucas, R.E. (1988) "On the Mechanics of Economic Development," *Journal of Monetary Economics* 22: 3–42.

Mankiw, N.G., D. Romer and D.N. Weil (1992) "A Contribution to the Empirics of Economic Growth," *Quarterly Journal of Economics* 107; May: 407–37.

Mason, A. (1987) "National Savings Rates and Population Growth: A New Model and New Evidence," in D. Johnson and R. Lee (eds.). *Population Growth and Economic Development: Issues and Evidence*. Wisconsin.

_____. (1988) "Saving, Economic Growth and Demographic Change," *Population and Development Review* 14; March: 113–114.

_____. et al. (1986) *Population Growth and Economic Development: Lessons from Selected Asian Countries*, Policy Development Study No. 10. New York: UN Fund for Population Activities.

_____. et al. (1980) *The Economic and Social Modernization of the Republic of Korea*. Cambridge, Mass.: Harvard University Press.

Morley, S.A. (1981) "The Effect of Changes in the Population on Several Measures of Income Distribution," *American Economic Review* 71: 285–294.

Musgrove, P. (1980) "Income Distribution and the Aggregate Consumption Function," *Journal of Political Economy* 88: 504–525.

Ohkawa, K. and H. Rosovsky (1973) *Japanese Economic Growth: Trend Acceleration in the Twentieth Century*. Stanford, Cal.: Stanford University Press.

O'Rourke, K. and J.G. Williamson (1992) "Were Heckscher and Ohlin Right? Putting History Back into the Factor-Price-Equalization Theorem," *Discussion Paper No. 1593.* Harvard Institute of Economic Research, · May.

Oshima, H.T. (1988) "Human Resources in East Asia's Secular Growth," *Economic Development and Cultural Change* 36, 3 Supplement; April: S103–S122.

_____. (1987) *Economic Growth in Monsoon Asia: A Comparative Study.* Tokyo: University of Tokyo Press.

Paglin, M. (1975) "The Measurement and Trend of Inequality: A Basic Revision," *American Economic Review* 65: 598–609.

Perkins, D.H. and S. Yusuf (1984) *Rural Development in China,* Baltimore, Md.: Johns Hopkins University Press.

Sachs, J.D. (1987) "Trade and Exchange Rate Policies in Growth-Oriented Adjustment Programs," *NBER Working Paper No. 2226.* NBER, Cambridge, Mass., April.

Schultz, T.P. (1987) "School Expenditures and Enrollments, 1960–80: The Effects of Income, Prices, and Population Growth," in D. G. Johnson and R. Lee (eds.). *Population Growth and Economic Development: Issues and Evidence.* Madison, Wisconsin.

Singh, S. (1975) *Development Economics: Some Findings.* Lexington, MA: D. C. Heath.

Taylor, A.M. and J.G. Williamson (1991) "Capital Flows to the New World as an Intergenerational Transfer," *Discussion Paper No. 1579.* Harvard Institute for Economic Research, December.

United Nations (1989) *Global Estimates and Projections of Population by Sex and Age: The 1988 Revision.* New York: UN ST/ESA/SER.R/93.

Williamson, J.G. (1968) "Personal Saving in Developing Nations: An Intertemporal Cross-Section from Asia," *Economic Record*: 194–210.

_____. (1979a) "Why Do Koreans Save 'So Little'?" *Journal of Development Economics* 6: 343–362.

_____. (1979b) "Inequality, Accumulation, and Technological Imbalance: A Growth-Equity Conflict in American History?" *Economic Development and Cultural Change* 44, 3; January: 231–253.

_____. (1985) *Did British Capitalism Breed Inequality?* London: Allen and Unwin.

_____. (1991) *Inequality, Poverty, and History: The Kuznets Memorial Lectures.* Oxford: Basil Blackwell.

_____. (1993) "Human Capital Deepening, Inequality and Demographic Events Along the Asia-Pacific Rim," in N. Ogawa, G. W. Jones and J. G. Williamson (eds.). *Human Resources in Development Along the Asia-Pacific Rim.* Singapore: Oxford University Press.

_____ and P.H. Lindert (1980) *American Inequality: A Macroeconomic History.* New York: Academic Press.

World Bank (1980, 1983, 1987) *World Development Report.* Oxford: Oxford University Press.

The Relationship Between Growth and Financial Markets: Some Outstanding Theoretical Issues

*Roberto S Mariano & Tayyeb Shabbir**

Introduction

After a long period of apparent neglect, the Schumpeterian idea that developed financial markets can positively affect economic growth by facilitating savings and more efficient allocation of capital has come to enjoy new popularity amongst academics and policy-makers alike. This renewed interest in the idea has spurred a flurry of theoretical work and a few interesting empirical studies both for the developed as well as the developing countries.

*Respectively, Professor of Economics, Department of Economics, University of Pennsylvania, and Senior Research Economist, Pakistan Institute of Development Economics, Islamabad and Department of Economics, University of Pennsylvania. An earlier draft of this paper was presented at the Sixth Biennial Conference on U.S.-Asia Economic Relations on 16–18 May 1994, Brandeis University. The authors are grateful to Gregory Chow, Malcolm Dowling, Richard Hooley, Lawrence R. Klein, and Hugh Patrick for insightful comments on this paper at the conference. The authors also acknowledge partial research support from the University of Pennsylvania Research Foundation. Tayyab Shabbir is grateful to Professor Syed Nawab Haider Naqvi, Director of the Pakistan Institute of Development Economics, for encouragement and providing an opportunity to work in this project.

Though it may appear as an intuitively appealing idea that the various financial intermediaries such as the money, bond, and foreign-exchange markets as well as the stock markets should be essential for economic growth, since they facilitate mobilization of savings, efficient allocation of capital, risk management through portfolio diversification and positive inducement for the society to increase its rate of savings, there has been a surprising lack of consensus among economists on the nature of the role of capital markets in economic growth. As a matter of fact, until recently, with the exception of the seminal papers of McKinnon (1973) and Shaw (1973), most economists generally dismissed as secondary at best the potential role of financial intermediaries in promoting economic development. A part of the reason for this state of affairs was conceptual—perhaps a lack of rigor in theories linking financial intermediation to growth—and part empirical—little reliable evidence establishing that finance causes growth. However, recent theoretical developments link more firmly finance with steady-state growth (Greenwood and Jovanovic 1990), and, concurrently, empirical evidence has been accumulating which implies that financial intermediation positively affects economic growth (Goldsmith (1969), King and Levine (1993), and Atje and Jovanovic (1993)). A related study of interest is Ratcliffe (1994) which uses the Lucas (1990, 1993) framework to address the issue of why capital does not flow from the rich to the poor countries when rates of return on it differ even after adjustments for degree of financial intermediation, human capital, and tax incidence.

On account of the great interest in the recent phenomenon of the emerging stock markets, the issue of the relationship between financial markets and growth and international capital flows has gained an additional measure of importance. Financial deregulation or liberalization and a tremendous inflow of portfolio investment in 1993 has spurred a phenomenal growth in emerging equities markets, especially in Asia, e.g., China, the Philippines, Malaysia, and India.

The main purpose of this paper is to characterize some of the recent theoretical developments in analyzing the relationship between financial intermediation and economic growth and offer some preliminary observations regarding the possible directions in which this literature could grow. The rest of the paper is organized such that Section 2 briefly notes the role or the major functions of financial markets; Section 3 characterizes two main representative models of the relationship between the financial sector and growth; Section 4 discusses the question of causality (or endogeneity) regarding the financial and real sectors; Section 5 contains a few observations; and finally Section 6 sketches a proposed theoretical framework and outlines empirical work we are considering to undertake.

Role of Financial Markets

In general, well-functioning financial markets play many important roles that affect economic growth:

First, by spreading the risks of long-term investment projects, the growth of the financial markets can lead to a lower cost of equity capital and thereby stimulate investment and growth.

Second, by acting as monitor and facilitator, these markets could lead to a greater efficiency of the available investment funds.

Third, by attracting foreign portfolio capital, developed financial markets can serve to enhance the supply of investible resources, particularly in the developing countries. This feature is particularly attractive for highly-indebted countries whose traditional sources of foreign financing, such as grants and concessional loans, are rapidly drying up.

Fourth, financial markets also play a role in domestic resource mobilization and the provision of fresh equity capital to the corporate sector. This is particularly important in emerging capital markets where the expansion of stock markets is often characterized by an increase in the number of companies going public.

For the developing countries, some useful preliminary work already has been done which tries to enumerate the nature of the linkages between financial development and economic growth (see Clemente and Mariano (1992, 1993) and Dailami and Atkin (1990)). However, there is a significant need to generate formal empirical evidence on this question.

Modeling the Relationship between the Financial Sector and Economic Growth

Physical Capital, Financial Development, and Economic Growth

Using a simple model, Greenwood and Jovanovic (1991) and Atje and Jovanovic (1993) formalize the above ideas regarding the effects of financial development and economic growth[1] with the following aggregate production function as a starting point:

$$Y = K \min (L, L^*)^a \quad a > 0 \tag{1}$$

where output (Y) is expressed in terms of physical capital (K) and labor (L); and L^* represents the labor capacity-constraint. At full employment of labor .we get the following constant returns to scale production function:

$$Y = K (L^*)^a = mK \tag{1'}$$

where $m = (L^*)^a = Y/K$ = output-capital ratio at full employment.

Capital accumulation in this economy is given by:

$$K_{t-1} = (1 - d) K_t + R (F_t) I_t \tag{2}$$

---

[1] In fact, much of the discussion in Atje and Jovanovic (1993) uses Greenwood and Jovanovic (1991) as its point of departure.

Here d represents the rate of depreciation of capital stock, I represents investment, F is the level of financial intermediation, and R is a function of F and is meant to formalize the positive impact of financial intermediation on the rate of return on investment. This impact essentially works through improved allocation of investible resources on account of portfolio diversification and informational efficiencies. Atje and Jovanovic (1993) assume $R(\bullet)$ to be an increasing function of F. A more general approach would be to model $R(\bullet)$ more explicitly, starting with a non-monotonic formulation to allow for an empirical test of the monotonicity of R.

Let $g_X = (X_{t-1} - X_t)/X_t$, i.e., the annual rate of growth of a variable X. Then g_K is given by the following expression:

$$g_K = -d + R(F_t)(I_t/K_t) \tag{3}$$

$$= -d + R(F_t)(Y_t/K_t)(I_t/Y_t)$$

$$= -d + mR(F_t) z_t$$

at full employment, where z_t is the investment-output ratio. At steady state, where output, capital, and labor are growing at the same rate, the growth rate of income per worker is then

$$g_Y - g_L = g_K - g_L = -d - g_L + mR(F_t) z_t \tag{4}$$

Using a first-order Taylor's expansion of R around $F = 0$ gives us

$$R(F_t) \approx R(0) + R'(0)F_t$$

$$g_Y - g_L = -d - g_L + mR(0)z_t + mR'(0)z_tF_t \tag{5}$$

One of the major issues of interest is the nature of the financial intermediation index, F, and numerical proxies for it. Though far from representing a consensus, Atje and Jovanovic (1993) considered the following indices (all normalized by GDP):

$B =$ (credit extended by private and government banks)/ GDP

F_1 = (annual value of all stock market trades)/GDP

F_2 = (value of stocks outstanding)/GDP

While each of the above indices can be used by themselves, $(B + F_2)$ can be used as a composite measure of bank loans and value of equity. However, adding B and F_1 is not feasible as the former is a stock and the latter is a flow.

In principle, once a decision is made regarding how best to measure F, one needs only to assume that m (the inverse of the capital-output ratio) is invariant across countries to be able to use equation (5) to estimate cross-country regressions.

Then the following derivative would give the estimated "importance of finance" in terms of the growth rate of per capita income:

$$\partial(g_Y - g_L) / \partial F = mR'(0)z = \beta z.$$

For an empirical implementation of this model, equation (5) suggests the regression of $(g_Y - g_L)$ on the growth rate of labor (g_L)m the investment-output ratio, and the interaction between financial intermediation and the investment-output ratio (Fz). Atje and Jovanovic ran regressions of this type, with the following numerical estimates of the impact of financial intermediation on the growth of per capita income:

$$\partial(g_Y - g_L)/\partial F = 0.05z.$$

Note that 0.05 is the estimated coefficient of Fz in the regression of $g_Y - g_L$ described above.

The Role of Human Capital in the Link between Finance and Economic Growth

Like much of the literature of the recent past, the Atje and Jovanovic (1993) paper discussed above by and large ignores the role of human capital while specifying the link between financial development and economic growth. However, lately endogenous growth models which formally "endogenize" the role of human capital (or technology) have become more common in the growth literature. In the context of the links between financial intermediation and economic growth, Levine (1990) is a recent theoretical attempt to analyze the issue in the context of an endogenous growth framework.

With relatively stronger microfoundations, Levine (1990) postulates an economy that consists of an infinite sequence of three-period lived generations with the same countable number of agents from each period. All income during age 1 is saved. During age 2 individual agents have a choice between "storing" their first-period wage, w_t, as a "liquid" asset with $n > 0$ return, or investing it in the risky and illiquid activity of forming and investing in "firms" that provide a higher expected return than the "liquid" option. However, what is really important is that along with consumption goods, human capital is produced within these firms, which positively affects the wage rate, the return to entrepreneurs, and the economy's output. (Incidentally, Levine's formal discussion is couched in terms of human capital alone, but exclusion of physical capital was motivated only by a desire to focus relatively sharply on the role of human capital.) Thus in this model, growth would be proportional to the stock of capital the society invests and maintains in firms that augment human capital (and technology). Embodied in an individual, human capital represents nontradable knowledge and skills that depend positively on his interactions with others, the amount of resources invested by him, and the average amount of capital invested and maintained in the firm.

Thus an important aspect of this model is the existence of a (positive) externality that depends on the average stock of investment in these firms. This stock of human capital is adversely affected if some of the agents prematurely withdraw (liquidate) their investments from these firms in order to meet short-term liquidity needs (liquidity shock). Thus enters financial intermediation, or the stock market which the paper focuses on, as an example of such intermediation. The stock market accelerates growth in this model essentially by helping agents manage liquidity and productivity risk. In the absence of financial markets, risk-averse investors may shy away from investing in firms on account of firm-specific productivity shocks. By allowing portfolio diversification across firms, stock markets ameliorate the effects of these idiosyncratic shocks, thus augmenting the fraction of resources allocated to firms.

In addition to discouraging firm investment, an absence of stock markets also reduces firm productivity, which can result from premature capital liquidation. The stock markets allow these agents affected by liquidity shock to sell their stock shares to other investors for more than the liquidation value of their firm capital.

Thus, in light of the above arguments, stock markets are postulated to accelerate growth *directly* by increasing firm productivity, and *indirectly* by encouraging firm investment.

More formally, consider the following two equations, which respectively give the economy's growth rate with and without stock markets:[2]

$$g_Y = Hqr$$

$$g_{YS} = Hq^S rp^{-b}$$

where g_Y (resp. g_{YS}) is the economy's equilibrium growth rate without (resp. with) stock markets; H is a constant representing the rate of human capital accumulation (or a shift parameter in the human capital production function);[3] q and q^S represent the fraction of age-1 wage (w_t) invested in the firm by an agent at time t under each regime; p is the number of initial members remaining in the firm at $t + 2$ (i.e., "non-premature liquidators"); $r = (1 - q) p^q$, $0 < q < 1$, where q is the share of output going to "entrepreneurs", i.e. age-3 firm members with human capital who hire age-1 workers and produce goods y ; and b is a

---

[2]For details, see Levine (1990).

[3]See Levine (1990: 6).

parameter representing the effect of the externality on account of the average stock of human capital in the firm.

When comparing the relative growth rate of the economy with and without stock markets, note that there are two channels through which stock markets influence growth—by increasing firm efficiency, and by increasing the fraction of resources allocated to firms. First, even when $q = q^s$, the stock-market economy would grow relatively faster by alleviating the incidence of premature liquidation of firm capital—agents who experience liquidity shocks sell their shares to agents who value deferred period-3 consumption; consequently, more capital is maintained in firms for two periods, which promotes growth.

Second, in an economy with stock markets, $q^s > q$, i.e., the proportion of resources devoted to firms is higher than in an economy without a stock market, as risk-averse agents are encouraged to invest a relatively greater amount in firms due to the possibilities of risk diversification, the potential for absorbing liquidity shocks, and increased efficiency of firms. Thus, the emergence of stock markets accelerates growth.

The Issue of Causality

In terms of the two models of the relationship between financial intermediation and growth outlined in Section 3 above, note that the Atje and Jovanovic framework focuses mainly on physical capital, while the Levine model moves a step further by calling attention to the important need for incorporating human capital into the analysis. However, both of these representative models implicitly assume that financial growth precedes or "causes" economic growth. In fact, the issue of causality is not trivial, since it is plausible that, rather than preceding growth, financial development may occur simultaneously or even lag behind economic growth. Though the literature has not completely ignored the causality question, the attention it has received is not commensurate with its importance.

Amongst the existing literature, the work by Patrick (1966), though over two decades old, remains perhaps the most significant analytical effort to address the critical question of whether the financial or the real sector leads in the process of economic growth. Patrick identifies two possible patterns in the causal relationship between financial development and economic growth—"demand-following" and "supply-leading." In the "demand-following" case, the growth in the real sector precedes the growth in the financial sector—as a matter of fact, the latter is characterized as perhaps no more than a "passive" response to meet the demand for financial sources generated by the real sector. On the other hand, according to the "supply-leading" scenario, the financial sector induces real-sector growth by essentially channeling investible funds of the savers to the investors and creating other informational efficiencies. In terms of the direction of the causality between financial intermediation and growth, the "Patrick Hypothesis" in effect postulates a nonlinear relationship—in the early stages of economic growth, financial development induces faster growth via the investment channel and "as the process of real growth occurs, the supply-leading impetus gradually becomes less important, and the demand-following financial response becomes dominant" (Patrick 1966: 177).

Despite its intuitive appeal, the "Patrick Hypothesis" has been subjected to little empirical testing. One notable exception is Jung (1986), who uses post-World War II data on 56 developed as well as developing countries to test the above hypothesis. Using ratios of M_1 or M_2 relative to GNP as proxies for financial development and based on Granger-causality tests, Jung reports "a moderate support for the supply-leading phenomenon in LDCs. The causal direction, both unidirectional and simple, running from financial development to economic growth, is more frequently observed than the reverse" (Jung

1986:341). Similarly, Jung notes only moderate support for reverse causal direction for the developed countries (Jung 1986: 344).[4]

As mentioned earlier, there are few empirical studies that explicitly address the issue of the direction of causality. Besides Jung, Spears (1992) reports some spotty evidence for five sub-Saharan African developing countries which suggests financial intermediation may promote economic growth. Robustness of conclusions from tests of the Granger-causality type further weakens evidence from this type of analysis. An alternative approach, which we will pursue further, is to treat financial intermediation as an endogenous variable (together with economic growth) in a wider econometric system. With enough detail in this expanded framework, tests can be constructed to determine the relative strengths of the feedback relationship between financial intermediation and growth.

Comments on Existing Models

In this section we offer some preliminary observations about existing models of the relationship between financial development and economic growth.

Specification of the Production Function

In the context of the appropriate specification of the aggregate production function, there are three (related) issues that are pertinent here: (i) what are the relevant inputs; (ii) what is the appropriate functional form; (iii) what assumptions are needed for a viable estimation that may pool data across countries and over time.

(i) In terms of the relevant inputs, in Section 3 we have already noted that, as demonstrated by the work of Levine

---

[4]In the case of DCs, even this support evaporates when the monetization rather than the currency variable is used to measure financial intermediation.

(1990), the awareness is growing that besides physical capital, human capital should also be included as a relevant determinant of national output. However, what is lacking is a comprehensive production-function framework which presents the physical and human capital aspects in a fully integrated fashion. Such a framework no doubt would present some new challenges in terms of estimation and data requirements.

(ii) Regarding the question of the appropriate functional form of the aggregate production function, one notices rather specialized specifications (for instance Atje and Jovanovic) which are nevertheless significant contributions as important first steps. However there is an obvious need to conduct the analysis in terms of more generalizable specifications.

(iii) Thirdly, often cross-country estimation is made feasible only after certain restrictive assumptions are invoked. These assumptions relate both to substantive phenomena (such as the assumption of "full employment" for all countries and for all time periods implied in Atje and Jovanovic) and to production-function parametrization, as is the case when production functions are assumed to be the same across countries. Now it is not clear that, when data on developed and developing countries are pooled, this last assumption especially in the sense of "realized" production technologies is tenable. In any event, at a minimum, the sensitivity of the empirical results to such assumptions should be ascertained.

The Question of Endogeneity

We have already discussed the issue of causality in Section 4. However, here we would like to reiterate the need to address the related question of endogeneity of financial intermediation and simultaneity of real- and financial-sector development. Atje and Jovanovic (1990) make an attempt to deal with this issue essentially by adding the lagged value of the dependent variable (growth rate of GDP per capita) as an additional explanatory variable to the specification—the robustness of the financial intermediation index is then taken as an indication of a lack of simultaneity. This is an important question, and a more extensive analysis can be developed through an expanded model which explains the simultaneous interaction between financial intermediation and the real sector.

Measuring Financial Development

When estimating financial development's relationship to economic growth, there is a relatively greater consensus in terms of how to measure growth (per capita), while financial development can be (and often is) measured by a disparate set of indices or their linear combinations. In order to arrive at something resembling a consensus on the empirical estimate of the nature of the relationship between financial development and economic growth, we would need to standardize measures of financial development, or at least ascertain the range of estimated effects as a function of these indices of financial intermediation.

A Proposed Theoretical Framework and Agenda for Future Empirical Work

To cater simultaneously to all the suggestions that we have noted in the previous section would certainly be a tall order. However, we propose to consider an aggregative production function which explicitly considers physical as well as human capital as amongst the relevant determinants, in order to derive a relationship between financial development and growth rate of output per capita. (This would be an integration of the Atje and Jovanovic (1993), Levine (1990), and Mankiw, et al. (1992) approaches.) Then, using a pooled time-series cross-section of a number of developed as well as developing countries, we want to estimate the extent to which financial development affects growth rate of per capita income. We propose to gauge financial market performance by such measures as market capitalization, annual turnover in the money and equity markets, and credit available to the private and public sectors. Again, in order to test the sensitivity of the results, the specified relationship may be estimated separately for such groups as DCs, LDCs, and subgroups thereof, such as highly indebted, Asian, or lowest-income countries. This should provide useful information regarding the structural aspects of the process by which financial intermediation may affect economic development.

A related framework that we propose is based on the approach taken by Lucas (1990, 1993), and Ratcliffe (1994), where certain assumptions about factor markets (perfect competition) and profit maximization allow us to address the question of the relationship between financial intermediation and international rates of return to capital without requiring explicit data on capital stock.

References

Atje, R. and B. Jovanovic (1993) "Stock Markets and Development," *European Economic Review* 37: 632–640.

Bencivenga, V.R. and B.D. Smith (1991) "Financial Intermediation and Economic Growth," *Review of Economic Studies*.

Chandravarkar, A. (1992) "Of Finance and Development," *World Development* 20: 133–142.

Clemente, L.C. and R.S. Mariano (eds.) (1992) *Asian Capital Markets.* Manila: Asian Securities Industry Institute.

_____ (eds.) (1993) *Asian Capital Markets—Dynamics of Growth and World Linkages.* New York: Asian Securities Industry Institute.

Dailami, M. and M. Atkin (1990) "Stock Markets in Developing Countries," *Working Paper Series No. 515.* Washington, D.C.: The World Bank.

Darrat, A. and T.K. Mukherjee (1987) "The Behavior of the Stock Market in a Developing Economy," *Economics Letters*: 273–278.

Drake, P.J. (1977) "Securities Markets in Less-Developed Countries" in P.C.I. Ayre (ed.). *Finance in Developing Countries*. London: Frank Cass and Co., Ltd.

Fischer, S. and R.C. Merton (1984) "Macroeconomics and Finance: the Role of the Stock Market" in K. Brunner and A.H. Meltzer (eds.). *Essays on Macroeconomic Implications of Financial and Labor Markets and Political Processes*. Carnegie-Rochester Conference Series on Public Policy, Vol. 21 (Autumn): 57–108.

Goldsmith, R. (1969) *Financial Structure and Development*. New Haven: Yale University Press.

Greenwood, J. and B. Ivanovic (1990) "Financial Development, Growth, and the Distribution of Income." *Journal of Political Economy* 98.

Jung, W.S. (1986) "Financial Development and Economic Growth: International Evidence," *Economic Development and Cultural Change* 34: 333–346.

King, R. and R. Levine (1993) "Finance and Growth: Schumpeter Might be Right," *Quarterly Journal of Economics* (August).

_____. (1993) "Financial Indicators and Growth in a Cross-Section of Countries," *World Bank Paper No. 819*, January.

Levine, R. (1990) "Stock Markets, Growth, and Policy," *Working Paper Series No. 484*. Washington, D.C.: The World Bank.

Lucas, R. (1990) "Why Doesn't Capital Flow from Rich to Poor Countries?" *American Economic Review Papers and Proceedings* 80: 92–96.

_____. (1993) "Making a Miracle," *Econometrica* 61: 251–272.

Mankiw, N., D. Romer, and D.N. Weil (1992) "A Contribution to the Empirics of Economic Growth," *Quarterly Journal of Economics* 107: 407–437.

McKinnon, R. (1973) *Money and Capital in Economic Development*. Washington, D.C.: The Brooking Institute.

Patrick, H.T. (1966) "Financial Development and Economic Growth in Underdeveloped Countries," *Economic Development and Cultural Change* 29:174-189.

Ratcliffe, R. (1994) "Why Doesn't Capital Flow from Rich to Poor Countries?" University of Pennsylvania Ph.D. dissertation in economics.

Shaw, E.S. (1973) *Financial Deepening in Economic Development.* New York: Oxford University Press.

Spears, A. (1991) "Financial Development and Economic Growth— Causality Tests Anthology" *Atlantic Economic Journal* 19.

World Bank (1989) *World Development Report.*

Impact of Technological Transformation on Income Distribution

*Harry T. Oshima**

This paper is concerned with the direct impact of technological changes on income distribution, not so much their indirect impact through changes in demographic, structural and other factors. It deals with very long-term relationships, comprising periods over several decades; specifically with the impact of three major technical transformations—the 19th century technologies powered by steam-engines; the 20th century technologies powered by electric-engines; and the electronic technologies, controlled and monitored by computers and robots emerging in the closing decade of the present century. These three technologies, designated as general purpose technologies, have served (are serving) as "engines of growth" in driving technological progress and economic growth since the 19th century in the West (Bresnahan and Tajtenberg 1992).

*Professor Emeritus of Economics, University of Hawaii. This paper is an extension of ideas outlined in my *Economic Growth in Monsoon Asia: A Comparative Survey*, Tokyo University Press, 1978, and in *Strategic Processes in Monsoon Asia's Development*, to be published by the Johns Hopkins University Press, August 1993. See also my paper entitled "The Kuznets Curve and Asian Income Distribution Trends," *Hitotsubashi Journal of Economics*, June 1992, Hitotsubashi University, Tokyo, Japan.

As Kuznets noted, the family instead of the individual or person is the proper unit in the study of income distribution and economic growth, even though it is the latter who participates directly in the production process. The reason is that much of incomes, especially proprietor's income, is generated collectively by members of the family (including women and children), not individually by the head of the household. This is the case not only with respect to work in farms, stores, restaurants, and workshops but also with respect to property incomes. Assets such as homes, farms, stores may be jointly owned by husband and wife, or their parents (Kuznets 1966: 139–140).

Analytically, we look into the impact of major technological changes on each distributive share such as proprietor's incomes, wages and salaries, and the various property incomes. These shares can change in part because of changes in the number of proprietors, wage earners, salary earners, and in part because of changes in the rate of return to property, the wage rate, monthly salary, and proprietor's income per year. Or the impact of technological changes can be on the distribution within each share, i.e., between large and small entrepreneurs, between unskilled, semi-skilled workers, and highly skilled technicians, between large and small property owners, and between middle and top management.

Thus, if the income share of proprietors rises against that of salary earners, this may contribute to greater inequality because the former's incomes are usually more unequally distributed. Or if the share of unskilled workers rises more than the share of skilled workers, overall income disparities increase because the unskilled workers occupy the lowest rung of the income distribution and the salaried worker, the middle ranges. And since property incomes are mainly received by those in the upper income brackets, their rise will imply greater overall inequality. Also, if the aggregate shares of lower-income sectors such as agriculture or retailing rise relative to higher-income manufacturing, the impact on distribution will be adverse. Or, the number of earners per family in the lower-income families may increase relative to upper-income families with the employment of housewives, then overall inequality will be improved.

Also, the changes in the shares of quintiles and deciles will denote changes in disparities, i.e., the rise in the share of the highest quintile and the fall in the share of the lowest quintile will signify increased inequality. In contrast, the rise in the third quintile shares of income together with those in the adjacent deciles will lessen inequalities.

Three Phases in Income Distribution Trends

In what follows, we shall contend that in the West, the steam-driven technologies of the 19th century raised income inequalities. In the second stage, technologies driven by electric motors from the early decades of the 20th century reduced income inequalities. And in the present period, the emergence of electronic technologies is raising income inequalities once again.

The statistical trends may be briefly outlined as follows. Kuznets noted that the data for the 19th century were scanty. Data from tax returns indicated that the income of the highest 20 percent of taxpayers rose from 58 percent in 1880 to 59 percent in 1913 in the United Kingdom, from 21 percent in 1854 for the top 5 percent in Prussia to 26 percent in 1875 and 30 percent in 1913. The share of Saxony's top 5 percent rose from 56 percent in 1880 to 57 percent in 1896. For Denmark, there was a decline for the share of the highest 10 percent from 50 percent in 1870 to 38 percent in 1903 (Kuznets 1966: 208–209). Looking at data from national income estimates, Kuznets (1966: 168–169) found that the proportion of property incomes in total national income rose from the 19th century to around World War II for the United Kingdom, France, Germany, and the United States. In Japan, inequality rose from the late 19th century and fell after World War II (Mizoguchi 1989).

Much more data are available for the second phase of declining trends, especially after World War I and into the 1960s. This was the case for the United Kingdom, West Germany, Netherlands, Denmark, Norway, Sweden, and the United States (Kuznets 1966: 208–209). The decline was widespread and clear-cut in all the industrialized countries for which data were available and for a period as long as over half a century.

From the 1970s, inequality began to rise, slowly at first in the United States from a Gini averaging 0.35 in the latter 1960s to 0.36 in the 1970s, and then accelerating to 0.38 in the 1980s and 0.40 in the early years of the 1990s.[1] Inequality of earnings of men heading families rose in West Germany, Canada, Sweden, and Australia (Green et al. 1992). Overall inequality of wages (including those of women) rose not only in the foregoing countries but also in Sweden, the United Kingdom, and the United States, although it was stable in France and Netherlands (Davis 1993).

First Phase: Steam-Driven Technology of the 19th Century

Kuznets' writings were largely on the 20th century, but he remarked that for the 19th century, "It seems plausible to assume that, in the process of growth, the earlier periods are characterized by a balance of counteracting forces that may have widened the inequality in the size distribution of total income for a while because of the rapid growth of the non-A (agriculture) sector and the wider inequality within it" (Kuznets 1966: 217). Elsewhere he mentions that the rise in inequality was due to the increase in the growth rate of population, the expansion of urbanization, and the low rate of national savings (Kuznets 1955). But for some reason, he did not pay much

---

[1]U.S. Bureau of Census, *Survey of Consumer Finances*, January 1992.

attention to the nature of 19th century technology as a major source of income disparity.[2]

The steam-driven technology, compared to that of the later electric-driven technology, was crude and cumbersome, lacking in precision, flexibility, and versatility, and costly, not affordable for most firms. Generating steam required large, coal-fed boilers; and for steam to be distributed throughout the factory, a complex maze of shafts, pulleys, and pipes had to be built overhead. This infrastructure was too costly for most of the smaller firms, which were owned and operated by families with accumulated capital that was too meager.

Cheaper were the water wheels run by water-power, but firms had to be located near rivers. Often far from urban centers, and being less powerful than steam-engines, only smaller numbers of machines could be handled. Thus, the vast majority of craft shops and domestic industries had to operate machines and other equipment by hand.

Major differences in labor productivity and earnings prevailed in latter 19th century England, with varying mixtures of large factories with steam-engines, medium factories with water-mills, and craft shops and domestic industries based on muscle power in each industry. With the exception of textiles, most firms were small, averaging about ten workers. Even in the metal-working industries, small furnaces with simple, hand-operated equipment were found in the home-based shops.

Not only did 19th century technologies fail to mechanize most firms in the various industries, but within each firm the extent of mechanization was limited. This is so even in the textile factory where skilled operatives worked side by side with even larger numbers of poorly-paid women and children, most of whom were involved in menial tasks such as handling,

---

[2]It may be that Kuznets was not fully aware of the unique character of the post-World War I period. He wrote before historical research has established the enormous impact of the shift from steam-engines to electric-motors as general purpose technologies.

hauling, cleaning, sweeping, and so on. The iron industry looked more like construction works, with most of the workers shovelling, digging, hauling, and pounding. Even in the most highly mechanized industry, textiles, only six of the production operations were mechanized, compared to 25 mechanized operations in the electric-powered factories of the 20th century. In 1851, modern industry employed 1.7 million workers compared to 2.5 million in traditional industry. Between 1860 to 1900, only 56,000 patents were taken out, in contrast with 184,000 between 1900 and 1940.[3]

Nor did 19th century technology succeed in mechanizing the agricultural and service sectors. The steam engines with their elaborate infrastructures were too expensive for the wide-open fields and were irrelevant for the small shops, stores, and offices, although they quickly replaced horses in construction and the railroads.

Organizationally, the variations in size were considerable in agriculture. There were large estates of big landlords, large and medium-sized capitalistic farms, free holders, and tenanted farmers, besides farm laborers without land. In retailing, department stores began to emerge toward the end of the century amidst a sea of small stores. In transportation, alongside the steam-engine railroads were the innumerable one- and two-horse-driven carriages, wagons, and carts (Crouzet 1982).

In such a heterogenous structure, per worker productivity and earnings ranged widely not only between industries, i.e., between the partially mechanized manufacturing, mining, and transport industries, and unmechanized agriculture, construction, and services, but also within industries, i.e., between mechanized factories, mines, railroads, and medium, small craft shops and domestic industries.

All this meant that the middle class, whose families occupied the middle deciles in the distribution of income and

---

[3]See Crouzet (1982, Chapter 4) for data and descriptions in the above paragraphs.

were the main contributors to income equalization, was a small group relative to the upper-income class of landlords, capitalist farmers, industrialists, merchants, and bankers, and the lower-income working families of small holders, tenants, craftsmen, laborers, and domestic servants.[4] The simple technology of the 19th century did not call for the large group of professional, technical, clerical, and public workers which the 20th century technologies gave birth to. Instead, it created a large group of unskilled workers who filled the 19th century work shops, plus the lumpen proletariat of Karl Marx, comprising casual workers with intermittent jobs, the technologically unemployed, and the beggars.

In such a stratified society as the above, property incomes and proprietor's profits in the highest deciles were large relative to the salaries of white collar workers and wages of technicians, skilled workers, and farmers in the middle deciles while the share of wages of the farm laborers, unskilled laborers, casual workers, and servants in the lowest deciles was relatively small.

Second Phase: Electric-Driven Technology of the 20th Century

In 1900, 80 percent of machines were driven by steam engines, but by 1929, 78 percent were driven by electric motors while horses were replaced by internal combustion engines on the farm and road. And the weird array of shafts, pulleys and pipes on the factory ceilings was replaced by wires on the factory floor (Devine 1983). The rapid spread of electric power was due to its superiority over steam-power—in speed, convenience, versatility, flexibility, precision, and cost. Electric power became affordable not only to owners of small factories

---

[4]Because of the failure to mechanize household operations, a large class of domestic servants, comprising 7.3 percent of the labor force in the U.S. Census of 1900 and probably much larger in the U.K., were employed in the households.

but also to owners of stores, offices, shops, and homes. More important, its versatility, flexibility, and precision spawned innumerable machines, especially small ones, superior to the cumbersome steam-driven machines. Mechanization spread across and within industries. Electric motors were inserted into machines hitherto manually operated. Internal combustion engines revolutionized transportation.

The productivity gap between and within industries narrowed, and variability in earnings fell. Productivity in agriculture rose as internal-combustion engines replaced horses in plows and carts, and electric wires were connected to farm equipment. This made it possible for small farm families to operate larger farms (or reduce farm workforce per acre), thereby raising output per worker. Earnings in agriculture moved closer to industrial earnings.

More important, the development of varieties of machines and other equipments facilitated the mechanization of most factory operations (as noted above with respect to the textile industry), and the number of unskilled jobs (such as handling, hauling, cleaning, drying, packing) were sharply reduced. Machine operators and tenders replaced the unskilled workers and laborers, and earnings differentials within factories were cut down (Jerome 1934).

Cheaper and more flexible machinery eliminated handicraft and domestic industries together with the reduction of small farmers, and the spread of department stores and supermarkets shrank the size of the proprietor class and narrowed its hitherto wide-ranging spread of incomes.

With the availability of small, light-handed equipment, job opportunities for females in factories opened up, especially for wives freed from much housework with the advent of electrical appliances and automobiles. More jobs became available in department stores and supermarkets, and in the mechanized offices. The number of earners in medium- and lower-income households rose.

These forces gave rise to a middle class which was much larger than in the 19th century. Many more engineers, architects, scientists, technicians, officials, clerks, and sales workers were needed for the more varied and complex technologies of the 20th century factories, stores and offices; more managers, supervisors, accountants, lawyers, and other professionals had to be employed to handle the functions of the corporations and their capital-intensive, mass-producing factories. A larger bureaucracy had to be recruited to regulate public utilities and large corporations, to construct and manage roads and other physical infrastructure, and to educate and train a skilled labor force.

In the U.S., the number of white collar workers (professionals, technicians, managers, officials, clerks, and sales workers) rose sevenfold from 1900–1929 while laborers, farm and household workers dropped by one-half. From 1920, industrial laborers fell from 4.9 million to 3.5 million in 1960, and machine operatives rose from 6.6 million to 12.8 million.[5]

The share of income of the top 5 percent of families dropped from 24 percent in 1913–1919 to 20 percent in 1955–1959 while the income of the lowest 60 percent rose from 26 percent in 1929 to 32 percent in 1955–1959. In the U.K., the top 20 percent share declined from 58 percent in 1880 to 42 percent in 1957 (Kuznets 1966:192, 208, 281).

In short, it was the replacement of the Marxian proletariat and the unskilled laborers of the steam-driven factories by the middle class of white collar and skilled workers of the electric-driven factories, offices, and stores in the 20th century which brought down the high inequalities of the 19th century to average levels of about 3.5 Gini by the 1960s (U.S. Census Bureau 1992).

---

[5]See Oshima (1984) and the *Historical Statistics* and the *Statistical Abstract of the US* 1975 and 1993, respectively.

Third Phase: The Emerging Electronic Technologies

The shift to the predominance of electronic technologies of automation, computers, and robots has begun. A survey of 500 manufacturers showed that by 1992 U.S. firms have spent $800 billion on automation. This shift is said to have a greater potential of revolutionizing the economy than the previous technological transformations, with extensive ramifications in the ways of working and living. When completely integrated control by computers of all production processes of the factories, including designing, engineering, transporting, packing, and storing is installed, the labor saving can amount to a ratio of 30 to 1 (*Fortune*, October 5, 1981). With the beginnings of automation, U.S. manufacturing productivity has been rising by 3 or 4 percent from the mid-1980s.

Technological changes are accompanied by changes in production processes. For example, middle managers, one of whose tasks was to gather and transmit information, became redundant when computers took over the job of collecting and transmitting information. Further, when this information became readily available to all workers on the factory floor, these workers, operating in teams, were able to solve problems as they came up and thus took over the problem-solving function of middle managers. From the 1980s, middle managers began to lose their jobs and hundred of thousands became unemployed in the U.S. Working in teams and empowered to make decisions, workers were motivated with greater incentives and have raised productivity.

Moreover, electronic technologies may produce changes in the mechanism by which productivity and growth have occurred. In particular, capital in the form of machines, conveyor belts, motorized and other equipment was the main agent of labor productivity gains in the past. Productivity was raised "directly through the more advanced technologies embodied in the new machinery, and indirectly (through) the skills of workers in handling and the experience of firms in organizing modern technologies."[6] The technology embodied in the electric, mechanical machines is being replaced as the prime engine of growth by the power, speed, and versatility of computers, the agility of robots and automated transports in controlling and guiding the electric-driven machines, vehicles, assembly lines and other equipment. Capital in the form of machines and other equipment (and its ability to substitute for labor) will then take a backseat to information gathered and dispensed through computers and telecommunication devices.[7]

Specifically, the impact of electronic technologies affected income distribution in a number of ways. The demand for manual workers to operate machines, to transport materials, parts, and products, and to assemble parts and components began to decline as systems of machines and vehicles were controlled and monitored by computers, as robots were brought in to handle objects and tools and assemble parts and components, and as automated warehouses and transport forwarded them through the various processes. In a typical, automated plant, it is said that only 5 percent of the total employees are needed (Davidow and Malone 1992). The complexity of the electronic technologies called for problem-solving, cognitive capabilities instead of physical, manual skills. The demand for college-educated workers with backgrounds in science and mathematics rose (Hazewindus and Tooker 1985). Their earnings rose, particularly in the 1980s, when there was a slowdown in the growth of the supply of college graduates (Katz 1992). A robust correlation was

---

[6]See De Long (1991). This kind of mechanism is said to be assumed in the growth models of Robert Solow and more recently in Paul Romer.

[7]See the article by Peter Drucker on "Post-Capitalism." It will be impossible to disentangle each factor of production and allocate the sources of growth in the automated, integrated plants of the future, as Denison did in his well-known Brookings study on growth accounting.

found between the hiring of well-educated workers and investment in computers.[8]

The new technology is making headway into the back offices of industrial enterprises, as well as the front offices of banks, insurance companies, professions, hospitals, governments, and department stores. As in the factory, offices mechanized with electric, mechanical equipment are being automated and computerized. Computers and information systems for handling data, invoicing, accounting, inventory control; facsimile, word processors, portable printers, laser scanners, and so on are reducing the need for clerks, secretaries, typists and supervisors. By ordering through computers and by using laser scanners, retailers reduce the length of time, quantity of inventory (with just-in-time retailing), and the number of middlemen. Sam Walton of Wal-mart, by investing in computers, got rid of many wholesalers, mom-and-pop stores, and other middlemen (*Fortune*, May 24, 1992).

Moreover, also constraining the rise in wages of blue collar workers was the shift of U.S. firms producing labor-intensive goods to developing countries in the 1970s and 1980s, together with increased immigration from low-wage countries such as Mexico. ·

There were other forces contributing to income inequality. There was the tendency of families to shift from husband and wife to single-person units, although this shift slowed down in the 1980s. Also, families headed by retired, elderly persons rose. And finally, there were more two-earner families in the higher income groups than in the lower income families in 1987 which was contrary to the situation in the previous period. This may have been due to well-educated wives taking on work using electronic technologies. About 70 percent of families with working wives have incomes greater than $50,000

---

[8]See Berman, Bound, and Griliches (1993). It is reported that workers using computers are paid 15 to 30 percent more than workers not using them though doing the same work.

compared to 25 percent in families with less ·than $15,000 (*Statistical Abstract of the U.S.*, 1989).

Workers losing jobs in manufacturing moved into lower-paying jobs in retailing and personal services. In 1988, annual earnings in manufacturing averaged $31,000 compared to $15,000 in retailing. Occupation-wise, machine operatives, tenders, fabricators, and assemblers earned $15,000 as against $6,000 for service occupations.[9] Also during the 1980s, the wage gap between college-educated and high-school educated workers widened sharply (Katz 1992: 11).

For the economy as a whole, the proportion of men earning less than $20,000 and earning more than $40,000 increased, while those in the middle decreased from 57 percent in 1979 to 46 percent in 1987 (Levy and Murmane 1992; Green et al. 1992). Evidently, the large middle class (the product of electrically-powered technologies) responsible for the lower-income inequalities from the early decades of the 20th century, is being squeezed by the electronic technologies, as the better-educated families move into the higher deciles while the less-educated middle class fall into the lower deciles. As the jobs in the mass production industries and in the offices become scarcer, those in the lower middle class will have to turn to the lower-paying service occupations. If this continues into the next century, we are likely to see the end of Kuznets' inverted U-curve. The declining portion, which was encountered in the early decades of this century,. may now come to an end and begin to turn up.[10]

Even though there is likely to be an increase in the growth rate of college graduates in the coming decades, it may not be able to catch up with the escalating demand for college graduates. The electronic revolution has gained momentum

---

[9]Estimated from data in the *Statistical Abstract of the U.S. 1990*, and *Survey of Current Business*, August 1990.

[10]Kuznets died in 1983, before the acceleration of the electronic revolution, and before the trend toward inequality became conspicuous.

only in the 1980s and may be expected to accelerate, as the costs of electronic technologies fall sharply and the global competition heats up.

Implications for Asia

Despite growing earning differentials among men, family income inequalities have not risen in Japan. This may have been due to the shortage of labor prevailing in Japan up to the present. The automating industries have been able to offset the labor-saving tendencies of electronic technologies with the expansion of output, while the tertiary sector has been able to generate jobs paying as much as the wages of small industries. Housewives have had no difficulty in finding jobs, increasing the share of the lower-income deciles. And the rise in the supply of better-educated labor has tended to constrain earnings differentials. But with the labor shortage easing in 1993, unemployment may begin to rise if the present recession continues; and with the exodus of labor-intensive industries to developing countries of Asia, income disparities may begin to rise in Japan in the coming years.

One consequence is discernible. The labor-saving nature of automation sharply reduces the manual-labor content of production, as noted above. It was cheap labor which enabled Asian countries to penetrate Western markets with labor-intensive exports in the postwar decades. Automation in the U.S. has begun to penetrate labor-intensive industries (such as textiles), and this will reduce the competitive advantage of Asian exports in the future. And to Western investors looking to move their factories into Asia, the lower wages of Asian workers will not be as attractive as before.

It is to be remembered that the fall in income disparities played a crucial role in the political and social stability in most countries of East and Southeast Asia. The exceptions were South Korea and the Philippines where disparities have either been rising (S. Korea) or remained constant at high levels (Philippines), with disruptive impact on social and political stability. From the mid-1970s and to the mid-1980s, rising inequalities have also had destabilizing effects on Malaysian and Thai society. (In South Asia, this was the case in Bangladesh in the 1970s and Sri Lanka in the 1980s.)[11]

While automation has barely made a dent in Asia outside of Japan and the NIEs, wages and per capita incomes are rising rapidly in ASEAN, and it will not take too long for incomes to approach present Japanese and the NIEs levels. With further declines in the prices of chips, computers, robots, etc., the costs of automation will fall and its spread in Asia will begin to have an unfavorable impact on Asian income distribution. Accordingly, plans to minimize the disruptive effects should be made now. Such plans should include the training of young people for computer usage and educating increasing numbers of college graduates for problem-solving capabilities. For those not trainable to handle electronic technologies and problem-solving capabilities, the modernization of small industries and services should generate good-paying jobs. The lesson of Japanese experience, noted above, in the maintenance of full employment to sustain the income of low-income families should not be lost. The technological unemployment from the use of electronic equipment may turn out to persist much longer than in electric-powered and steam-powered revolutions in part because the automated machines and equipment are likely to be capital-saving but also they replace labor much more extensively, as noted above.

Finally, related to the electronics revolution sweeping Japan and Western industries are their growing productivity and competitiveness. Close attention should be paid to the ways in which they are being revitalized, and lessons learned from the movement to reduce corporate hierarchies, slim down

---

[11]See details in Oshima (1992).

and become more agile by out-sourcing and networking, to improve quality, variety, and customer satisfaction, to motivate employees by team work, empowerment, and through increased worker participation in decision-making, besides cost-cutting through automation, computerization, and robotization, re-engineering, and so on.[12] For in the long run the loss of competitiveness of Asian economies can affect not only per capita income growth but its distribution through unemployment and poorly paying jobs, so that some of the methods being adopted by Western and Japanese enterprises should be incorporated by Asian enterprises.

---

[12]Particularly useful are the various publications of the Asian Productivity Organization which have attempted to describe the various ways in which Japanese industries achieved high levels of productivity. Also see Davidow and Malone (1992); Pine (1991); Burt and Doyle (1980); Forrester (ed.) 1980; and Best (1990).

References

Best, M. (1990) *The New Competition: Institutions of Industrial Restructuring.* Harvard.

Bresnahan, T.F. and M. Tajtenberg (1992) "General Purpose Technologies: Engine of Growth," National Bureau of Economic Research, *Working Paper No. 4148*, August.

Burt, D.N. and M.F. Doyle (1993) *The American Keiretsu.* Irwin. Illinois: Business One.

Crouzet, F. (1982) *The Victorian Economy.* New York: Columbia University Press: Chapter 4.

Davidow, D. and M.S. Malone (1992) *The Virtual Corporation.* N.Y.: Harper Collier.

Davis, S. (1993) "Cross-Country Patterns of Change in Relative Wages," *National Bureau of Economic Research, Working Paper No. 4085,* May.

De Long, J.B. (1991) "Productivity and Machinery Investment: A Long-Run Look, 1870–1980," *NBER Working Paper No. 3903,* November.

Devine, W.O. (1983) "From Shafts to Wires: Historical Perspectives on Electrification," *Journal of Economic History,* June.

Forrester, T. (ed.) (1980) *The Microelectronic Revolution.* Oxford.

Fortune (1992) "The Next Industrial Revolution Is on the Way," October 5, 1981; May 24.

Green, G., J. Coder and P. Ryscarvage (1992) "International Comparisons of Earnings Inequality of Men in the 1980s," *Review of Income and Wealth,* March.

Hazewindus, N. and J. Tooker (1982) *The U.S. Microelectronics Industry.* New York: Pergamon Press.

Jerome, H. (1934) *Mechanization in Industry.* NBER: New York.

Katz, L.F. (1992/93) "Understanding Recent Changes in the Wage Structure," *NBER Reporter,* Winter: 10–15.

Kuznets, S. (1955) "Economic Growth and Income Inequality," *American Economic Review,* March.

_____. (1966) *Modern Economic Growth*. Yale. New Haven, pp. 139–40.

Levy, F. and R. J. Murmane (1992) "U.S. Earnings Levels and Earning Inequality: A Review of Recent Trends and Proposed Explanation," *Journal of Economic Literature*, September.

Mizoguchi, T. (1989) *Economic, Sociological, and Institutional Factors Relating to Changes in Size Distribution of Household Income: Japan's Experience in a Century*. Institute of Economic Research, Hitotsubashi University, Kunitachi.

Oshima, Harry T. (1978) *Economic Growth in Monsoon Asia: A Comparative Survey*. Tokyo University Press.

_____. (1984) "Growth of Factor Productivity in the US: the Significance of New Technologies in the Early Decades of the 20th Century," *Journal of Economic History*, March.

_____. (1992) "The Kuznets' Curve and Asian Income Distribution Trends," *Hitotsubashi Journal of Economics*. Tokyo, Japan: Hitotsubashi University, June.

Pine, B. Joseph III (1991) *Mass Customization, the New Frontier in Business Competition*. Boston: Harvard Business School.

GOVERNMENT DOCUMENTS

"Changes in Family Finances from 1983 to 1989," Survey of Consumer Finances, *Federal Reserve Bulletin*. Washington, D.C., January 1992.

Historical Statistics. Washington, D.C.: Government Printing Office, 1975.

Statistical Abstract of the United States. Washington, D.C.: Government Printing Office, 1989, 1990, 1993.

Survey of Current Business. Washington, D.C., Commerce Department, August 1990.

U.S. Bureau of Census (1992) *Current Population Reports*. Series P-60, No. 180. Washington, D.C.: US Government Printing Office.

Conditions of Agricultural Diversification for Economic Development

*Yujiro Hayami**

In a decade since the "green revolution" achieved self-sufficiency in staple food cereals such as rice and wheat in many countries in tropical areas, agricultural diversification has increasingly been emphasized as a key to sustained agricultural development in a manner compatible with overall economic development. The task of this paper is to identify basic conditions under which developing countries can achieve significant progress in agricultural diversification. For this task, I will attempt to advance a perspective on the current problem mainly in terms of the historical experience of Japan. History is a mirror on which the image of the present comes into focus by comparison with similarities and differences with the past. The historical overview in this paper hopes to facilitate proper focusing of policy designers on the strategy of agricultural diversification.

*Professor, Aoyama Gakuin University. This paper originally appeared as Working Paper No. 9201 at the Center for Agricultural Economic Research, Hebrew University. It draws heavily on Hayami (1989) and Ruttan (1985, chapter 12) and Nghiep and Hayami (1979).

Nature and Significance of Agricultural Diversification

First, for a proper policy choice it is critically important to understand the nature of agricultural diversification that is being required in developing economies today. Agricultural diversification defined broadly as "the increased variety of agricultural commodities produced" can be achieved by (a) planting new crops in newly opened lands beyond the lands used for traditional crops, and (b) adding new crops to traditional crops in the same lands through more intensive crop rotation or intercropping.

Several developing economies in the past had records of remarkable success in agricultural diversification along the first approach. The history of Southeast Asia in the nineteenth to the early twentieth century represents a typical example. Corresponding to rising demands from the West for tropical agricultural commodities, large outputs of export cash crops such as sugar, coffee and tea were added to those of subsistence food crops. These additions were produced mainly in the lands newly opened by either native peasants or colonial planters (Myint 1965). Since this process was based on abundant availability of unused land resources, it was bound to end as virgin lands were exploited. In the post-colonial period, too, some significant developments along this line were recorded, e.g., corn and cassava in Thailand, and banana and pineapple in Mindanao, Philippines. Yet, by now the scope of agricultural diversification through new land opening has been severely narrowed.

Clear recognition must be established that the significant scope of agricultural diversification in Southeast Asia is now left only in the direction of intensifying cropping systems and crop-livestock combinations on the farm lands already in use. It must also be recognized that new policy requirements are added corresponding to a shift from agricultural diversification through new land opening to diversification through intensification of land use. In the traditional process, there was little possibility of tradeoff between old and new crop outputs since new land resources were added for the production of new crops. Provision of transportation and communication infrastructure facilitating market linkage between external demand and producers as well as migration of labor force was largely sufficient for the support of traditional development.

In the new regime the tradeoff becomes very serious. Unless major innovations are developed to overcome this tradeoff, significant diversion of fixed land resources from traditional food cereals to new commodities will result in reduction in the supply and increases in prices of food cereals relative to the new crops, making production of the latter unprofitable. Therefore, in addition to the traditional requirements, new policies become indispensable for facilitating increases in the productivity of lands in order to prevent this self-defeating process.

One such requirement has been met by the successful development and diffusion of modern rice technology. Indeed, recent enthusiasm for agricultural diversification in Asia has stemmed mainly from this technological breakthrough that has achieved self-sufficiency in cereal food staples in many countries in this region. As a result, a need has arisen to divert land and labor resources to non-cereal activities in order to prevent cereal prices and incomes from declining sharply.

This need has been exacerbated by rapidly rising per capita incomes in middle-income economies, especially the NIEs, followed by the ASEAN countries, where consumption has been shifting away from low income-elastic commodities such as cereals, to high income-elastic ones such as fruits, vegetables, pulses, and livestock products. Both production and consumption effects have combined to cause a major imbalance between cereal and non-cereal sectors in agriculture. For example, Indonesia was able to move from being the largest rice importer in the world to self-sufficiency in rice within a decade ending in the mid-1980s, based on the diffusion of modern rice technology. Meanwhile, Indonesia's self-sufficiency ratio for soybean (a major source of protein foods such as *tofu* and *tempe*) declined from 100 to almost 50 percent, partly because of rapidly rising demand for protein foods and partly because of significant diversion of land from soybean to rice (CGPRT Center 1985).

On the other hand, in most countries in Southeast Asia the urban industrial and service sectors have not yet reached the stage of absorbing incremental labor. The rapidly growing labor force following population explosion has been pressing hard on limited land resources with the result of decreasing returns to labor relative to land. In order to maximize the labor-absorptive capacity in the rural sector, it is important to add extra farm production activities to traditional cereal production by developing more intensive crop rotations and crop-livestock combinations. Agricultural diversification in this direction represents a powerful counteractive force against population pressure that threatens to result in growing poverty and inequality in developing economies.

Furthermore, agricultural diversification geared for increasing labor absorption can be so designed as to earn foreign exchange needed for economic development. While world demands for traditional tropical export crops, such as sugar, coconut, and tea, have been rather stagnant, demands from high income countries for tropical fruits, vegetables, and flowers have been rising rapidly. The export of these horticultural products from developing countries increased at 8.3 percent per year from 1975 to 1985, while total agricultural export of developing countries and horticultural export of developed countries increased 5.2 and 5.5 percent, respectively (Islam 1990). Horticultural production is known for its high labor absorptive capacity and small requirements for land relative to the value produced. In this, densely populated parts of Asia have a comparative advantage. Moreover, horticultural products require major marketing and processing activities before they reach urban consumers, both domestic and foreign.

Not only horticultural products but also many upland crops produced in remote unfavorable areas such as cassava and soybean, if adequately processed and marketed, can be important foreign exchange earners either through increased exports or reduced imports. Processing, if done in rural-based industries, will add significant employment and income to local economies. A case study for soybean in Indonesia shows that local employment and income generated from processing and marketing activities relative to those of farm production activities were as much as 140 percent and 56 percent, respectively, in an upland area of Java (Hayami, and Kawagoe 1993, Ch. 2).

Thus, agricultural diversification, defined as diversification of agricultural production, marketing, and production activities from the major cereal sector, can contribute significantly to both growth and equity in developing economies. However, it must be pointed out that diversification to new crops and livestock products is not likely to be successful unless it is based on major technological advancements in either farm production or processing and marketing. In the past, the role of agricultural diversification has been emphasized repeatedly, especially in the periods of relatively abundant supply of food cereals, e.g., the so-called "green revolution" bandwagon period in the late 1960s to the early 1970s. Usually, however, policy efforts toward agricultural diversification waned soon after the euphoria of staple food affluence was over. Significant progress in agricultural diversification cannot be expected unless it is supported by technological innovations to make new crop rotation and crop livestock combination profitable in normal product and factor market conditions. New technology must be designed so as to minimize the tradeoff between traditional and newly-introduced commodities. Technological innovations must be supported by major institutional innovations. This contention is borne out by the historical experience of agricultural diversification in developed countries to be reviewed in the following sections.

Western Experience

First, we review two classical examples of agricultural diversification in Western economies.

British Case

Britain experienced a major agricultural transformation from the mid-eighteenth until the mid-nineteenth century. The transformation in eighteenth-century Britain is commonly called the agricultural revolution. Its technical basis was the Norfolk crop-rotation system including new fodder crops such as clover and turnip. This system intensified the recycling of nutrients among plants, livestock, and soil, thus permitting a rise in output per unit of land area, while maintaining soil fertility. The institutional basis was the enclosure—the consolidation of communal pasture and farmland into single private units—which facilitated the introduction of an integrated system of crop-livestock production.

The technology associated with the agricultural revolution was consistent with the conditions of demand and supply of factors and products. The increase in population since the second quarter of the eighteenth century expanded the demand for food and raised the price of food grains. The increase in population was followed by an increase in the labor force. Both food demand and labor supply pressed on land. It was technically feasible and economically profitable to adopt an intensive integrated crop-livestock system of agricultural production.

A second agricultural transformation in Britain occurred following the repeal of the Corn Laws and the Navigation Acts. Confronted with competition from foreign grains, British agriculture successfully transformed itself into efficient large-scale farming based on the trinity of landlord, capitalist tenants, and wage laborers. The development of "high farming" in mid-nineteenth-century England involved the substitution of industrial inputs such as farm machinery and fertilizer for labor. This process was consistent with the rapid absorption of labor by manufacturing industries in the "Workshop of the World."

High farming was supported technically by advances in soil conservation techniques, including underground drainage, application of guano and commercial fertilizers, and the traditional excellence of British livestock-breeding techniques, which produced numerous improved breeds. Institutionally, the establishment of an entrepreneurial tenant farming system based on the common law conventions of the compensation by landlord for tenants' investments, including soil improvements, facilitated the rational adjustment of agriculture to the changing economic environment.

In contrast to the pattern developed during the agricultural revolution, in which the primary value of livestock was the dung produced for restoring soil fertility, meat and milk became the major value of livestock production in the high farming of the mid-nineteenth century. This was, of course, a rational response to rising animal prices relative to cereal price in this period.

The British experience is considered a classical "ideal type" of agricultural diversification. Except as an illustration of effective response of technology to economic opportunities, however, the British experience is of limited value to the developing counties today because of the extreme differences in the economic environment and technological possibilities as compared to eighteenth and nineteenth century Great Britain. The agricultural revolution in the eighteenth century occurred in an environment in which agriculture was a relatively self-contained system. The linkage of industry to agriculture through the supply of industrially produced inputs was not yet established. The agricultural transformation of the nineteenth century occurred at a time when the labor supply to agriculture was contracting, a situation diametrically opposite to that in developing countries today, where the absolute increase in agricultural labor force presses hard on limited land resources.

Danish Case

The Danish agricultural transformation experience, particularly the developments associated with the invention of the cream separator and the establishment of cooperative creameries, represents a more relevant case for developing countries.

Agricultural development in Denmark during the last quarter of the nineteenth century and the first quarter of this century represents a case of remarkable agricultural diversification in response to changes in product and factor market conditions. Denmark was traditionally a grain exporter to the British market. When large quantities of grains began to be imported into Britain from the new continents and grain prices fell, the traditional economic base of Danish agriculture came under severe pressure. In response to this challenge, Denmark successfully transformed itself into a major exporter of butter and bacon. An important point is that this transformation was carried out while the agricultural labor force was expanding. The absolute size of the agricultural labor force in Denmark did not begin to decline until the late 1920s.

A number of technological advances facilitated the transformation of Danish agriculture. These included tile drainage, increases in the application of fertilizer and lime, and improvements in seed and livestock varieties. The innovations that were most critical to the agricultural transformation were the invention and diffusion of the cream separator and the cooperative creamery system. Practically usable centrifugal cream separators were developed by the Danish inventor L.C. Nielsen in 1878 and the Swedish physicist, Carl Gustav Patrik de Laval in 1879. Both were immediately used in production, and by 1881 there were eighty separators operating in Denmark. Prior to this invention the production of butter was dominated by large farms or manors, which could build a "skimming hall," a large ventilated room where milk was kept fresh twenty-two to forty-six hours while the cream was rising. Small farmers who could not afford such a large capital investment were unable to participate in the profitable butter production; therefore, the expansion of dairy production was limited. The invention of the cream separator removed this constraint. The new potential that emerged from this technical invention was exploited by an institutional innovation—the cooperative creamer. With this combination of technical and institutional innovations, "*the profitableness of milk production was raised on middle-sized farms and even on small holdings to the level of the big farms*" (Jensen 1937: 176).

This innovation also contributed to the integration of dairy and hog operations. Large quantities of skim milk, a by-product of butter production, provided cheap feed for hogs. Production of lightly cured bacon based on this integrated system was developed in Denmark, and its export to Britain came to exceed the export of bacon to Britain from the United States; "*this is an outstanding example of an 'old' agricultural country entering a market fully occupied by the new overseas competitors*" (Jensen 1937: 191).

The Danish experience demonstrates the critical role of technical and institutional innovations for agricultural diversification. This experience is relevant to the developing countries today because the technology and institutions were so developed as to absorb a larger number of workers in agriculture and to use farm labor more fully by reducing the seasonality of agricultural production.

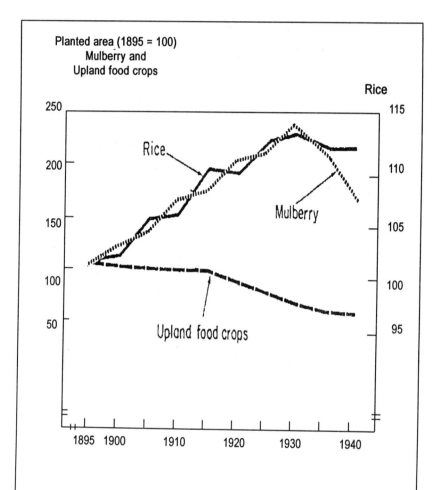

Figure 1

Trends in the indices of areas planted to selected crops, 1985–1940 (five-year averages centering the years shown).

Note: Upland crops include barley, naked barley, rye, soybean, Irish and sweet potatoes.

Source: N. Kayo (ed.) (1977) *Kaitei Nihon Nogyo Kiso Tokei* (The Basic Statistics of Japanese Agriculture, revised edn). Nihon Tokei Kyokai.

Development of Sericulture in Japan

An even more relevant example of agricultural diversification to developing countries today was the development of sericulture in the early period of modern Japanese economic growth.

Role of Sericulture in Economic Development

The development of sericulture is one of the most dramatic stories in the history of modern economic growth in Japan. From the 1880s to the 1930s, cocoon production increased tenfold from the level of 30,000 metric tons to more than 300,000 tons. Meanwhile, the share of sericulture in the total value of agricultural output rose from about 8 to 15 percent. This development was critical for Japanese economic growth because silk was a major source of foreign exchange earnings. It accounted for more than 40 percent of the value of total commodity exports before 1900, and its share continued to be higher than 30 percent before World War II.

This role of cocoon production as a cash sector in Japanese agriculture was similar to that of tropical cash crops, such as sugar and rubber, in developing countries today. However, there was a critical difference in the pattern by which the development of the cash sector was related with the subsistence sector. First, in Japan cocoon production was carried out strictly within the framework of traditional family farming, mostly as a sideline in addition to the production of food crops. Large-scale production organization of the plantation type did not emerge.

Second, the dramatic increase in sericultural production did not sacrifice the production of rice, the major food staple in Japan. The increase in the area planted with mulberry trees in Japan was parallel to those of the area planted with rice (Figure 1). In this process the output of upland food crops such as barley and potatoes was reduced. However, those were the inferior commodities with negative income elasticities, for

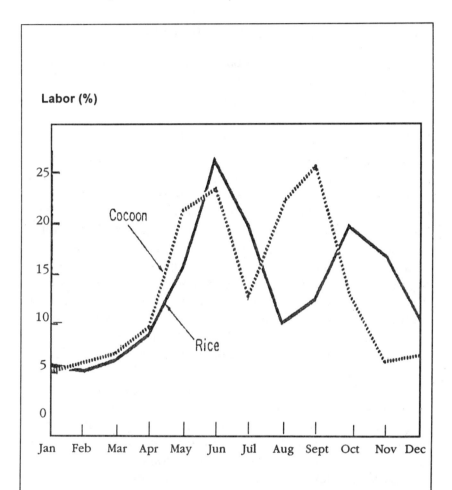

Figure 2

Monthly distributions of labor inputs for rice and cocoon production.

Source: Le Thanh Nghiep and Yujiro Hayami (1979) "Mobilizing Slack Resources for Economic Development: The Summer-Fall Rearing Technology of Sericulture in Japan," *Explorations in Economic History* 16 (April): 163–81.

which the demands contracted as urban population increased and per capita income rose. In fact, the competition in the use of land resources between cocoon and food crops was not so strong, especially in earlier years, because a large portion of mulberry orchards was developed on the steep slopes of hills and mountains that had hitherto been unused for farm production.

Thus, the dramatic development of sericulture in Japan was achieved without major changes in agrarian structure and without reducing the output of basic food staples for which domestic demand expands in response to population growth and income increase in the process of modern economic growth.

Significance of the Summer-Fall Cocoon Rearing Technology

The major innovation underlying the expansion of the Japanese sericulture industry can be identified as the development and diffusion of summer-fall rearing technology. Traditionally, spring (April to June) was the period of cocoon culture. However, this period coincided with the peak of the labor requirement for rice production and was hence competitive in its demand for labor. Therefore, cocoon production was initially limited to mountainous areas and was not commonly practiced by farmers cultivating lowland rice fields. For the major expansion of sericulture, technological innovations were required to enable cocoon culture during summer-fall months (July to September) so that labor standing idle between rice planting and harvesting periods could be mobilized for cocoon production.

Such relations are evident in the pattern of monthly labor allocations of a typical farm for rice and cocoon production during the 1930s (Figure 2). The labor requirement for the spring cocoon culture coincided almost exactly with the peak of labor use for rice transplantation and labor preparation. On the other hand, the summer-fall culture demanded labor when

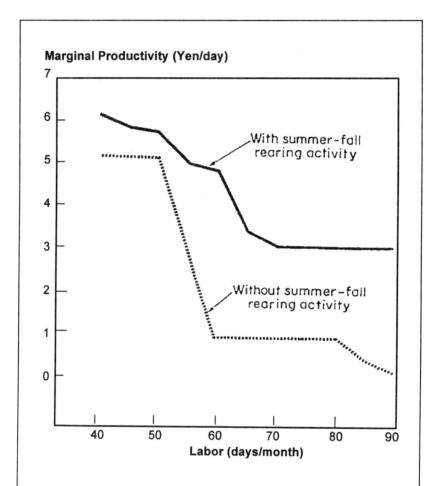

Figure 3

Marginal value productivities of labor in the linear-programming solutions for different levels of labor endowment for a typical sericulture farm in Japan during the 1930s.

Source: Le Thanh Nghiep and Yujiro Hayami (1979) "Mobilizing Slack Resources for Economic Development: The Summer-Fall Rearing Technology in Sericulture in Japan," *Explorations in Economic History* 16 (April): 163–81.

the labor requirement for rice production was low. With the development of summer-fall rearing technology, the possibility opened for the majority of small farmers producing rice to introduce sericulture into their farming system within the constraint of family labor.

Summer-fall cocoon culture, using the nonhibernating bivoltine varieties, had been practiced on a very small scale before the Meiji period. It was only after the discovery in 1875 by Mototada Odaka, a manager of the Tomioka Silk Reeling Mill, of a method of postponing the hatching of hibernating varieties by storing the silkworm eggs in cool caves that the summer-fall culture became practical for many farmers. Later a method of artificial hatching by chemical processing was developed. Finally, a hydrochloric acid processing method was established in 1912/13 at the Aichi prefectural Egg Multiplication Station. The summer-fall culture was greatly facilitated by the development of F_1 hybrid varieties (originally by Kametaro Tooyama in 1906). The hybrids prove much more vigorous, resulting in a dramatic improvement in the survival rate of summer-fall-reared silkworms.

There were a number of advantages to summer-fall rearing in the use of resources. It increased the efficiency of capital use for farmers because rearing equipment and utensils could be used more than once a year. Also, reelers could economize on the use of circulating capital because they were able to divide payments for cocoons between the spring and summer-fall seasons. It reduced the risk of frost on mulberry leaves, which often damaged early spring culture. The most critical contribution, however, was the increase in the efficiency of labor use resulting from the employment of seasonally idle labor. Labor that was idle between the rice planting and harvesting periods could be mobilized for cocoon production. The result was a substantial increase in the number of work days per year per person engaged in agricultural production and an increase in labor income.

Further, the summer-fall-rearing technology was biased in favor of small peasants whose family labor endowments were large relative to land endowments, as indicated by the linear-programming (LP) analysis of a typical farm in Japan for the 1930s (Nghiep and Hayami 1979). The calculations of the marginal product of labor in the LP solutions for different levels of family labor endowments for a given land endowment indicate that up to a labor input of 50 man-days per month per hectare, there was little difference on labor's marginal productivity between the cases with and without summer-fall rearing (Figure 3). As labor inputs without summer-fall rearing increased, however, marginal productivity declined sharply to zero, whereas with summer-fall rearing, marginal productivity declined more moderately and remained positive up to a labor endowment of 90 man-days. These observed relations are consistent with the hypothesis that the contribution of the summer-fall-rearing technology to the increase in labor's marginal productivity was largest on small farms where the endowments of labor were high relative to the endowments of land.

Cocoon production from summer-fall culture rose from a negligible level at the beginning of the Meiji period (1868) to 12,000 tons in 1890—about 25 percent of total production—and to 119,000 tons in 1920—about half of total production. This innovation of summer-fall culture enabled the Japanese sericulture industry to surpass France, Italy, and China in production. It contributed to the simultaneous achievements of two major roles assigned to the agricultural sector for economic development: (a) to supply food (rice) for the growing urban population, and (b) to provide a material basis (cocoon) for foreign exchange earnings. Those goals were achieved while the incomes of small-scale family farms were improved through increases in the efficiency and the intensity in the use of their labor.

It must be emphasized that this technical innovation was supported by a number of institutional innovations, including the establishment of silk inspection stations (1895), national and prefectural silkworm egg multiplication stations (1910/11), and sericultural colleges in Tokyo (1896), Kyoto (1899) and Ueda (1920). The development of sericulture cooperatives was also important. Their activities ranged from the transmission of technical information and the cooperative rearing of young worms to the management of cooperative silk reeling mills and even the training centers.

Policies for Agricultural Diversification

The historical experiences in developed economies indicate clearly that a key to the success of agricultural diversification is technological and institutional innovations consistent with the conditions of product and factor markets. The scope of success for an agricultural diversification strategy is limited if it simply attempts to divert resources from the production of basic cereals to other crops and livestock products with no major technological innovation in either farm production or processing and marketing. If this resource reallocation would be enforced by government programs such as price supports and input/ credit subsidies, it would prove to be counterproductive for the purposes that agricultural diversification tries to achieve. For example, without a major breakthrough in summer-fall rearing technology, the development of sericulture in Japan would have been seriously constrained by the seasonal profile of labor use in rice production. If the government attempted to intervene in markets to divert resources from rice to sericulture without developing appropriate technology to remove this constraint, the increase in sericultural production would have been met by sharp declines in rice production; this would have resulted in high rice prices and high cost of living for urban consumers or serious drain of foreign exchange due to large-scale rice imports, both unfavorable to national economic development. Therefore, the effective policy of agricultural diversification must include as a critical component the major effort to strengthen and expand research and development not only on farm production technology but also on processing and marketing technologies.

Indeed, in order to support the introduction of new commodities, not only technological innovations but also major institutional reorganizations in production, processing and marketing systems are often required. A typical example was the development of the cooperative creamery in response to the invention of the centrifugal cream separator in the history of Denmark. In Southeast Asia today, if the commodities of rapidly increasing demand, such as vegetables and fruits, are to be introduced to traditional rice or corn areas, a new marketing system that enables much tighter coordination between production and marketing shall be required for marketing of the storable commodities, so as to retain the freshness, the perishable commodities delivered to consumers.

It must be cautioned, however, that the substitution of governmental or semi-governmental organizations such as marketing boards or government-sponsored cooperatives, for private marketing channels if attempted for this reason, is likely to reduce rather than improve both efficiency and equity as it tends to promote corruption and rent-seeking activities. Accumulated empirical evidence in the past indicates that private marketing in developing economies is largely competitive and efficient; contrary to the myth of the monopolistic exploitation by middlemen and moneylenders, exploitation by government monopoly is often more devastating (Hayami 1990). Moreover, I have encountered cases in which indigenous marketing/processing systems were able to adjust remarkably well under private initiatives to major innovations in farm production. For example, I was impressed by a case observed in West Java, in which local entrepreneurship was able to achieve effective coordination between production and marketing when commercial vegetable production was newly introduced to an unfavorable rainfed environment where corn and upland rice were traditionally grown (Hayami and Kawagoe 1993, Chapter 4).

Thus, I am convinced that appropriate innovations in marketing and processing industries in support of agricultural diversification can best be achieved by private initiatives in free markets. Governments must support these private initiatives by providing education and training services to management and workers as well as information services such as crop reporting, market price quotations, grading and standardization of weights and measures, in addition to investments in transportation and communication infrastructure.

Finally, I would like to emphasize again that the basic condition for significant diversion of agricultural production resources from the rice to the non-rice sector is sustained increase in the supply of rice outpacing its demand growth so that diversion of resources to non-rice crops continues to be profitable. In this respect, sustained growth in rice yields is vital for the success of agricultural diversification in Southeast Asia. A disquieting aspect is that growths in both total rice output and average yield per hectare in this region decelerated significantly for the recent decade as compared with the previous two decades. In order to achieve genuine progress in agricultural diversification, efforts must be intensified to reverse the present trend in yield together with the efforts to search for appropriate cropping systems to combine rice with other commodities. Otherwise, agricultural diversification will soon be trapped by the tradeoff between food and cash crops as was repeated in the past.

References

CGPRT Center (1985) *The Soybean Commodity System in Indonesia.* Bogor, Indonesia: ESCAP-CGPRT Center.

Hayami, Y. (1990) "Community, Market, and State," Elmhirst Lécture, in Allen Maumder and Albert Valdes (eds.). *Agriculture and Governments in an Interdependent World.* Aldershot, U.K.: Dartmouth Publishing Co. 3–14.

_____. (1989) "Conditions of Agricultural Diversification: A Historical Prespective," paper presented at APO Study Meeting on Agricultural Diversification. Tokyo: Asian Productivity Organization.

_____. and V.W. Ruttan (1985) *Agricultural Development: An International Prespective,* Revised edition. Baltimore: Johns Hopkins University Press.

_____. and T. Kawagoe (1993) *The Agrarian Origins of Commerce and Industry: A Study of Peasant Marketing in Indonesia.* London: MacMillan and New York: St. Martin's Press.

Islam, N. (1990) "Horticultural Exports of Developing Countries: Past Performance, Future Prospects and Policy Issues," *IFPRI Research Report No. 80.* Washington, D.C.: International Food Policy Research Institute.

Jensen, E. (1937) *Danish Agriculture: Its Economic Development.* Copenhagen: J.H. Schultz Forlag.

Myint, H. (1965) *The Economics of the Developing Countries.* New York: Praeger.

Nghiep, L. T. and Y. Hayami (1979) "Mobilizing Slack Resources for Economic Development: The Summer-Fall Rearing Technology of Sericulture in Japan," *Explorations in Economic History* 16 April: 163–81.

Land Reform in the Philippines: Lessons from the Past and Direction for the Future

Keijiro Otsuka*

Introduction

Land reform programs in Asia typically consist of tenancy reform and land redistribution programs (Otsuka 1993). Tenancy reform rules out the practice of share tenancy, regulates the leasehold rent at a low level, and prohibits the eviction of tenants. The land redistribution policy sets the ceiling on the maximum landholding and transfers the ownership right of land in excess of the ceiling to the actual cultivators. In order to "protect" or preserve the status of land reform beneficiaries, transaction in cultivation rights including subleasing is prohibited by law. Another common feature is that area under owner cultivation with employment of agricultural laborers is exempted from land reform. These features of the Asian land reform programs are also to be found in the Philippines (see, e.g., Hayami *et al.* 1990).

*Professor of Economics, Tokyo Metropolitan University.

Land reform programs have the twin objectives of enhancing social equity by transferring wealth from the landed class to landless tenants and achieving higher production efficiency by converting share tenancy to owner cultivation as well as leasehold tenancy. The presumptions are that the tenants belong to the poorest segment of rural society and that share tenancy is less efficient than leasehold tenancy and owner-cultivation, the latter being operated even with employment of hired labor. These presumptions, however, are empirically incorrect. First, the poorest of the rural poor are landless laborers. Second, share tenancy is not generally inefficient compared with leasehold tenancy and owner cultivation, unless tenancy contracts are distorted by land reform laws themselves. Third, by suppressing the option of tenancy and subtenancy contracts, land reform tends to induce cultivation with employment of laborers, which is less efficient than tenant-cultivation. Fourth, in this way land reform tends to block the agricultural ladder for landless laborers to ascend, thereby perpetuating their status.

The purpose of this article is to identify the basic flaws of conventional land reform programs and to seek better alternatives, based mainly on my own empirical research conducted in the Philippines. Since my previous research mostly pertains to the rice sector, the analysis in this article is particularly relevant for rice and other crop sectors where scale economies are largely absent. Specifically I would argue that the conventional land reform regulations should be abolished and replaced by the progressive land tax scheme for the sake of achieving the social justice with minimum sacrifice of production efficiency.

Was Land Reform Successful in the Philippines?

The whole Philippines was proclaimed a land reform area under Presidential Decree No. 2 in 1972. Particular importance was attached to the land redistribution policy by Presidential Decree No. 27, which proclaimed "the emancipation of the tiller from the bondage of the soil." The Philippine land reform applies only to tenanted areas growing rice and corn, with exclusion of owner-cultivated areas and areas growing crops other than rice and corn. Landlords are allowed to retain seven hectares of land, to which the Operation Leasehold (LHO) program applies, and lands in excess of the retention limit are subject to the Operation Land Transfer (OLT) program. Under the LHO program, share tenancy is converted to leasehold tenancy with rent fixed at 25 percent of average output, net of the costs of seeds, harvesting and threshing for three normal crop years preceding the Presidential Decree. Under the OLT program, excess lands are to be sold to former tenants at a price 2.5 times the gross normal output. The Certificate of Land Transfer (CLT) is distributed to eligible tenants, identifying their cultivated areas and promising them the right to purchase the land, with CLT holders required to pay amortization fees to the Land Bank over 15 years. The annual amortization fee, if paid equally for 15 years by installment, amounts to about 25 percent of the gross value of normal production in the early 1970s. Thus, there is not much difference between the status of leaseholder and of CLT holder in the Philippine land reform program.

With respect to implementation, the common view in the Philippines seems to be that the land reform in the 1970s was unsuccessful, not to mention the more recent comprehensive agrarian reform program. Indeed, a comparison of agricultural census data for 1971 and 1980 indicates no major change in tenure distribution occurred in the 1970s.

However, according to an extensive survey of 50 rice-growing villages, encompassing Northern, Central and Southern Luzon, and Panay Island, conducted by myself in 1987, land reform was surprisingly well implemented (Otsuka 1991). Table 1 compares the distribution of rice areas by tenure and by rice production environment between 1970 and 1986. Note that the unfavorable rainfed area is either a low-lying flood-

	Irrigated		Favorable Rainfed		Unfavorable Rainfed	
Table 1 Comparison of Rice Areas by Land Tenure and by Rice Production Environment, 1970 and 1986 (Percent)						
	1970	1986	1970	1986	1970	1986
Owner	22	22	19	19	46	46
CLT	–	34	–	34	–	17
Leasehold	10	35	7	34	13	12
Share Tenancy	68	9	74	13	41	25
Total	100	100	100	100	100	100
(Sample Size)	(17)		(17)		(16)	

Source: Otsuka (1991)

prone area or a hilly drought-prone one, whereas the favorable rainfed area is the shallow rainfed environment common in the Philippines.

It is clear that the incidence of share tenancy drastically declined from 1970 to 1986 in irrigated and favorable rainfed areas, and somewhat less so in unfavorable areas. In contrast, the ratios of leasehold and CLT areas increased dramatically in the former areas. The beneficiaries of land reform in favorable areas have been capturing a large economic surplus because rice yields have been increasing significantly due to the adoption of modern high-yielding rice varieties (Otsuka and Gascon 1992) while leasehold rents and amortization fees have been fixed. Otsuka, Cordova, and David (1992), conclude that not only CLT holders but also leaseholds are legitimately considered to be land reform beneficiaries.

The data on the implementation of land reform provided by the Department of Agrarian Reform are largely consistent with our data (Hayami *et al.* 1990).[1] Thus, it seems reasonable to

---

[1]How to resolve the inconsistency of the data on the implementation of land reform between the Census statistics and other information remains an important issue.

conclude that the land reform in the Philippines was successful in terms of the implementation of the LHO and OLT programs.[2] Successful implementation, however, does not necessarily imply that the basic objectives of enhancing production efficiency and achieving greater social justice have been realized.

Is Share Tenancy Inefficient?

The conventional view of share tenancy asserts that since the marginal return to the work effort for the tenant is proportionally less than the marginal product of his effort (conventionally called the marginal product of labor) under the share contract, the work incentives to the tenant are thwarted. In contrast, it is commonly accepted that the fixed-rent leasehold contract, in which the tenant pays a fixed sum to the landlord and claims the residual, and owner farming do not distort work incentives.

An implicit assumption of the inefficiency view of share tenancy is that it is prohibitively costly for the landlord to observe and enforce the tenant's work effort, so that the tenant determines his effort to maximize his own utility without fear of punishment for labor shirking. In practice, like owner-cultivators, tenants engage in care-intensive activities such as fertilizer application and water control. In other words, the tenant's effort represents his conscientious effort to apply his labor even for allocative decision-making. Given a spatially dispersed and ecologically diverse production environment in agriculture, it will not be an easy task for a landowner to supervise a tenant's effort. It is therefore no wonder that the inefficiency view of share tenancy is widely accepted.[3]

---

[2] I found that most CLT holders never paid any amortization fees, presumably because of the small penalty on deferred payments. This seems to represent the critical defect of the OLT program.

[3] See Otsuka, Chuma, and Hayami (1992) and Hayami and Otsuka (1993a) for recent reviews of the tenancy literature.

The source of the incentive problem lies in the difficulty the landlord has in observing the tenant's work effort. If the work effort is observable and enforceable without cost, the landlord can specify and enforce the tenant's work effort at the desired level. In equilibrium, no inefficiency is shown to arise under share tenancy in this situation.

While the assumption of costless enforcement is unrealistic, the assumption of prohibitively costly enforcement seems too restrictive. A recent model of Otsuka, Chuma, and Hayami (1993) introduces the monitoring function of tenant's work effort, which posits that the probability of detecting tenant's shirking is increasingly a function of the degree of his shirking (i.e., the difference between actual effort level and the level specified by the landlord) and landlord's supervision time. The monitoring efficiency will depend on the landlord's ability (e.g., associated with his farming experience, size of landholding, and residential proximity to his tenant farms) and the technological characteristics of production (e.g., traditional vs. new technology and food crops vs. commercial crops). So long as the monitoring of tenant's work effort is feasible but costly, as certainly it is, the equilibrium effort level will lie in-between the "second-best" and the "first-best" optimum levels of work effort conventionally examined in the literature.

Whether the equilibrium effort level is closer to the first-best or second-best optimum depends not only on the probability of detecting tenant's shirking but also on the amount of punishment. Thus, the controversy on the efficiency of share tenancy must be settled by determining whether, in practice, landowners have sufficient ability to enforce share tenancy contracts and whether sufficiently strong penalties, such as loss of personal reputation, exist in rural communities to enforce contractual performance.

To test the hypothesis of inefficient resource allocation under share tenancy, a large number of case studies have been conducted in South and Southeast Asia. They compared average output, and also inputs in some cases, per unit of land between share tenancy and owner cultivation and between share and leasehold tenancy. The production data were often classified by the presence of irrigation and the size of cultivated area, to control the quality difference in land and the effect of scale of farm operation. According to an exhaustive survey of the empirical studies by Otsuka and Hayami (1988), updated by Hayami and Otsuka (1993a), the physical quantity of output per unit of land tends to be equalized between share tenancy and owner farming and between share and leasehold tenancy. In the case of the Philippines, too, no significant inefficiency of share tenancy is reported by Castillo (1975), Hayami and Kikuchi (1982), Mangahas *et al.* (1976), and Roumasset (1987), among others.

Otsuka, Chuma, and Hayami (1992) attribute the absence of significant inefficiency of share tenancy to the landlord's ability to enforce the share tenancy contract. According to their survey of the empirical literature, small resident landowners, who are also experienced farmers, tend to choose share tenancy, whereas large absentee landlords and widows, who have no farming experience, tend to prefer leasehold tenancy. Needless to say, a small resident landowner offering a couple of share tenancy contracts has an advantage in monitoring his tenants' work effort over a large absentee landlord. Because of the high monitoring ability of the landowner offering the share contract, the probability of detecting tenant's shirking is likely to be high. Moreover, the penalty on the share tenant's behavior is also likely to be high because landowners and share tenants are often relatives and close friends. Given such personal relationships, the cost of losing one's reputation in a relatively closed agrarian community may be sufficiently high to deter the tenant's opportunistic behavior. Thus, it is not surprising to find that share tenancy is not generally inefficient.[4] The

---

[4]It is also considered in the tenancy literature that share tenancy retards the speed of innovation. Such dynamic inefficiency, however, is not generally found by empirical studies. See David and Otsuka (1990) for the Philippine case.

178 Choice, Growth and Development

implication is that the abolition of share tenancy cannot improve production efficiency to a significant extent.[5]

It is theoretically established that in order to justify the choice of share tenancy rather than fixed-rent tenancy, the merit of sharing production risk under this contract in the presence of tenant's risk aversion must be taken into account (Hayami and Otsuka 1993a). If the tenant is risk averse, he will prefer share to fixed-rent tenancy because of the smaller variability of his income under the former than the latter arrangement. So long as share tenancy is preferred by risk-averse tenants for the sake of reducing income risk, its abolition will impair their welfare.

Who are the Rural Poor?

While most people in rural areas are poor, owner-cultivators are richer than tenants and tenants are richer than landless agricultural laborers. It is the landless laborers who belong to the poorest segment of the poor rural society in Asia (David and Otsuka 1993). As in other countries of Asia, the number of poor landless agricultural laborers has been increasing in recent decades in the Philippines.

Table 2 compares annual income per capita among members of owner-cultivator, tenant, and landless laborer households by production environment based on the household survey of five selected villages in Nueva Ecija and Iloilo province conducted by the International Rice Research Institute. All villages are "typical" rice-based villages. It is confirmed that landless laborers are poorer than tenants and tenants are poorer than owner cultivators. This is particularly the case in the irrigated areas. This is because the return to land is higher in the irrigated environment owing to higher productivity of land. In

---

[5]Otsuka, Chuma, and Hayami (1992) argue that the tenancy regulations in India and Bangladesh distort the tenancy transactions, thereby resulting in production inefficiency.

fact, the difference in income between environments as well as between tenure classes can be explained mostly by the difference in the return to land (Otsuka, Cordova, and David 1992). Therefore, the difference in income among the tenure classes is smaller in less favorable production environments.

	Irrigated Village[a]	Favorable Rainfed Vill[b]	Unfavorable Rainfed Vill[c]
Table 2 Comparison of Annual Income Per Capita Among Members of Owner, Tenant, and Laborer Households (₱1,000), by Production Environment, 1985			
Owner	6.0	4.0	1.4
Tenant	4.6	3.0	1.6
Laborer	2.6	2.3	1.4
Proportion of landless households (%)	3.2	22	15

[a]Average of two irrigated villages in Nueva Ecija and Iloilo provinces.
[b]Average of two shallow rainfed villages in Nueva Ecija and Iloilo provinces.
[c]Drought-prone rainfed village in Iloilo province.

It is also remarkable to observe that the income of landless laborers is almost equal between irrigated and favorable rainfed areas. The demand for labor increased particularly in irrigated areas when modern rice varieties (MVs) were introduced, which raised not only labor use per hectare per season but also labor use per year as MVs facilitated double cropping of rice. The "equalization" of laborers' income can be explained largely by labor migration from less favorable to favorable production environments, which tends to equalize wages in agricultural activities in the Philippines (Otsuka, Cordova, and David 1990). The higher proportion of landless laborer households in irrigated areas reflects the migration of landless households. On the other hand, the income of agricultural laborers in unfavorable rainfed village is particularly low. This will be explained, at least partly, by the lower education level of laborers in this village, which limits their labor earnings from nonfarm sources.

	Irrigated		Favorable Rainfed		Unfavorable Rainfed
	N. Ecija No. (%)	Iloilo No. (%)	N. Ecija No. (%)	Iloilo No. (%)	Iloilo No. (%)
Eviction	11 (22)	0 (0)	14 (31)	7 (29)	0 (0)
Former tenants	21 (41)	3 (5)	26 (58)	11 (46)	2 (18)
No. of landless laborers	51	57	45	24	11

Table 3
Incidence of Tenant Eviction Since 1972 and the Number of Former Tenants Among Landless Laborers in Five Selected Villages in the Philippines, 1985

Source: Otsuka (1991).

If the major objective of land reform is to improve the welfare of the poor, it must be so designed as to confer benefits to landless agricultural laborers. Since the existing land reform program has no such provision, its impact on social equity is deemed to be limited. The conventional land reform ought to be "reformed" so as to transfer income from the landed class to the poor landless laborers.

The Conventional Reform Creates the Landless

While land reform ought to have improved the income of landless laborers, its actual impact is shown to be the opposite. First, land reform induced the eviction of tenants, which increased the landless labor population. Second, by prohibiting new tenancy and subtenancy contracts, the land reform perpetuated the status of landless laborers.

If the rents and amortization fees were fixed at a level significantly lower than the rental value of land, landlords would have been motivated to evict tenants in order to undertake "their own-cultivation." This would be particularly the case in those villages where the leasehold rents and amortization fees have significantly diverged from the rental value of land. In my survey of landless laborers' households in five selected villages in Nueva Ecija and Iloilo province, I tried to obtain data on the incidence of tenant eviction (Otsuka, 1991). It is, however, difficult to obtain accurate information simply because eviction is illegal. Therefore, questions are asked not only about eviction but also about tenure status before land reform. According to Table 3, a number of landless laborers in the Nueva Ecija villages and the unfavorable rainfed villages in Iloilo are former tenants and some of them explicitly reported having been evicted. No single case of eviction, however, was reported in the other two villages. These observations are consistent with a priori expectation, as leasehold rents and amortization fees were significantly different from the estimated rental value of land in the former three villages.[6]

Moreover, the present land reform has prevented the so-called agricultural laborers from becoming tenants, since land reform beneficiaries and landlords who still administer sizable areas have lost incentives to rent out their land under the tenancy regulations. If they engage in illegal tenancy transactions, they may lose their cultivation rights. Thus, there

---

[6]In those three villages, high-yielding rice varieties were introduced after land reform was implemented, which have made the rental value of land significantly higher than fixed rents and amortization fees computed on the basis of yield with traditional varieties. In the irrigated village in Iloilo, leasehold rents were high because high-yielding varieties were already introduced before 1972.

is virtually no possibility for landless laborers to become tenants. While the possibility to climb up the agricultural ladder has been lost, the possibility to climb down has been left open. It is common to observe that small leaseholders and amortizing owners mortgage out their titles to large farmers and wealthy agricultural traders for urgently needed cash. Nagarajan, Quisumbing, and Otsuka (1991) argue that part of the reason why some land reform beneficiaries mortgage out their land is that their cultivation right is not transferable and, thus, cannot be used as collateral for formal credit. To obtain credit, they mortgage out their lands and virtually suffer from a lowering in status to become landless laborers, forced to make a meager living from unstable farm work.

Tenancy Transactions Should Not be Suppressed

It must not be overlooked that tenancy transactions play an important role in the transfer of land from land-abundant households to households with little or no land. Thus, the prohibition of tenancy transactions prevents many socially desirable transactions. One good example is the case of Japan, where tenancy transactions, including share tenancy, have been suppressed by law. This has resulted in a decrease in the number of tenancy cases, despite the recent relaxation of the tenancy regulations (Otsuka 1992). As a result, average farm size remains as small as 1.2 hectares. This is inefficient because significant economies of scale have emerged with the introduction of medium-size machinery.

In the Philippines, the tenancy regulations led to the substitution of inefficient labor contracts for tenancy contracts. Hayami and Otsuka (1993b) observe that a "new" labor contract called *kasugpong* has recently become common in Central Luzon. The *kasugpong* contract itself existed even before the land reform. Traditionally, the *kasugpong* laborer was a young boy who stayed in a farmer's house and helped with the farming tasks as well as the household activities of the master-farmer. Typically he worked together with his master on the farm and took care of draft animals throughout the year. The *kasugpong* contract practiced in recent years, however, is different in the sense that the laborer is assigned the obligation of performing major farm tasks. Under this contract a laborer receives either a fixed sum of paddy or 10 percent of ·gross output at the end of a crop season in exchange for his continuous labor service throughout the season. The *kasugpong* contract is usually renewed, like the permanent labor (or attached labor) contract widely practiced in South Asia. Although the payment of a proportional share of the output resembles that which is practiced under share tenancy, a *kasugpong* contract (alternatively called *porsiyentuhan*) is not usually considered a tenancy contract because of the low output sharing rate. Yet tasks performed by the *kasugpong* laborer are essentially the same as those done by tenants and owner cultivators, e.g., land preparation, water control, and supervision of casual laborers.

The *kasugpong* contract is considered a substitute for tenancy or subtenancy contracts. In fact, large farmers and agricultural traders, who have accumulated cultivation rights by land mortgaging, employ *kasugpong* laborers. Because of the payment of fixed wage or low output sharing rates, the *kasugpong* workers have little incentive to work. Otsuka, Chuma, and Hayami (1993) advance the hypothesis that in order to prevent labor shirking, employers of *kasugpong* laborers offer them more lucrative contractual terms than their alternative jobs. If a laborer's shirking is detected, not only will his current contract be terminated but he also loses the opportunity to be offered a *kasugpong* contract in the future. To the extent that the landlord assures a laborer utility higher than the latter's opportunity utility, the fear of losing lucrative future contractual opportunities may represent a potentially heavy penalty on laborer's shirking. In practice, a *kasugpong's* alternative job opportunity is casual labor employment.

	Kasugpong Laborers	Casual Laborers
Table 4		
Labor Income and Workdays of *Kasugpong* and Casual Laborers in the Nueva Ecija Village by Source, 1989 Dry Season		
Sample size	23	25
Labor income (₱ per season)		
Rice production	7,594	802
Non-rice production	1,138	3,533
Total	8,732	4,335
Income per workday:		
Rice production	106.7	38.6
Non-rice production	49.5	44.5
Average	92.7	43.3
Source: Otsuka, Chuma, and Hayami (1993).		

According to an intensive survey of an irrigated village in Nueva Ecija, *kasugpong* laborers are better-off than casual laborers (see Table 4). In this village, nearly half of landless laborers are engaged in *kasugpong*. The major source of income of the landless laborers are *kasugpong* and casual labor employment in rice production and unskilled off-farm jobs, such as carpentry and tricycle operation. The total labor income of a *kasugpong* laborer per season is found to be twice as large as that of casual laborers, and the difference is significant. In terms of non-farm labor earnings per day there is no significant difference between *kasugpong* and casual laborers, because they are largely homogeneous. The significant difference in total income arises mainly because the earnings per day under the *kasugpong* contract are far greater than the daily wage rate for casual laborers. Thus, it seems clear that *kasugpong* laborers are better-off than casual laborers, owing to the superior terms and conditions of the *kasugpong* contract. Needless to say, however, their income is much smaller than the income of the land reform beneficiaries.

Table 5

Average Value of Rice Output, Costs of Production, and
Residual Profit Per Hectare in Farms With and Without
Kasugpong Labor in the Nueva Ecija Village,
1989 Dry Season (1,000 Pesos)

	With *kasugpong*	Without *kasugpong*
Sample size	26	71
Value of output (A)	22.4	25.5
Current input cost (B)[a]	3.0	3.1
Capital input cost (C)[b]	1.7	1.8
Labor Cost (D)[c]	4.9	4.1
Labor supervision cost (E)[d]	0.6	0.2
Residual profit (A - B - C - D - E)	12.2	16.4

Source: Otsuka, Chuma, and Hayami (1993).

[a]Total costs of chemical fertilizer, other chemical inputs, fuel, and seeds.

[b]Total costs of draft animal, tractor, and thresher services, including both actual and imputed costs.

[c]The sum of hired labor costs, including the payment of the *kasugpong* laborers, and imputed family labor costs.

[d]Mandays of supervision time multiplied by the estimated time costs per day. 80 pesos per day was applied for resident farmers and 120 pesos for non-resident managers of farms.

Yet, *kasugpong* laborers still shirk because of the inadequate work incentives. Table 5 compares output values of rice production, production costs, and residual profit per hectare between farms with and without *kasugpong* laborers.[7] We consider the value of output rather than the physical yield because there were marked differences in prices of paddy among varieties grown in this village. The average value of output on farms with *kasugpong* laborers is significantly lower than on farms without *kasugpong* laborers (or farms operated

[7]We exclude from the comparison here farms with *kasugpong* laborers managed by "professional managers" (Otsuka, Chuma, and Hayami 1993) who are non-residents, college graduates, and exceptionally efficient full-time managers of farms.

by family labor of tenant and owner-cultivator households). This observation is consistent with the hypothesis that *kasugpong* laborers shirk because of weak work-incentives.

The value of output depends not only on the work-effort but also on the application of other inputs and the supervision of *kasugpong* laborers by their employers. Table 5 also compares costs of current inputs, capital, and labor inputs, and the residual profit. The residual profit is obtained by subtracting those costs and the time cost of supervision from the output value. For the evaluation of the time cost of supervision per day, we applied ₱80 for resident farmers and ₱120 for non-resident employers of *kasugpong* laborers. The imputed cost of ₱80 corresponds to the average daily earnings of harvesters, which is the highest hired-labor wage in rice production in this village. The estimated time cost of non-resident employers of *kasugpong* laborers is obtained from interviews.[8] The costs of current inputs and capital inputs are largely the same between the two types of farms. Labor costs are higher on farms of *kasugpong*-labor operation largely because of the larger wage payment to *kasugpong* laborers. There are also significant differences in supervision costs.

As a result, the residual profit on farms of *kasugpong*-labor operation amounts to only 74 percent of the profit on farms of family-labor operation. Such results support the hypothesis that, being an imperfect substitute for tenancy, farming under the *kasugpong* labor contract is less efficient than under tenant- and owner-cultivation because of the insufficient work incentives under the fixed-wage or very low output-sharing contracts.

The emerging agrarian structure in the Philippine rice sector resembles that of India where farmers in upper castes do not work but only supervise the work of permanent laborers in

---

[8]Because of the substantial difference in supervision time, the assumed time costs per day do not make much difference in the comparison of total costs and the residual profits between farms with and without *kasugpong* labor.

lower castes, with no agricultural ladder bridging them. If the current trend continues, the incidence of *kasugpong* contract may become widespread and the Philippine rice sector may be eventually beset with both production inefficiency and social inequity. This suggests that the tenancy regulations should be abolished to reopen the agricultural ladder for both efficiency and equity.

Towards New Land Reform Program

Needless to say, I am not arguing that land reform is socially undesirable. My view is that it must be so designed as to avoid the loss of production efficiency and the welfare loss of the rural poor. Before considering the issue of a desirable land reform design, we have to examine the experience in Asia on what determines the success and the failure of land reform implementation. The Japanese case does not provide any lesson because its land reform was strictly implemented by the strong power of the US occupation forces. In South and Southeast Asia, the history of the land reform program is replete with failed experiences, despite the popular support for reformism. Perhaps it is fair to say that land reform in the Philippines during the 1970s was one of the most successful. Otsuka (1991) demonstrates that one of the reasons for the successful implementation of land reform in the Philippines was the introduction of modern rice varieties, which raised the rental value of land, thereby increasing tenants' incentives to acquire the status of leaseholders and CLT holders.

There are a number of factors that affect the fate of land reform. If I have to choose one key factor, I would dare to choose the simplicity of the program. Complicated laws create loopholes and invite corruption among government officials. For example, the Marcos land reform programs applied only to tenanted areas of rice and corn lands. Therefore, some landlords converted rice lands for the production of other crops and others evicted tenants to resume own cultivation by employing laborers, including *kasugpong* workers. Even worse is the case in which discretion is left to government officials who can be brought over to the side of landlords for reasons of local politics. Thus, I am in agreement with a leading land reform specialist in the U.S. who strongly advocates "the importance of simple rules in the effective implementation of land reform programs" as a necessary condition for successful land reform (Prosterman and Riedinger 1987).

My task now is to delineate the features of a desirable land reform program. It follows directly from the flaws of the present land reform that the tenancy regulations should be abandoned. Simply to do so, however, may lead to the emergence of new landlordism. In fact, large farmers and wealthy traders have already accumulated large tracts of land through land mortgaging. Land mortgaging is illegal and, hence, suppressed by law to some extent. If large farmers and traders are allowed freely to purchase the cultivation rights, they will continue to accumulate the lands, as they did historically in this country. Therefore, liberalization of tenancy regulations is likely to conflict with the social goal of greater social justice. Herein lies the difficulty of achieving greater social justice and production efficiency within a framework of the traditional land reform. In the first place, because of the complexity of rules, there is little assurance that the traditional programs will succeed. What is needed is a simple mechanism which prevents the holding of large areas in the hands of a few and which at the same time allows free transaction in cultivation rights.

I cannot conceive of any way other than the scheme of a very simple progressive land tax proposed by Hayami *et al.* (1990) that can improve social equity with a minimum sacrifice of production efficiency. This scheme meets the objective of attaining greater equity; as larger landholdings become increasingly more costly, large landowners have more incentives to sell their excessive lands. The efficiency loss associated with land tax is expected to be small, as the supply of land is inelastic. It is simple and, hence, effective. It does not suppress tenancy transactions and, hence, is non-distortionary. It is beneficial for the landless laborers partly because the agricultural ladder is opened and partly because small-scale farming demands more labor inputs. The tax revenue can possibly supplement the land taxation scheme by being used to provide extension service and credits for production and land purchase for the poor—measures which facilitate the landless laborers' climb up the agricultural ladder.

There is, however, a critical defect in this scheme. Knowing that it is effective, the landed class will express fierce opposition to such a policy. But if land reform is to improve social justice by improving the well-being of the landless poor with the minimum sacrifice of production efficiency, we must clearly recognize that the appropriate choices are extremely limited.

References

Castillo, G. T. (1975) *All in a Grain of Rice: A Review of Philippine Studies on the Social and Economic Implications of the New Rice Technology.* Laguna, Philippines: Southeast Asian Regional Center for Graduate Study and Research in Agriculture.

David, C. C., and K. Otsuka (1990) "The Modern Seed-Fertilizer Technology and Adoption of Labor-Saving Technologies: The Philippine Case," *Australian Journal of Agricultural Economics* 34 August: 132–46.

_____ (1993) *Modern Rice Technology and Income Distribution in Asia.* Boulder, Col.: Lynne Rienner.

Hayami, Y. and M. Kikuchi (1982) *Asian Village Economy at the Crossroads.* Baltimore, MD: Johns Hopkins University Press, 1982.

Hayami, Y., A. M. Quisumbing, and L. S. Adriano (1990) *Toward an Alternative Land Reform Paradigm: A Philippine Perspective.* Quezon City, Philippines: Ateneo de Manila University Press.

Hayami, Y. and K. Otsuka (1993a) *The Economics of Contract Choice: An Agrarian Perspective*. Oxford: Clarendon Press.

_____ (1993b) "Kasugpong in the Philippine Rice Bowl: The Emergence of New Labor Institutions after the Land Reform," in *The Economics of Rural Organization: Theory, Practice, and Policy*, edited by Karla Hoff, Avishay Braverman, and J.E. Stiglitz. Oxford: Oxford University Press.

Mangahas, M., V. A. Miralao, and R. P. de los Reyes (1976) *Tenants, Lessees, Owners: Welfare Implications of Tenure Change*. Quezon City, Philippines: Ateneo de Manila University Press.

Nagarajan, G., A. M. Quisumbing, and K. Otsuka (1991) "Land Pawning in the Philippines: An Exploration into the Consequences of Land Reform Regulations," *Developing Economies* 29 June: 125–44.

Otsuka, K. (1991) "Determinants and Consequences of Land Reform Implementation in the Philippines," *Journal of Development Economics* 35 April: 339–55.

_____ (1992) "Agricultural Reforms and Development in Asia: A Comparative Perspective," edited by Ross Garnaut and Liu Guoguang. *Economic Reform and Internationalisation: China and the Pacific Region*. Sydney and London: Allen & Unwin.

_____ (1993) "Land Tenure and Rural Poverty in Asia," M.G. Quibria and T.N. Srinivasan (eds.). *Rural Poverty in Asia*. Oxford: Oxford University Press.

Otsuka, K., H. Chuma, and H. Yujiro (1992) "Land and Labor Contracts in Agrarian Economies: Theories and Facts," *Journal of Economic Literature* 30 December: 1965–2018.

_____ (1993) "Permanent Labour and Land Tenancy Contracts in Agrarian Economies: An Integrated Analysis," *Economica* forthcoming.

Otsuka, K., V. Cordova, and C. C. David (1990) "Modern Rice Technology and Regional Wage Differential in the Philippines," *Agricultural Economics* 4 April: 297–314.

_____ (1992) "Green Revolution, Land Reform, and Household Income Distribution in the Philippines," *Economic Development and Cultural Change* 40 July: 719–41.

Otsuka, K., and G. Gascon (1992) "Two Decades of Green Revolution in Central Luzon," *Southeast Asian Journal of Agricultural Economics* 1 June: 45–62.

Otsuka, K., and Y. Hayami (1988) "Theories of Share Tenancy: A Critical Survey," *Economic Development and Cultural Change* 37 October: 31–68.

Prosterman, R. and J. Riedinger (1987) *Land Reform and Democratic Development.* Baltimore and London: Johns Hopkins University Press.

Roumasset, J. A. (1976) *Rice and Risk: Decision Making among Low Income Farmers.* Amsterdam, Netherlands: North-Holland.

Ability, Schooling and Occupational Choice in Philippine Rural Households

*Robert E. Evenson**

Introduction

The schooling of children is regarded as being of high importance in Philippine households. International comparisons show that both rural and urban schooling attainment levels in the Philippines have been higher than in other countries with comparable per capita income.[1] The motives for investment in schooling by both parents and children include both the attainment of higher skills (and hence higher incomes) within a chosen occupation *and* the attainment of options for entry into higher income occupations (and locations). Parental motives for investment in schooling include the desire to make a "bequest" to their children by supporting and financing schooling.

Most "return to schooling" studies in the Philippines are based on estimates of schooling-income relationships, often

*Professor of Economics, Yale University.

[1]See King (1982) for a review of Philippine experiences. Pshacharopoulos review schooling attainment and returns to schooling in a number of countries.

within a single occupation (e.g., farming). These studies did not examine household investment behavior. Later studies of household schooling investment decisions in the Philippines (King 1978) have addressed this investment decision, but none to date have incorporated child ability measures in the analysis. And no studies to date have studied the role of ability and schooling investments in an intergenerational structure including the occupational choice of the second generation.

In this paper an empirical intergenerational study of schooling decisions and occupational choice is undertaken. The first generation (parents) are in rural households in Laguna Province in the Philippines. A sample of these households was drawn in 1975 and has been subsequently resurveyed in 1976, 1977, 1982, 1985, 1990, and 1992. "Ability" tests for a subsample of children in these households were administered in 1976. Schooling completion has now been attained for most of the second generation, i.e., the children of the original respondents. Occupational choice has also been observed for a large part of the second generation. This exceptional data set thus enables a systematic study of both schooling attainment and occupational choice.

Part 2 of this paper discusses the economic logic underlying the specification of the schooling and occupation choice decisions. Part 3 discusses the data and variables. Part 4 reports estimates of the schooling decision specification. Part 5 reports estimates of the location and occupational choice specification. Part 6 discusses the economic implications of these estimates.

Family and Individual Decisions to Invest in Schooling and to Choose Occupations

Decisions to invest in schooling typically precede but anticipate occupational search and migration decisions. Both parents and children have a stake in these decisions and we can generally regard the schooling decisions in most rural Philippine households to be a collective family decision. The occupational choice, migration and marriage decisions are best seen as individual decisions but as having been conditioned by the prior household schooling investment decision.

The "household model" (see the Symposium on "Household Economics," *The Philippine Economic Journal*, Volumes 1 and 2, 1978) provides considerable guidance to both the schooling choice problem and the occupational choice problem. It must be noted, however, that this model, which has guided a number of studies of Philippine household behavior, does not offer a complete structural characterization of this behavior. One of the difficulties with the model is the specification of a collective household utility function over a time span when the weight of the second generation is changing. The relative weight of the child in the schooling completion decision increases over time. That is, when a child drops out of school in the fourth grade this may reflect parental choice. Dropping out in the ninth or tenth grade, on the other hand, is likely to reflect more strongly the child's preference for school activity and both the child's and parents' assessment of the productivity of the child in school (which in turn is related to ability).

In this paper I will deal with this issue by treating the schooling decision as primarily a household decision and the occupational choice decision as primarily a child decision conditioned by household expectations (as reflected by predicted schooling).

Consider the household model as it applies to the schooling decision. Let the household utility function be:

$$U = U(C_1, C_2, ..., C_n, S_1, S_2, ..., S_n, Z) \qquad (1)$$

where $C_1, C_2, ..., C_n$ are child services from each of n children, $S_1, S_2, ..., S_n$ are schooling investments in each of n children and Z represents other home produced goods.

The "home production" constraints facing the household are:

$$C_i = C_i(X_i, t_{ij}, K) \qquad i = 1,2,...,n \tag{2}$$

$$S_i = S_i(t_{si}, A_i, S) \qquad i = 1,2,...,n$$

$$Z = Z(X_z, t_{zj}, K^*)$$

These production constraints specify that child services require vectors of purchased goods X_i, (including basic food, clothing and medicine) and child care time t_{ij} of one or more other household members as well as household capital K (shelter, kitchens, etc.).

Schooling acquisition for each child is specified to depend on the child's time in school, t_{si}, the child's innate academic ability A_i and schooling resources S, (which may be "rented" by the household). Ability in this model is specified as an input into the schooling achievement production function. It is specified to be a normal factor of production so that more able students achieve more schooling per unit of child time and other schooling resource.

Other home produced goods Z, also require time, t_{zj}, and purchased goods, X_z and community infrastructure, K^*.

The time constraint for this problem for each household member j is:

$$T_j = \sum_i t_{ij} + t_{zj} + t_{sj} + t_{wj} + t_{lj} \tag{3}$$

That is, for each household member total time, T_j, is allocated to child care t_{ij}, home goods production t_{zi} school time t_{sj}, work for wages t_{wj} and leisure t_{lg}.

The budget constraint for this problem is where V is non-labor income:

$$V + \sum_i t_{wi} W_i = \sum_i X_i P_x + \sum_i S_i P_s + X_z P_z \tag{4}$$

The full income constraint is obtained by substituting the time constraint (3) into the budget constraint (4).

$$V + \sum_i T_i W_i = \sum_i X_i P_x + \sum_j \sum_i t_{ij} W_j + \sum_i S_i P_s + X_z P_z + \sum_i t_{li} W_i \quad (5)$$

This household will maximize its utility function (1) subject to the production constraints (2) and the time (3) and budget constraints (4). This is equivalent to maximizing utility subject to the full income constraint (5) under certain conditions.

The endogenous (choice) variables are:

a) the number of children, n, (we will presume X_i and t_{js} to be the same for each child).

b) schooling per child, S_i (because ability varies by child we cannot presume that all children within the household will receive the same schooling).

c) other household goods, Z.

d) time allocation for each individual (parents and children t_{ij}).

The exogenous variables and relationships in the model are:

e) prices of goods, P_x, P_z and schooling P_s.

f) abilities, A_i.

g) household capital, K, and community infrastructure K^*.

h) wages, w_j, which in turn may be determined by past schooling.

Children's earnings are included in the budget (full income) constraint. At some age the child will leave the household and then may "remit" a certain proportion of his earnings back to the household. Each individual in the household can be seen as choosing an occupational, migrational and remittance program upon departure.

The household does form expectations as to these decisions before they are actually made. And they influence schooling, and time allocation decisions in the household. The focus of the empirical work in this paper is on schooling and on occupational and locational choices. Other endogenous variables will not be examined and no attempt to estimate structural parameters will be made. The procedure will be to first estimate the "reduced form" dealing with the schooling decision. (Estimation of only part of the reduced form system is valid, although estimation of the full system might give improved efficiency). Then occupational choice decisions are analyzed.

I will not develop first and second order conditions for this problem but the following logic is motivated by the model. If it is assumed that there are no biases in the utility gained from child services and schooling investments, i.e., that all children are equal on utility grounds, differences in schooling within a family will be determined by differences in abilities A_i. To the extent that the bequest motive holds this will mean that families will attempt to compensate children who obtain lower than average schooling in other ways.[2] Differences in all endogenous variables (including average family schooling) between families will be determined by prices, household capital including parent's education, and community capital. Parents play a key role in this decision because they observe (and thus project forward) schooling, occupation and migration patterns.

The occupation-migration choice is typically made after schooling is completed although for some occupations (e.g., nursing) schooling is an integral part of the career trajectory. The pursuit of this choice is not simply a matter of choosing among options. More often it is a matter of searching for and

---

[2]Beth King provided an analysis of the determinants of education in the Laguna province. She finds that the schooling rates have been increasing and there has been equalization between males and females. Female drop rates are lower and education rates have been increasing faster than male rates. Her model is in the Becker Quality-Quantity trade-off framework. She finds that having a high school in the community raises education. She also finds that households will invest in schooling based on what returns they can expect from their adult children.

actually creating options. It entails trial and error. Marriage options are part of the process and men and women are affected differently by marriage. In most societies the occupational and locational choice of the husband dominates that of the wife. Indeed, in many traditional societies, women do not have (or at least do not exercise) career choices other than that of "housewife."

As will be noted below, this is not the situation in the rural Philippines where most women pursue occupations, even though most are married, and their migration from their birth place may have been dominated by their husband's occupational opportunities.

The economic factors that enter into these decisions are thus quite complex. Economic opportunities at home, as reflected by the wage rates and job opportunities, as well as farm and business opportunities, will be compared with those in other locations including overseas locations.[3] Completed schooling and ability will affect success in pursuing these options. They will also affect success in the marriage market.

Life-cycle models of earnings and savings decisions inform these decisions but are not adequate structural models for the problem. In the empirical work reported here, the basic logic of the household model guides the first-generation schooling choice specification and some of these questions are addressed in detail below. That specification is also guided by the life cycle, marriage and career expectations that dominate second-generation career and occupational choices.

Data and Econometric Specifications

The Laguna Household Study was initiated in 1975. A sample of 496 households in 31 barrios (barangays) was surveyed in

---

[3]In fact this reinforces the relationship between schooling and occupational choice because provision of credit and support for a farming occupation may be major form of compensation.

the initial survey.[4] In 1976 three specialized surveys in a subsample of 100 households were undertaken. The first of these measured individual dietary intake. The second measured individual time allocation. The third measured individual "abilities" through the administration of an internationally recognized "non-verbal" intellectual ability test. The test was the "Test of 'g' Culture Fair, Scale 2" test developed by the Institute for Personality and Ability Testing in Champaign, Illinois, USA, and licensed to and administered by the Philippine Psychological Corporation in Makati, Rizal, Philippines. The test is the non-verbal "matrix" type. Administration of the test includes examples discussed in local languages. The first three of four parts were administered to Laguna Household respondents.

In 1977 a resurvey of households in the 20 lowland rice barangays was undertaken. Further resurveys in 1979, 1982, 1985, 1988, 1990 and 1992 were undertaken. As households "aged" they were dropped from the survey. The 1992 survey included 140 households and 704 children for which data were available for all previous survey periods. Of these households virtually all had completed child-bearing. Four hundred seventy eight of the children (second generation) were over 21 years of age and had completed schooling and made career choices. Of the 227 second generation females, 128 had completed the 1976 ability test. Of the 251 second generation males, 144 had completed the 1976 ability test.

For stage 1 of the analysis (the schooling completion decision) years of schooling completed was related to characteristics of the individuals, to characteristics of their families and to characteristics of their communities. This stage utilized the OLS regression procedure. For the second stage migration, and occupational choice decisions, probit and multinomial logit methods were utilized. The "predicted" years

---

[4]Information sources (e.g., through relatives) are a crucial part of the career choice decision. In this study data are inadequate to address this issue.

	Table 1 Variables and Definitions		
		Means	
		Males	Females
Individual Variables			
(END) YRS SCHOOL: Years of Schooling Completed		7.32	8.71
(END) LOCATION: See Table 3			
(END) QCCHOICE: See Table 4			
SEX: Female = 0, Male = 1		1	0
YR BORN: Year of Birth		63.5	63.4
ABILITY: Score on 1976 IPAT Test		17.54	18.28
Family Variables			
FATHERS EDUC: Years of Schooling of Father		4.41	4.85
MOTHERS EDUC: Years of Schooling of Mother		4.51	4.56
FARM SIZE: Land Farmed (owned plus rented) (ha)		1.35	1.35
LAND OWNED: Land Owned (ha)		0.38	0.44
Community Variables			
DIST SECSCA: Distance (kms) to Nearest Secondary School		4.86	3.28
DIST POB: Distance (kms) to Nearest Poblacion (Market Center)		5.12	5.35
BARRIO WAGE: Median Daily Agricultural Wage (1982-1990) Pesos		28.44	28.58
TRANS COST: Index of Transactions Costs (see text)		2.21	2.28

of schooling from the first stage was utilized in the second stage estimates.

Table 1 reports a summary of the individual, family and community variables used in the analysis. A brief discussion of each is presented in the table, but some further elaboration is offered in the following discussion of "expected" effects.

The schooling decision specification included as independent variables, SEX, YRBORN, and for observations where ABILITY was measured, the ability test score. All family variables DISTSECSEH, BARRWAGE and TRANSCOST were also included. SEX was interacted with parental education to estimate sex specific coefficients for these effects. Sex was also interacted with the ABILITY variable.

The following "expected" effects are consistent with the logic of the household model and related life cycle models.

SEX: Mean schooling is higher for females (see Table 1). This implies a possible sex difference is related to parental education and that females have a higher sensitivity to parental education than males. (Note most explanatory variables differ little for males and females because SEX is randomly distributed over sample households. Accordingly, coefficient differences are required to explain higher schooling for females.) (See below for SEX-ABILITY effects.)

YRBORN: It is possible that changes in community attitudes and related factors have occurred over time so that children born in later years might have more schooling. These time effects are not captured by other variables, none of which varies over time.

FATHERS EDUC, MOTHERS EDUC: Parental education effects are expected for at least two reasons. First, higher levels of parental schooling are associated with the value of parent's time. (Note that BARRIO WAGE is the average wage in the barrio) and this is expected to have both an income and time cost effect which operates on the quality-quantity tradeoff and causes more investment in schooling. Since the mother's time effect is more important in child costs than the father's time effect, it is expected that mother's education will have the larger coefficient for this reason. Second, parental education influences parental assessment of occupational options and leads parents to shift "bequests" to their children toward educational support. To the degree that the schooling of children enhances earnings contributed to the household before their departure and remittances after, this effect is further heightened. Thirdly, parental education is correlated with child ability and is likely to have a positive impact in the estimates excluding ability for that reason.

ABILITY: Ability is expected to be related to school completion for both males and females. Ability enhances learning and more able students are more productive in school. Low ability students are often both unproductive and unhappy in school and their voice is heard in family councils. The ability effect is likely to differ by sex in that males typically see themselves as somewhat more occupation-oriented than females, i.e., they do not have the "housewife" option. Accordingly low ability males may stay in school longer.

DIST SECSH: Sixteen of the 20 barangays in the study have a primary school. And most children in the sample complete at least primary school. (See Table 1.) Three of the 20 barangays have secondary schools, but most children must travel some distance to a secondary school (up to ten kilometers). Thus distance is a "price" and is expected to have a negative impact on schooling.

LAND OWNED: Land owned is the best available proxy for wealth in the data set. It is expected that land ownership will have a positive effect on schooling.

The variables, DIST POB FARM SIZE, BARRIO WAGE and TRANS COST represent economic opportunity variables that affect the occupation-migration decision and are included in the second-stage occupational choice estimates. These variables also reflect a "derived" demand for schooling because schooling is either required or valued for some occupations. (The variable TRANS COST discussed below is not included in the schooling equation.)

DISTPOB: The distance from a major market town is expected to have information and job prospect effects. In general the more remote barrios offer few local job opportunities and this would be a factor leading to a demand for more schooling to facilitate occupations outside the barrio. Not all occupations outside the barrio have high education requirements (or value schooling highly) but on average they do.

FARM SIZE: Farming activities (whether owned or rented) are associated with the ability of parents to offer bequests to children in terms of assistance with capital and learning to enable the children to farm. However, modern farming itself provides opportunities for educational income differences through managerial skills. Earning opportunities by children on farms are expected to be better for households with land and this raises the opportunity cost of school attendance. This effect would lead to a negative impact of FARM SIZE on schooling. It might also be noted that this variable is effectively a tenanted land variable and since tenants do have property rights it also serves as a wealth variable.

BARRIO WAGE: Barrios with relatively high daily agricultural wages offer better short-term earning opportunities. Children can often find better earning opportunities and this raises the opportunity cost of being in school. This should produce a negative impact on schooling. This is reinforced by the fact that high local wages also encourage children to remain at home in occupations with lower schooling content.

Further discussion of occupation choice variables is deferred to Part 5 of the paper.

Estimates: Schooling Decisions

Table 2 reports OLS estimates of the schooling specification for the full sample of children over 21 with completed schooling and for the reduced sample with ability scores. Since the ability sample is a random sub-sample of the larger sample no selectivity bias procedures are required.

The estimated equation without ability appears to have a relatively low R^2. For the ability sample the R^2 is higher largely because of the high significance of the ABILITY variable. The "F" tests for significance of the group of independent variables shows high statistical significance for both equations.

The estimated coefficients obtained in both equations generally meet expectations. I do not find a significant YRBORN effect though it is positive. This in all likelihood reflects the fact that economic and institutional conditions in these barangays changed little over the past two decades.

Parental education has the expected impacts. In the equation without ability, mother's education has the stronger impact for both males and females. Parental education effects on males are lower (but not significantly) than for females. In

Table 2

Schooling Choice Estimates

Dependent Variable: YRS SCHOOL

Independent Variables	Estimated Coefficients*			
	Full Sample		Ability Sub-Sample	
Constant	9.585	(4.28)	5.11	(1.64)
YR BORN	0.0069	(0.23)	0.0140	(0.34)
SEX	0.0116	(0.02)	2.064	(1.70)
FATHERS EDUC	0.2728	(3.34)	0.1751	(1.96)
MOTHERS EDUC	0.3355	(3.02)	0.1723	(1.45)
(FATHERS EDUC) × (SEX)	-0.1704	(1.42)	-0.0756	(0.60)
(MOTHERS EDUC) × (SEX)	-0.1242	(0.88)	0.0115	(0.08)
FARM SIZE	0.0987	(0.91)	0.0929	(0.84)
LAND OWNED	0.5381	(2.45)	0.2672	(1.18)
DIST SECSCH	-0.0719	(0.70)	-0.2083	(1.86)
DIST POB	-0.0463	(0.36)	0.1817	(1.33)
BARRIO WAGE	-0.1363	(3.91)	-0.1110	(2.94)
ABILITY	–	–	0.2581	(6.10)
(ABILITY) × (SEX)	–	–	-0.1697	(2.87)
Obs, R², (F)	553, 0.162, (9.5)		289, 0.326, (10.3)	
*adjacent figures in parentheses are t-statistics				

the ability sample, the addition of the ABILITY variable lowers parental education impacts as expected. And when the SEX differential is in the ABILITY coefficient, (males have a lower coefficient as expected), there are no sex differences in parental impact though there is some indication that other things equal, males do complete more schooling than females.

Distance from secondary school has a negative impact on schooling (significant in the ability sample and substantial—a 5-km distance reduces schooling by one year).

The wealth effect (LAND OWNED) is positive in both samples (but not significant in the ability sample) as expected.

The occupation-related variables are generally as expected. Farm size (tenanted land) has a positive but not significant effect on schooling. This is probably because tenants have considerable property rights in these barangays and so this is a combination of wealth effects and opportunity cost effects.

Distance from the poblacion has no effect in the general sample but a weak positive effect in the ability sample. This appears to be reflecting an "escape" motive (see Part 4).

The BARRIO WAGE effect has a strong and significant negative effect on schooling. This is probably due both to the fact that it is an opportunity cost measure for time in school and that it also measures economic opportunities influencing children to choose occupations "at home" with lower perceived schooling requirements.

Perhaps of most relevance is the ABILITY variable. It is a highly significant determinant of schooling. Its effect is large. A 2 standard deviation increase in ability scores produces a 3-year increase in schooling for females and a 1.1-year increase in schooling for males. The significantly lower impact for males is consistent with the fact that males may be more concerned with school completion at the lower levels of ability and school completion because they do not have the same options to be dependent on a spouse that females may perceive themselves to have.

I will return to these occupation-related effects after examining occupation and migration choices in the next section.

Occupational (Locational) Choices

We now turn to location and occupational choice by second-generation respondents. Tables 3 and 4 provide a descriptive summary of these choices.

Table 3 reports relatively high rates of location shifts. Approximately one-half of the respondents report locations other than their parents' barrio and 30 percent have moved out of Laguna province including more than 10 percent who have moved overseas.

Table 4 reports occupational choices. For males one-third are farmers, one-fourth are wage workers and most others are engaged in commerce, jeepney driving, etc. with a substantial entrepreneurial role.

Table 3

Location Choices (Second Generation)
Laguna Respondents

Current Residence	Males	Females
Same Barrio	89	93
Same Town	16	20
Laguna Province (other)	15	12
Abroad	17	20
Manila	14	32
Other Locations	10	11
Total	161	188

Table 4

Occupational Choices (Second Generation)
Laguna Respondents

Occupation	Males	Females
Farmer, Same Barrio	69	7
Farmer, Other Barrio	36	5
Housewife, Same Barrio	na	35
Housewife, Other Location	na	49
Government, Professional	7	23
Wage Employment	81	83
Driver	44	0
Commerce	57	58
Overseas Employment	20	14
Total	314	274

Thirty percent of the female respondents classify themselves as "housewives" (13 percent remain in the same barrio whereas 22 percent of the farmers remain in the same barrio). Almost 10 percent are government employees or professionals. Thirty percent work for wages. More than 20 percent work in commerce and many of these are self-employed. A significant number work abroad.

In order to analyze the factors influencing these choices we have two tools available to us. The first is to analyze several binary choices (either A or B) using binary probit methods. The second is to analyze multiple choices (relative to a reference choice) using multinomial logit methods. Both methods are utilized and discussed below. Some discussion as to expected consequences of several independent variables on these choices was given in the schooling decision discussion. All of the statistical choice analyses reported here use a common set of independent variables. These are: SEX, FARM SIZE, DIST POB, BARRIO WAGE, TRANS COST, PRED EDUC and for the ability subsample, ABILITY. The variables TRANS COST and PRED EDUC require further discussion here.

TRANS COST is a variable that attempts to measure transaction costs at the barrio level. It is based on the differences between prices of rice paid by consumers and received by farmers in the barrio. It is thus a price "wedge" reflecting market efficiency. The prices in question were measured in local market stores (in most cases in "sari-sari" stores and obtained from rice buyers and farmers). An attempt to control for rice quality was made. Price observations from the 1982, 1985, 1988 and 1990 barrio surveys were averaged. Then the barrios were clustered into 3 classes and assigned indexes of 1 for low transaction costs, 2 for medium and 3 for high in the TRANS COST variable.

The effect of high transactions costs, to the extent that they are measuring market imperfections, is to give family enterprises an advantage over more commercial enterprises and to discourage wage employment in local activities. High transaction costs would thus be expected to encourage local self-employment but may well also encourage out-migration to better functioning markets.

The second variable, PRED EDUC is the years of schooling "predicted" from the regressions in the analysis reported in Table 2. If one concluded that a clear and definite "break" existed between the schooling decision and occupational decisions one could argue that years of schooling is an exogenous variable from the occupational and locational choice perspective. That is, one could consider actual years of schooling completed to be exogenous in a recursive decision-making framework. But many of the occupational choice decisions are not made in this fashion. This is particularly true for many of the lower skill choices and the farming and housewife choices. Local work experience results in joint decisions regarding occupations and schooling. The predicted schooling variable addresses this endogeneity program in the same way that two-stage least squares procedures address it in a full regression framework.

Binary Probit Analysis

I turn first to binary probit evidence. This requires that respondents be classified into two categories. In Table 5 evidence for four such categorization is reported. In each case the binary probit coefficients can be interpreted as scaled probability impacts and the probability of being in the class (positive coefficient) or of being in the reference class (negative coefficients). Each classification is independent of the others and should be interpreted for each classification separately.

The four classifications are (1) respondents in the· same location (or other locations in the reference class), (2) respondents who work overseas (respondents in the Philippines are the reference group), (3) respondents in government or professional occupations (other occupations are the reference

Table 5

Probit Analysis of Location and Occupation Choices Second Generation Laguna Respondents

Independent Variable	Same Location		Government and Work Overseas		Professional		Farmers (Males)	
	FS	AS	FS	AS	FS	AS	FS	AS
Sex	-0.326	-0.371	0.318	0.143	-0.357	-0.275	0.195	0.144
	(2.42)	(1.90)	(1.51)	(0.47)	(1.50)	(0.68)	(2.89)	(1.97)
Farm Size	0.054	0.016	0.004	0.021	0.080	0.156	0.061	0.118
	(1.50)	(0.33)	(0.08)	(0.34)	(1.60)	(2.11)	(1.54)	(2.36)
Dist Pob	0.025	0.044	-0.047	-0.054	0.029	0.007	0.043	0.067
	(1.05)	(1.35)	(1.37)	(1.17)	(0.66)	(0.08)	(1.70)	(1.74)
Barrio Wage	-0.118	0.004	0.0004	0.027	0.039	0.202	0.240	0.324
	(0.78)	(0.21)	(0.21)	(0.80)	(1.32)	(1.89)	(1.90)	(1.74)
Trans Cost	0.033	0.096	0.050	0.477	0.409	1.770	-0.240	-0.264
	(0.39)	(0.84)	(0.39)	(0.28)	(2.33)	(1.81)	(1.78)	(1.50)
Pred Educ	-0.163	-0.193	0.108	0.115	0.102	0.379		
	(3.17)	(2.39)	(1.60)	(1.08)	(1.26)	(1.99)		
Ability		0.025		0.008		-0.071		0.028
		(1.23)		(0.29)		(1.37)		(1.12)
Constant	1.03	0.269	-2.26	-3.42	4.67	-14.30	-1.29	-2.46
	(1.19)	(0.25)	(1.91)	(2.08)	(3.10)	(2.40)	(0.76)	(1.30)
Chi²	18.16	15.39	9.29	7.57	21.17	31.85	33.20	29.74
Prob > Chi²	0.0058	0.0313	0.1581	0.371	0.0035	0.0001	0.0006	0.0001
Pseudo R²	0.0263	0.0437	0.0363	0.0540	0.0981	0.3004	0.0985	0.1678

Note: FS = Full Sample; AS = Ability Sample

group) and (4) male respondents who are farmers (males in other occupations are the reference group). Two sets of estimates are presented, one for the full sample, one for the reduced ability sample.

The Chi square tests show that the OVERSEAS estimates are not reliable. They are reported here for purposes of comparing them with the multinomial logit estimates reported below. Other estimates will be discussed by independent variable.

It is useful to begin with the effects of the PRED EDUC variables. This is for two reasons. First, it is the most important variable from the perspective of this paper. Second, since it is predicted using some of the other variables (notably SEX, FARM SIZE, DIST POB and BARRIO WAGE and ABILITY) the interpretation of these variables is that their impacts are "in addition" to their impacts on schooling. It is thus useful to have first discussed the PRED EDUC impacts when discussing them.

Schooling investments do have impacts on these choices. More schooling leads to a decreased likelihood of staying in the same barrio. There is weak evidence that it increases the likelihood of overseas employment. There is also evidence that it increases the likelihood of a government or professional occupation. And the results indicate that more schooling makes it less likely that males will be farmers.

The SEX variable (males = 1) shows that males are less likely to remain in the same location and less likely to be government or professional workers than females when other factors are controlled for.

Higher family wealth (FARM SIZE) increases the likelihood of staying in the same location, of obtaining government and professional employment and of being a farmer. The effect on being a farmer is clearly more than a wealth effect. Larger farm enterprises provide experience and apprenticeship to children to enable them to become farmers. And parents with substantial farm activities are in a position to better provide support and bequests to sons who become farmers than to sons who do not.

Distance from market centers, a measure of remoteness, appears to increase the likelihood of staying in the same location and of becoming a farmer. There is an indication that it reduces the likelihood of overseas employment as well.

Higher barrio wage levels are associated with higher likelihood of government and professional careers and of becoming a farmer. It appears that farm income prospects are correlated with rural wages.

Higher transaction costs have little effect on location or overseas employment but do appear to increase the likelihood of government and professional careers and of becoming a farmer. The latter effect is consistent with the family enterprise argument (i.e., family farms have a comparative advantage in high transaction costs environments. But they may also lead to more intensive escape strategies).

Ability appears not to have strong impacts on these choices over and above its contribution to schooling.

Multinomial Logit Evidence

The multinomial logit procedure allows one to examine the effects of the independent variables on multiple choices relative to a reference class. This allows a richer set of comparisons than afforded by the sample 2 class probit analysis.

Locational Choice

Table 6 reports estimates for five alternative locations relative to the reference group which is that the second generation members remain in the same barrio as their parents. All comparisons are with the reference group although the size of the coefficients and the Z scores (approximately "t" ratios) are comparative interpretations. (Note that the CHI square test results indicate statistical significance.)

Consider the schooling impacts on location. choice. The PRED EDUC coefficients indicate that higher schooling levels

			Table 6			

Table 6

Locational Choice Multinomial Logit Analysis Second Generation Laguna Respondents Reference Class in Same Barrio

Variables	Independent Time	Same Province	Laguna Manila	Abroad	Other
SEX	0.136	0.382	0.411	0.820	0.264
	(0.29)	(0.68)	(0.86)	(1.68)	(.43)
FARM SIZE	-0.042	-0.184	-0.048	-0.101	-0.034
	(0.31)	(1.22)	(0.50)	(0.87)	(0.24)
DIST POB	0.069	-0.189	-0.052	-0.132	-0.231
	(0.80)	(1.97)	(0.61)	(1.68)	(2.16)
BARRIO WAGE	0.035	0.121	0.200	0.019	0.082
	(0.66)	(1.69)	(3.03)	(0.35)	(0.95)
TRANS COST	0.087	-0.084	0.206	0.067	0.445
	(0.31)	(0.23)	(0.64)	(0.23)	(0.97)
PRED EDUC	0.204	0.382	0.700	0.561	0.0006
	(1.07)	(1.82)	(4.06)	(3.34)	(0.002)
Constant	-4.83	-7.38	-13.52	-6.47	-4.63
	(1.56)	(1.93)	(3.87)	(2.12)	(1.02)
No. of Observations	324				
Chi² (30)	63.28				
Prob > Chi²	0.0004				
Pseudo R²	0.0690				

increase the likelihood of moving to the town or poblacion, of moving elsewhere in the province, of moving to Manila and of moving abroad, all with reference to staying at home. The strongest impacts are on the move to Manila, next on the move abroad.

There are few sex differentials in location decisions with some evidence that males are more likely to work overseas.

Farm size or wealth effects are not strong in this specification. (They are stronger in the probit analysis.)

Distance from the poblacion tends to reduce the likelihood that respondents will move elsewhere in the province, abroad, or elsewhere in the Philippines. Remoteness seems to retard mobility.

Respondents from high wage barrios are more likely to move to Manila and elsewhere in Laguna province.

Transaction costs have little or no effects on geographic mobility.

Occupational Choice

Occupational choices are analyzed separately for male and female second generation respondents using the multinomial logit procedure. Results are reported for females in Table 7, for males in Table 8.

Consider the analysis for females first. The reference group here is the class of housewives who stayed in the same barrio. One of the other classes is housewives who are located elsewhere in the Philippines. Results are reported for both the full sample and the ability subsample.

Here again we begin with the schooling impacts. Higher schooling leads to increased likelihood of government and professional careers, wage employment, commerce, overseas work, and housewifery in another location. The strongest effects are for overseas work and housewifery in other locations. We appear to be observing two somewhat different types of effects (and motives). Schooling appears to enhance skills and also to open up marriage opportunities.

Ability has few effects on occupational choice over and above its strong contribution to schooling. The negative sign on the ability term for housewifery in another barrio suggests that females who are in some sense over-educated relative to ability are penalized in the marriage market.

Farm size (wealth) appears to induce females toward government and professional careers.

Living in a remote barrio (DIST POB) appears to discourage overseas employment.

Barrio wage conditions have relatively weak effects. Higher wages may stimulate housewifery in another barrio.

Table 7

Occupational Choice, Multinomial Logit Analysis: Second Generation Female Laguna Respondents Reference Class is Housewife in Same Barrio

Independent Variables	Government and Professional		Wage Employment		Commerce		Overseas Work		Housewife in Other Barrio	
	FS	AS	FS	AS	FS	AS	FS	AS	FS	AS
FARM SIZE	.169	.767	-.094	-.066	-.071	.006	-.071	.211	-.071	.326
	(1.19)	(2.40)	(.64)	(.25)	(.51)	(.02)	(.40)	(.68)	(.53)	(1.24)
DIST POB	.15	.153	.044	.090	-.044	-.168	-.375	-.456	-.091	-.325
	(1.06)	(.40)	(.48)	(.63)	(.50)	(1.24)	(2.64)	(2.40)	(.89)	(2.04)
BARRIO WAGE	.095	.629	-.074	-.079	-.046	.086	-.059	.081	.096	.223
	(.96)	(1.83)	(1.38)	(1.08)	(.83)	(1.08)	(.54)	(.60)	(1.33)	(1.97)
TRANS COST	1.174	5.13	.308	-.074	-.327	-.177	.200	.188	.067	.647
	(2.21)	(1.72)	(1.01)	(.18)	(1.05)	(.43)	(.35)	(.79)	(.18)	(1.15)
PRED EDUC	.388	.571	.307	.383	.220	.416	.411	.514	.485	.668
	(1.83)	(.86)	(1.94)	(1.13)	(1.36)	(1.26)	(2.08)	(1.25)	(2.79)	(1.79)
ABILITY		-.030		-.098		-.080		-.063		-.168
		(.14)		(.90)		(.75)		.44		1.37
CONSTANT	-11.00	40.09	.287	.379	.664		-.203	-5.57	-6.99	-10.20
	(2.27)	(2.21)	(.10)	(.11)	(.23)		(.43)	(.94)	(1.96)	(1.96)
No. of observations	.227	128								
Chi²	53.75	72.91								
Prob > Chi²	.0007	.0000								
Pseudo R²	.0703	.1688								

Note: FS = Full Sample; AS = Ability Sample

Table 8

Occupational Choice, Multinomial Logit Analysis: Second Generation Male Laguna Respondents
Reference Group: Farmer, Same Barrio

Independent Variables	Government, Professional, Wage Employment		Commerce-Employment and Self Employment		Driver-Employment and Self Employment		Overseas Work		Farmer in Other Barrio	
	FS	AS	FS	AS	FS	AS	FS	AS	FS	AS
Farm Size	-9.06 (4.16)	-0.636 (2.39)	-0.665 (3.30)	-0.462 (2.09)	-0.068 (0.43)	-0.089 (0.44)	-0.358 (1.55)	-0.264 (1.13)	-0.171 (1.19)	-0.199 (1.13)
Dist Pob	0.040 (0.36)	-0.107 (0.72)	-0.060 (0.55)	-0.204 (1.43)	0.032 (0.28)	0.079 (0.50)	0.093 (0.70)	0.017 (0.09)	0.193 (1.67)	0.099 (0.60)
Barrio Wage	0.073 (1.10)	0.078 (0.81)	0.058 (0.85)	0.102 (1.05)	-0.067 (0.96)	-0.054 (0.52)	0.109 (1.31)	0.189 (1.50)	0.228 (2.95)	0.306 (2.60)
Trans Cost	-0.310 (0.90)	-0.477 (1.01)	0.001 (0.01)	0.027 (0.06)	-0.054 (0.16)	0.102 (0.20)	0.086 (0.21)	0.193 (0.32)	0.616 (1.68)	1.024 (1.96)
Pred Educ	1.412 (4.01)	1.874 (3.46)	1.186 (3.42)	1.277 (2.45)	0.517 (1.43)	1.066 (1.89)	1.327 (3.28)	1.611 (2.51)	1.249 (3.53)	1.584 (2.79)
Ability		-0.204 (2.57)		-0.129 (1.67)		-0.077 (0.93)		-0.105 (0.08)		-0.107 (1.36)
Constant	-10.01 (2.27)	-10.04 (1.75)	-8.45 (1.91)	-8.00 (1.37)	-1.54 (0.33)		-13.27 (2.47)	-16.65 (2.20)	17.49 (2.59)	-20.77 (3.15)
Number of Observations	251	144								
Chi²	81.23	71.45								
Prob > Chi²	0.0000	0.0000								
Pseudo R²	0.0929	0.1453								

Note: FS = Full Sample; AS = Ability Sample

Higher transaction cost environments are associated with government and professional work.

Now consider the evidence for males (Table 8). Much stronger effects are observed for most variables than was the case for females. The education impacts are quite strong. Higher schooling induces males to choose government, professional and wage employment, commerce, overseas work, and farming in another barrio relative to farming at home. When ability is included in the specification it takes on a negative sign indicating that holding schooling constant, higher ability males (i.e., those who have high ability relative to their predicted schooling), are more likely to farm in their home barrio. This may be indicating that the ability measure is reflecting some entrepreneurial ability.

Farm size clearly holds males in the farming occupation in the same barrio class and discourages other occupation (except for the driver occupation).

Remoteness of the barrio (DIST POB) has little effect on the occupational choice of males. High barrio wage levels and high transaction cost environments hold males in farming occupation, but in other barrios.

Implications

The statistical analysis of the schooling decision found that variables proxying occupation opportunities influenced schooling choice. Ability levels also influenced schooling choice and this influence was stronger for females than for males.

The locational choice analysis showed that educational decisions were important to location choice. Higher schooling is clearly associated with locational mobility including moves to Manila and overseas.

The occupational choice analysis also confirmed that schooling was an important determinant of these decisions.

The probit analysis showed that higher schooling led to higher likelihood of overseas work, and government and professional work and to lower likelihood of farm work.

When analyzed by sex, using the multinomial logit procedure, education was the dominant variable associated with occupational choice for both females and males. For females, high levels of schooling increased the likelihood of all forms of employment including government and professional and overseas employment. It also appears to be associated with higher likelihood of housewifery in another location (including Manila).

Several other factors were important to the occupational decision for females, but the stronger pattern of correlates was observed for schooling.

The results for males were similar: Higher schooling led to more government, professional and wage employment, more commerce and overseas work, and more farming careers outside the home barrio. Again schooling was the dominant variable in occupational choice.

It appears then that rural Philippine households invest in schooling with a view toward occupational options in a number of locations including overseas locations. And occupational choices confirm the merit of these investment decisions. Investment in schooling does open opportunity doors.

References

Behrman, J.R. (1990) "Interactions Among Human Resources and Poverty: What We Know and What We Do Not Know," unpublished mimeo, The World Bank.

_____. and A. Deolalikar (1988) "Unobserved Household and Community Heterogeneity and the Labor Market Impact of Schooling," unpublished mimeo, University of Pennsylvania.

_____. and B. Wolfe (1984) "The Socioeconomic Impact of Schooling in a Developing Country," *Review of Economics and Statistics* 66: 2, 296–303.

Boissiere, M., J.B. Knight, and R.H. Sabot (1985) "Earnings, Schooling, and Ability, and Cognitive Skills," *American Economic Review* 75: 1016–1030.

King, E.M. (1982) "Investment in Schooling: An Analysis of Demand in Low-Income Households," unpublished Ph.D. dissertation, Yale University.

Competitiveness

*H. W. Arndt**

The notion of international "competitiveness" has been prominent in public and professional discussion of Australia's current account and foreign debt problem. There is a large technical literature on the subject but most of it is mathematical and intelligible only to the initiated. The object of this article is to explain what is meant by competitiveness in a way that is acceptable to the profession but intelligible to Paul Keating and Paul Kelly.

Preliminaries

Some economists (Corden 1977, 1991; Pitchford 1989, 1990) question whether Australia has a current account and foreign debt problem. They regard the current account deficit (CAD) as generated by normal capital inflow, mainly private, and therefore presumptively self-servicing. They treat the current account as, in the main, driven by the capital account. This view is not shared by all economists and by hardly anyone else. Those who disagree with the Corden-Pitchford view believe that a country, no more than an individual, can indefinitely overspend its income and live on tick. If export earnings are insufficient to pay for imports of goods and

*Professor Emeritus, Australian National University.

services, whether because of a slump in overseas markets for exports or a domestic boom spilling over into imports or for longer-term structural reasons, and the deficit has to be financed by running down international reserves or borrowing, it is the current account that drives the capital account. (The problem cannot be assumed away by a floating exchange rate since, rather than permit the drastic consequences of a massive depreciation, the authorities tend to step in to manage the float.) The actual situation, of course, is usually a mixture of the two cases. Part of Australia's CAD of the 1980s can be attributed to normal capital inflow, but much of it has been due to inability to make ends meet on current account.

There is general agreement among economists about the twin causes of the longer-term problem: inadequate domestic saving and inadequate international competitiveness. The interaction between these two causes is most simply explained by the Swan (1963) diagram: to achieve two objectives, internal and external balance, requires two instruments, demand management and the real exchange rate; or, in Corden's terminology, "expenditure-cutting" and "expenditure-switching" (Corden 1960). If a CAD is due to domestic excess demand spilling over into imports, demand management (expenditure-cutting) is the appropriate policy. (Expenditure-cutting is the short-term, promotion of saving, i.e. reducing consumer spending relative to income, the longer-term aspects of demand management.) But if the CAD is due to a fall in world demand for a country's exports or inadequate international competitiveness, expenditure-cutting alone will not do; it will cause underemployment at home (upsetting internal balance) before external balance is restored. Expenditure-cutting needs to be accompanied by expenditure-switching, i.e., by a real depreciation.

Some contributors to the discussion forget or ignore one or other of the two factors. Kelly (1992) at various points focuses on competitiveness alone, forgetting about the saving aspect.

Forsyth (1990), on the other hand, ignores competitiveness on the ground that, since $X - M = S - I$, it is all a matter of the saving-investment imbalance. Whitelaw and Howe (EPAC 1992) argue that growth alone can do the trick: if consumption lags behind more rapidly growing income, the saving rate rises while growth of productivity improves competitiveness. One instrument, after all, is enough. But this rests on a large "other things equal" assumption. If faster growth results from more investment and higher productivity is passed on to consumers in higher wages, the net increase in saving and competitiveness will be small, and increased aggregate demand, unless adequately restrained, will spill over into imports.

With these preliminaries out of the way, we can turn to the question: what is meant by competitiveness?

External and Internal Competitiveness

The technical literature distinguishes two concepts of price competitiveness:

(i)   external (the relative prices of domestic and foreign goods); and

(ii) internal (the relative domestic prices of tradables and non-tradables).

The general view is that internal competitiveness is more fundamental because it determines the ability of tradable goods industries to attract resources (e.g. Martin-Nguyen 1989; Dwyer 1991). I shall argue that external competitiveness, the ability of domestic firms or industries to maintain or increase their market share relative to that of foreign competitors, is just as important. It is of little use attracting resources into your industries if you cannot sell the extra output.

External competitiveness is what people have in mind in public discussion and what businessmen themselves mean by competitiveness. The Australian coal industry becomes more competitive with its American rivals in the Japanese market if it can increase its market share. An Australian manufacturer becomes more competitive with imports if he can increase his share in the domestic market. The ability of a firm or industry to maintain or increase its market share depends on its profitability, the relation between prices and costs. The competitiveness of Australian tradables producers improves if their profitability increases because their product prices rise or their costs fall, relative to those of their foreign competitors. In the case of competition in the domestic market, this may occur through a nominal depreciation or tariff or in the longer-term if the Australian producers' unit costs fall relative to those of their foreign competitors, e.g. through a lower rate of inflation or faster growth of productivity. It is this relation between the prices of tradables and their costs of production (which are largely determined by the prices of non-tradables) that links external price competitiveness, the ratio of the prices of domestic and foreign goods, with internal price competitiveness, the ratio of the domestic prices of tradables and non-tradables.

External Competitiveness

External competitiveness does not depend on relative prices alone. There has been much emphasis in trade theory recently on non-price competitiveness (e.g. Porter 1990; Hoffman 1989). It derives from the view that non-price competitiveness has played a major part in Japanese success in export (and also domestic) markets. It is said that Japanese manufacturers compete primarily through quality, not price. Stringent quality control, attention to consumer tastes and flexible adjustment to changing market trends (aided by a "just in time" inventory policy), product innovation and skilful marketing, all these, it is said, enable Japanese producers to compete internationally on reputation (Kasper-Nguyen 1992) rather than prices, with the inference that American and other producers must follow the Japanese example if they are to hold their own. Warr (1992) has recently made the plausible suggestion that, in the course of economic development, the emphasis shifts from price competition to non-price competition, from comparative advantage in labour-intensive products to competitive advantage in skill and technology intensive products.

There can be no doubt that non-price competitiveness is important. But even for Japanese firms, prices and costs matter. Non-price competitiveness supplements but does not supplant price competitiveness.

If external price competitiveness depends on the relative prices of domestic and foreign goods, it seems natural to measure it by comparing indices of the general level of prices, such an index of wholesale prices or a cost of living index or GDP deflator, at home and abroad, converted at the nominal exchange rate. This is a widely used measure of external competitiveness, exemplified by the Morgan Guaranty estimate of the real exchange rate index (Morgan Guaranty 1978), where changes in the index are interpreted as deviations from purchasing power parity (cf. Dwyer 1991). The weakness of this measure of international competitiveness is that it focuses on just one determinant, though admittedly an important one, the relative rates of inflation at home and abroad. It neglects both relative productivity growth and the crucial distinction between tradables and non-tradables.

Where trade takes the form of sale of homogeneous products in a perfect world market, the law of one price holds. To the extent that the world wheat market approximates this situation, Australian wheat farmers are price takers. They sell at the given world price, and their profitability depends on this price in domestic currency relative to their costs. It is increased by nominal depreciation of $A and reduced by rising domestic wages and other costs (in effect, the prices of non-tradables). If demand is perfectly elastic (for a relatively small supplier) any increased output can be sold at the world price. This, therefore, is a case of internal competitiveness; the only relevant price ratio is that between the domestic prices of tradables and non-tradables.

The situation is very different in the case of exports of manufactures by a large country which has some market power over foreign-currency prices. A depreciation of the pound sterling, it used to be said in the textbooks, reduces the prices of British exports in $US. It "reduces the cost to foreigners of a bundle of commodities denominated in domestic currency" (Dwyer 1991: 54). Provided US demand is elastic, the volume of British exports (i.e., their market share) increases; their external competitiveness has improved. The British balance of payments improves once the favourable volume effect outweighs the unfavourable price effect (the J-curve case, cf. Arndt-Dorrance 1987). British external competitiveness here improves through a change in the relative prices of British and foreign goods, that is, through a worsening of Britain's terms of trade.

This is the neoclassical theory of exchange rate adjustment, from Marshall to Meade (Arndt 1976, 1979). It underlies the Marshall-Lerner rule (according to which a depreciation improves the balance of payments provided the sum of the price elasticities of domestic and foreign demand is greater than one). It goes back to Hume's specie-flow model: Two goods, domestic (exports) and foreign (imports); no non-tradables; gold the only money. An adverse trade balance causes specie to flow out, the money supply declines; domestic prices fall; external balance is restored through a decline in the terms of trade. Since there are no non-tradables, the only price ratio that can change is that between domestic and foreign prices; in other words, external competitiveness.

Even in the case of the small country which lacks the market power to influence the foreign-currency prices of its exports and imports and must take these (and therefore its terms of trade) as given, external competitiveness matters because the law of one price does not hold in the short-run, even for perfectly substitutable goods, because of price adjustment lags. Depreciation (or a tariff) raises the domestic prices of imports. If domestic import-competing manufacturers rely on cost-plus pricing of their products, they can undercut imports and increase their market share. Their profitability has improved through external competitiveness. It is this improvement which to the businessmen themselves constitutes the modus operandi of (tariff or exchange rate) protection (Arndt 1979). The improvement is temporary since depreciation raises domestic costs (wages and imported inputs) and thus erodes the real depreciation. But the temporary benefit which may last 2–3 years (cf. Gregory 1978) may be significant since it allows time to attract resources into tradable goods industries and expand production and marketing.

Internal Competitiveness

It was economists from a "small country," T.W. Swan (1963), anticipated by Roland Wilson and elaborated by Salter and Corden, who demonstrated that exchange rate adjustment of the balance of payments depends on the domestic price ratio of tradables to non-tradables, i.e., on internal competitiveness. Since profitability depends on the relation between product prices and costs, anything that raises the domestic prices of tradables relative to those of non-tradables (which largely constitute the cost of producers of tradables) will improve the profitability of producers of tradables, thereby enabling them to attract resources into their industries and thus improve the current account.

Some authors (e.g. Dwyer 1992) speak of "traded" rather than tradable goods. This is somewhat misleading since a good which is not traded at one set of prices and transport costs may be traded at another. As is now generally recognized, the distinction between tradable and non-tradable goods is not clear-cut. If tradables are defined, with Corden (1981), as goods (and services) the prices of which are influenced by international prices, all goods (and services) in an open market economy are tradable in the long run. They all shift over time from the non-tradable to the tradable end of the spectrum (Arndt 1979).

In the small-country case, with foreign-currency prices given, a nominal depreciation raises the domestic-currency prices of exports and imports, while the prices of non-tradables remain initially unaffected. (If the prices of domestic import-competing products are cost-plus priced, external competitiveness, as we have seen, also improves.) But the improvement is temporary. As domestic costs (the prices of non-tradables) rise, the nominal depreciation is offset. The same applies in principle to the large-country case, although the large country's producers may have enough market power to influence export and import prices in foreign currency, at least for a time. That is why the Swan emphasis on the domestic price ratio as the mechanism of exchange rate adjustment of the balance of payments is now generally accepted for large as for small countries.

The improvement in the balance of payments effected by a fall in the real exchange rate is temporary, both in the case of the wheat farmers, whose internal competitiveness improves for a time and in the case of the cost-plus pricing producers of import-competing manufactures whose external competitiveness improves for a time. In both cases the erosion occurs through domestic costs (non-tradables prices). But this way of putting it shares some of the weakness of the Morgan Guaranty type of real exchange rate index. It focuses purely on domestic inflation. Erosion of the relative profitability of tradable goods industries may be held off by productivity growth (in tradables and non-tradables) which slows the rise in costs and may improve non-price competitiveness. It also neglects the fact that what matters for a country's external competitiveness is its *relative* rates of inflation and productivity growth, relative to those of its trade partner countries. Australia's international competitiveness is affected by the domestic price ratio of tradables to non-tradables in its trade partner countries because a rise in their relative unit costs of production (whether because of faster inflation or slower growth of productivity) depresses the profitability of their tradable goods industries and therefore their market share.

Finally, a brief comment on two broader interpretations of a country's international competitiveness. One is that the notion of international competitiveness of a country, as contrasted with a firm of industry, makes sense only if it is defined in terms of its stage of economic development (Melville 1993). Germany is more competitive than Turkey, Japan than India, Mexico than Haiti. No doubt, a country with ample capital, advanced technology and high-quality manpower is likely to be successful in competition, particularly non-price competition, in world markets with countries less well endowed. But it is not plausible to treat competitiveness as correlated simply with per capita GDP, regardless of the real exchange rate. Hong Kong, for instance, has long been highly competitive with the United Kingdom, despite its much lower per capita GDP.

The second is a recent suggestion that the overall competitiveness of an economy in the longer term should be defined as its "ability to attract internationally mobile factors of production, especially capital and entrepreneurship" (Kasper-Nguyen 1992). Certainly, a country which is internationally competitive because it enjoys a favourable real exchange rate is likely to be able to attract internationally mobile capital and entrepreneurship and these will in turn tend to improve its real exchange rate through productivity growth. But the case of Japan suggests that this is not the only, or even the major, source of productivity growth.

Summary

The argument of the preceding pages can be summed up in five propositions.

1. The international competitiveness of a firm, industry or country refers to its ability to maintain or increase its market share relative to its foreign competitors.

2. This ability depends on both non-price and price competitiveness. The latter, in turn, requires both external competitiveness (a favourable ratio of domestic and foreign prices) and internal competitiveness (a favourable ratio of domestic prices of tradables to non-tradables), since to gain market share producers of tradables must be able not only to attract resources from non-tradable goods industries but also to expand sales.

3. Where the law of one price holds, as in perfectly competitive world markets for homogeneous commodities, internal competitiveness is enough; sales can be expanded indefinitely if demand is perfectly elastic. In trade in manufactures, where cost-plus pricing prevails, competitiveness means in the first instance external competitiveness, i.e. the ability of domestic producers to gain market share by undercutting their foreign competitors. In export markets, this involves worsening terms of trade (the Marshall-Meade case).

4. Any improvement in price competitiveness, external and internal, attained by a nominal depreciation of the currency is temporary. Sooner or later, it will be eroded by rising domestic costs (prices of non-tradables), generally within 2–3 years. But the temporary improvement may give a lasting fillip to the country's competitiveness and external balance.

5. In the long-term, a country's international competitiveness will improve if it enjoys a lower rate of inflation and/or faster growth of productivity than its trade partners.

Policy Implications

If Australia's CAD and foreign debt are a problem, what can be done about it?

Since the causes of the problem are inadequate saving and inadequate competitiveness, a two-pronged approach is needed. The problem of inadequate saving essentially turns on minimizing the public sector borrowing requirement and maximizing private (especially household) saving. At bottom, both aspects involve the political problem of reining in (public and private) consumption.

To improve competitiveness, it is necessary to promote non-price competitiveness which is a matter of the Australian business culture. Withdrawal of protection helps and there are other things government can do—labour market reform, research and development, education, competition policy—but it is mainly up to the private sector, enterprise and management.

Price competitiveness depends on the real exchange rate and therefore on its three determinants—apart from the terms of trade which in the "small country" are beyond policy control or influence—the nominal exchange rate, the (relative) rate of inflation and the (relative) growth of productivity.

There is now much doubt about the capability of national governments to control the nominal exchange rate in an environment of open capital account and international capital mobility. There may be a case for some constraint, e.g., through a withholding tax, but this is not favoured by the monetary authorities.

Inflation as a threat to external balance is partly a longer-term problem; this largely overlaps with the problem of inadequate saving. In a climate of inflationary expectations, it is also an aspect of countercyclical demand management; the danger is that excessive reliance on monetary policy, because of political constraints on fiscal policy, has counterproductive effects on the exchange rate, high interest rates attracting capital inflow. There is, finally, the inflationary effect of currency depreciation itself, the erosion of the real depreciation as the rise in domestic prices of tradables feeds into the CPI and wages. The danger here is that depreciation becomes a let-out: the Latin-American syndrome of an indexed exchange rate; loss of the international discipline of a fixed exchange rate.

The two approaches to productivity growth are "productive investment" and "microeconomic reform." A higher rate of investment, in physical and human capital, requires business confidence; but it is also liable to widen the $S - I$ (Savings - Investment) imbalance. Microeconomic reform is mainly a political problem: how to secure trade union acceptance of inroads into customary work practices.

Both inadequate saving and low productivity are basically symptoms of the determination of Australians to maintain higher living standards than their productive capacity can sustain; in other words, to live above their means and cover the gap by borrowing other people's savings—while they can.

References

Arndt, H.W. (1976) "Non-Traded Goods and the Balance of Payments," *Economic Records*, March.

_____. (1979) "The Modus Operandi of Protection," *Economic Record*, June.

_____. (1989) "Australia's Current Account and Debt Problem: A Skeptical View of the Pitchford Thesis," *Discussion Paper 219*, Centre for Economic Policy Research, Australian National University.

_____ and G. Dorrance (1987) "The J-Curve," *Australian Economic Review*, 1st Quarter.

Corden, W.M. (1960) "The Geometric Presentation of Policies to Attain Internal and External Balance," *Review of Economic Studies*, Vol. 28.

_____. (1977) *Inflation, Exchange Rates and the World Economy.* Oxford: Clarendon Press.

_____. (1981) "Exchange Rate Protection," in R.N. Cooper (ed.). *The International Monetary System under Flexible Exchange Rates.* Ballingen, Cambridge, Mass.

_____. (1990) "Does the Current Account Matter? The Old View and the New," mimeo, Washington, DC, December.

Dwyer, J. (1991) "Issues in the Measurement of Australia's Competitiveness," Economic Record, Supplement, *International Economics Postgraduate Research Conference.*

_____. (1992). "Real Exchange Rates as Indicators of Competitiveness: The Australian Experience 1970–1990," Ph.D. Thesis, Griffith University.

_____. and P. Lowe (1992) "Alternative Concepts of the Real Exchange Rate: A Reconciliation," mimeo, Reserve Bank of Australia.

Forsyth, P.J. (1990) "Why Microeconomic Reform Won't Reduce Foreign Debt," *Policy*, Vol. VI(2), Winter.

Gregory, R.G. (1978) "Determination of Relative Prices in the Manufacturing Sector of a Small Open Economy: The Australian Experience" in W. Kasper and T.G. Parry (eds.). *Growth Trade and Structural Change in an Open Economy.* University of New South Wales.

Kelly, P. (1992) *The End of Certainty.* Sydney: Allen and Unwin.

Kasper, W. and T. Nguyen (1992) "What Does Competitiveness Mean for Australia?" mimeo, University College ADFA & Griffith University.

Martin, W.J. and T. Nguyen (1989) "The Terms of Trade and Real Exchange Rates," *Working Paper No. 89/6, National Centre for Development Studies.* Australian National University.

Melville, L.G. (1993) Personal Communication.

Morgan, Guaranty (1978) "Effective Exchange Rates: Nominal and Real," *World Financial Markets,* May.

Pitchford, J.D. (1989) "A Skeptical View of Australia's Current Account and Debt Problem," *Australian Economic Review,* 2nd Quarter.

_____. (1990) *Australia's Foreign Debt: Myths and Realities.* Sydney: Allen & Unwin.

Porter, M. (1990) *The Competitive Advantage of Nations.* New York: Free Press.

Swan, T.W. (1963) "Longer-Term Problems of the Balance of Payments" in H.W. Arndt and W.M. Corden, *The Australian Economy: A Volume of Readings.* Cheshire, Melbourne.

Warr, P.G. (1992) "Comparative and Competitive Advantage in Manufactured Exports," Working Paper, *Economic Development Institute.* World Bank, Washington, D.C.

Whitelaw, R. and J. Howe (1992). "Current Account Adjustment: Options for the 1990s," *EPAC Council Paper No. 50,* Canberra, May.

Export Tax as Income Stabilizer under Alternative Policy Regimes: The Case of Philippine Copra

*Romeo M. Bautista**

Introduction

One of JE's early papers investigates analytically "the use of an export tax...in reducing fluctuations in export income" (Encarnacion 1962: 92). The export tax is variable—and can be negative (i.e., an export subsidy)—since "part of the tax is calculated on the difference between current price and the average price over a number of preceding periods" (p. 93). "For simplicity," the average levels of price and income are assumed constant, an assumption that is acknowledged as "extremal" (p. 97).

The present study provides an analysis of variable export taxation as an income stabilizer in the wider context of government interventions affecting agricultural prices directly and indirectly. The effects of alternative policy regimes, with

*International Food Policy Research Institute, Washington D.C. The author is indebted to Clemen Gehlhar for valuable research assistance.

and without an explicit price stabilization program, are examined empirically for an important export commodity (copra) in the Philippines during 1960–82, taking into account long-run (average) price incentives and short-run price stability as well as the further repercussions on producer income and welfare. In contrast to most existing studies on agricultural pricing policies in developing countries that focus on either price stability or producer incentives as the central policy goal, the analysis considers the simultaneous effects of the alternative policy scenarios on those two objectives.

Copra being only one of several competing sources of vegetable oil, the small-country assumption of an exogenous foreign price reasonably applies to Philippine exports despite the country's large contribution to world trade in copra and coconut oil. The period 1960–82 is significant in at least one respect: There was a marked increase in the volatility of world commodity prices, including those of coconut products, during the second half of the period. The year 1982 is a good cutoff point for the present study in view of subsequent policy developments that can be considered transitional or in the nature of emergency measures associated with the advent of the external debt-related foreign exchange crisis in 1983.

Government interventions that create a wedge between domestic and foreign prices affect producer welfare through the induced changes in long-run incentives and in the short-run instability of domestic prices. The latter consideration merits special attention in low-income rural areas where the capital market is highly imperfect and the management of consumption risk is costly. For small-farm households and tenant families the variability of copra price can be a threat to income and food security. Price stabilization for export crop producers may reduce the riskiness of income and thereby promote consumption smoothing over time. Insulating domestic producers from world price movements can lead however to a lower average price of copra than would prevail otherwise. Indeed, government price interventions in the Philippines have tended to disprotect (tax) the production of coconut and other export crops (Bautista 1987).

Section 2 describes the sector-specific and economywide policies affecting the domestic relative price of copra and evaluates their production incentive effects, including both direct and indirect effects; the consequences on domestic price variability are also examined, making comparisons of the actual (historical) price variability with the variability of the corresponding foreign (border) prices alternatively expressed in terms of the official and "equilibrium" exchange rates. In Section 3 the comparative effects on price stability are examined and the average relative price of copra simulated during the study period in the context of a variable export tax subsidy scheme, considered "in principle, the most suitable" mechanism for copra price stabilization (Habito and Intal 1990: 178). Section 4 extends the comparative analysis to the effects on crop output and revenue, followed in Section 5 by an assessment of the transfer benefit and risk premium for copra producers associated with a hypothetical change from the historical case to each of the other four policy scenarios. The paper ends with a brief statement of findings and some concluding remarks.

Price Effects of Government Intervention

Direct government intervention in the coconut sector was insignificant during the 1960s (Intal and Power 1990: 78). In 1970 a temporary stabilization tax was imposed on traditional exports (6 percent for copra, 4 percent for other coconut products), which after three years was incorporated in the customs and tariff code.[1] In February 1974, an additional tax, ranging from 20 to 30 percent, was levied on the premium

---

[1]Export taxes were abolished, except on logs, in 1986 by the new Aquino government.

derived from export price increases beginning 1973. These tax measures served to partly siphon off the significant gains for coconut (and other major export crops) producers from the February 1970 devaluation and the 1972–74 world commodity boom.

The government also imposed a levy on coconut production in 1973, initially set at 5.50 pesos per ton of copra. It evolved into a variety of special levies which financed, among other things, the acquisition of a major share of the country's total coconut milling capacity and operation of the Coconut Industry Development Fund to promote replanting of coconut farms with hybrid varieties.[2]

Such sector-specific policies led to a divergence of the domestic price from the border price evaluated at the official exchange rate. The latter price would have faced copra producers in the absence of government interventions specific to the coconut sector. The terms of trade for copra corresponding to the policy scenarios with and without sector-specific interventions can be represented by $P_1 = P_{cb}/P_{na}$ and $P_2 = P_{cbo}/P_{na}$, respectively, where P_{cb} is the historical (actual) domestic price of copra, P_{cbo} is the border price evaluated at the official exchange rate (r_0), and P_{na} is the nonagricultural price index.

Domestic relative prices of tradable agricultural products in developing countries are influenced not only by sector-specific policies but also—and often more importantly, as shown in recent research (e.g., Krueger et al. 1988)—by industrial, trade, and macroeconomic policies that affect the real exchange rate. In the Philippines, import restrictions to protect domestic industry effectively caused the real exchange to be overvalued (relative to that under unrestricted trade) by about 20 percent on average during the 1970s (Bautista 1987: 50); this rendered

[2]As pointed out by Intal and Power (1990: 60), the latter activity "was controversial because the government's top coconut administrator was the only Philippine franchisee of the variety and his coconut seed nut farm stood to profit handsomely from the arrangement."

the production of agricultural export and import-competing goods significantly less profitable. Also, the country's heavy foreign borrowing and expansionary fiscal policy in the face of the large current account deficit after the 1973–74 oil price shock contributed to the worsening exchange rate overvaluation in the second half of the 1970s and 1980s (Bautista 1988).

The foregoing considerations suggest a third measure of the terms of trade, or relative incentives, for copra producers—represented by $P_3 = P_{cbe}/P_{nae}$, where P_{cbe} is the border price of copra evaluated at the "equilibrium" exchange rate (r_e), and P_{nae} is the nonagricultural price index with the tradable goods component calculated at border prices using the equilibrium exchange rate. The policy scenario associated with P_3 and r_e is one in which both sector-specific and economywide price interventions are absent. The equilibrium exchange rate is defined as the exchange rate that would have prevailed under a free trade regime (i.e., no restrictions to foreign trade) and balance-of-payments equilibrium (i.e., no unsustainable imbalance in the current account).

The time profiles of P_1, P_2 and P_3 for the period 1960–82 are shown in Figure 1, based on the estimates of Intal and Power (1990). Two contrasting periods of low and high degrees of price instability can be discerned; they correspond roughly to the first and second halves of the period, the early 1970s marking the beginning of the increased instability. The average relative price levels, trends, and instability values are contained in Table 1. The trend is calculated as the slope of the regression line. Our measure of price instability is the detrended coefficient of variation, representing the dispersion of observed annual values around the trend line.[3]

In terms of both the average level and trend of the relative price of copra during 1960–82, domestic producers would have been better off without the sector-specific and/or economywide

---

[3]As shown by Cuddy and Valle (1978), this instability index can be calculated as the ratio of the standard error of the estimate in the trend regression to the mean value.

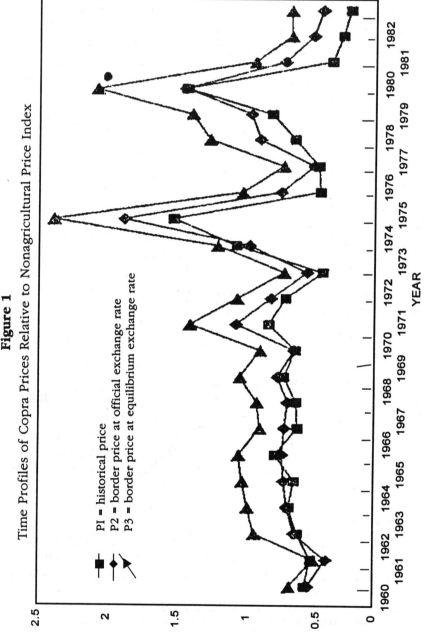

Figure 1

Time Profiles of Copra Prices Relative to Nonagricultural Price Index

PI = historical price
P2 = border price at official exchange rate
P3 = border price at equilibrium exchange rate

interventions of the government. Table 1 also indicates that the indirect price effect of macroeconomic policies through exchange rate overvaluation was relatively quite significant: the average value of P_3 exceeded by 30.6 percent the average P_2, whereas the latter was higher than the average P_1 by only 12.5 percent.

Did government interventions lead to a less unstable domestic price of copra? Somewhat surprisingly, they did not. The last column of Table 1 shows an even higher instability of

Table 1 Average Level, Trend Coefficient, and Instability Index of Relative Copra Prices, 1960–82			
Relative Price	Average (Pesos/100 kg)	Trend (Pesos/100 kg)	Instability (Percent)
P_1	68.6	0.00	39.1
P_2	77.2	0.99	35.8
P_3	100.8	1.51	36.2

Source: Calculated from annual estimates derived in Intal and Power (1990).

Note:

P_1 = producer price of copra deflated by P_{na}.

P_2 = border price of copra evaluated at the official exchange rate deflated by P_{na}.

P_3 = border price of copra evaluated at the equilibrium exchange rate deflated by P_{nae}.

P_{na} = nonagricultural price index (1972 = 100).

P_{nae} = nonagricultural price index with the tradable goods component calculated at border prices using the equilibrium exchange rate (1972 = 100).

P_1 relative to both P_2 and P_3. Doing away with the price biases of sector-specific and economywide policies would therefore have benefitted copra producers in terms of both increased long-run price incentives and reduced short-run price instability. It is also notable that the additional instability arising from the use of r_e instead of r_0 in the representation of the border price is relatively small, implying that economywide policy liberalization would not have been significantly price-destabilizing for copra producers.

Domestic Price Stabilization

One of the major concerns of developing country (LDC) governments in moving towards a liberalized trade regime relates to the instability of world commodity prices that, under a less restrictive policy, would be transmitted more fully to domestic prices. Free trade is politically unattractive in part because world commodity markets are perceived to be incapable of providing a satisfactory degree of price stability.

Domestic prices of agricultural crops in many LDCs have indeed been more stable than their border prices (Schiff and Valdes 1992). Evidently, this empirical generalization does not apply to Philippine copra in which direct and total government interventions, instead of dampening world price fluctuations, even accentuated their transmission to domestic producers (as shown above).

There has been a wide variety of domestic price stabilization schemes used in developing countries to deal with the price risk faced by agricultural producers in the context of uncertain and volatile international markets (Knudsen and Nash 1990). Many LDCs have employed a system of variable tax rates for primary product exports (i.e., high rates when export prices are high) to reduce the domestic price instability for export producers. This approach to agricultural price stabilization avoids the high fiscal costs associated with interventions that involve government handling and storage of commodities. The progressiveness of such export tax schemes is not always explicitly or even systematically applied. While a few countries have made use of a predetermined structure of rates (e.g., Colombia on coffee exports), others have simply waived the fixed export tax rate when world prices declined significantly. In all cases, the government budget is rendered more unstable.

Governments can avoid the adverse budgetary effect by operating a variable export tax/subsidy scheme in conjunction with a buffer fund—in which the tax proceeds are placed when export prices are high and on which subsidies to producers are drawn when export prices are low. Some LDCs use ·buffer funds, including Papua New Guinea (for cocoa, coffee, copra and palm oil). In that country, each fund has an annual reference price for the commodity based on the average of world prices in the previous 10 years; an export tax or subsidy rate is applied equal to one-half the difference between the reference price and actual price for the year.

In having the reference price determined by a moving average of past world prices, a variable export tax/subsidy-cum-buffer fund program in principle will not only dampen the short-run variability of world prices but also ensure that domestic prices do not deviate substantially from the long-run trend in world prices. In the latter sense, this price stabilization scheme can promote allocative efficiency, and is superior to others that do not give due attention to the longer-term relationship between domestic and foreign prices.

In what follows we examine the effects on long-run incentives and short-run instability of a Papua New Guinea-style stabilization scheme for Philippine copra. Had such a scheme been in place during 1970–82, what would have been the annual values of the relative price of copra facing domestic producers? Two "stabilized" price variables are determined for each year as follows:

$$P_4 = P_2 - 0.5(P_2 - P_{ro})$$

and

$$P_5 = P_3 - 0.5(P_3 - P_{re})$$

where P_{ro} and P_{re} are the reference prices (10-year moving averages of P_2 and P_3, respectively) based on the official and equilibrium exchange rates, respectively, and a 50 percent tax or subsidy is applied on their divergence from the current-year border prices. The calculated annual values are contained in Appendix Table 1.

The average levels and instability values of P_4 and P_5 for the period 1970–82 are presented in Table 2 together with the corresponding figures for P_1, P_2, and P_3. The average price incentive for copra producers is seen to be lower under the price stabilization scheme relative to the free trade regime with or without economywide interventions—by about 22 percent in either case. However, domestic price instability would have

Table 2

Average Level and Instability Index of
Relative Copra Prices, 1970-82

Relative Price	Average (Pesos/100 kg)	Instability (Percent)
P_1	71.4	48.3
P_2	85.6	40.4
P_3	112.1	41.4
P_4	67.2	24.1
P_5	87.4	25.2

Source: Author's calculations.

Note: P_4 and P_5 are the "stabilized" prices of copra based on border prices evaluated at the official and equilibrium exchange rates, respectively; see Note to Table 1 for definitions of P_1, P_2, and P_3.

been reduced considerably, the index decreasing from 40.4 (for P_2) to 24.1 (for P_4) and from 41.4 (for P_3) to 25.2 (for P_5). In comparison with P_1 (associated with the historical policy regime), the stabilized prices P_4 and P_5 show (i) average levels slightly lower and higher, respectively, and (ii) significantly lower instability in both cases.

A final observation is that three of the four alternative policy scenarios (different from the historical) would have resulted in a higher average price incentive, and that all four would have led to a lower price instability for copra producers. The sole exception is the case of stabilization around the border price at the official exchange rate, the average value of the stabilized price P_4 being about 6 percent lower than that of the historical price P_1. It is remarkable, however, that the instability index for P_4 (24.1) is only one-half that for P_1 (48.3).

Effects on Copra Production and Revenue

Crop price changes may affect producer welfare only if they influence the average level and variability of income. The supply response to the price movements associated with each policy scenario is therefore a relevant consideration. In this paper, producer income is simply represented by the value of crop output, i.e., copra revenue, computed for each year as the producer price multiplied by quantity produced.

It is well known that domestic price stabilization does not necessarily stabilize producer income, and may even lead to greater income instability (Newbery and Stiglitz 1981). The latter would be true, at least in the comparative static context, if price variability were the result of domestic supply shocks involving a nontradable good for which the price elasticity of demand is greater than 0.5. In the case of a tradable good, the domestic price under free trade is unaffected by changes in the level of output; indeed, the direction of causality is reversed in that the producer price is a determinant of domestic supply. Based on comparative static, partial equilibrium analysis, a reduction in price instability in a tradable good market will necessarily result in a lower variability of producer income. However, if one incorporates dynamic and general-equilibrium price effects in the supply response, and also trade restrictions that relate systematically to the level of domestic production, the correlation between price and income instability becomes tenuous.

To derive the annual quantities of copra production during 1970–82 associated with each of the four alternative policy scenarios (different from the historical), we make the assumption of a constant-elasticity supply function and use the price elasticity values employed by Intal and Power (1990) to estimate the "cumulative output effects" of direct and total government intervention. The cumulative effect takes into account the producer response to relative price changes in terms of the number of coconut trees (which have a gestation period of 5 to 10 years) and the average yield per bearing tree. The results of the four sets of calculations, together with the actual (historical) quantities of copra production, are contained in Appendix Table 1. Multiplying by the corresponding annual prices yields the annual values of copra revenue, shown in Appendix Table 2. The calculated average level and instability index for each policy scenario are given in Table 3.

Table 3		
Average Level and Instability Index of Copra Revenue, 1970-82		
Revenue	Average (Million Pesos)	Instability (Percent)
R_1	1,431	40.4
R_2	1,695	59.9
R_3	2,873	35.3
R_4	1,457	57.0
R_5	1,964	20.3

Source: Calculated from Appendix Table 1.
Note: R_1, ...R_5 denote copra revenue corresponding to the prices P_1, ...P_5 and quantities Q_1, ...Q_2.

Unsurprisingly, copra producers would have earned a higher average revenue during 1970–82 without the direct (sector-specific) government interventions (18.4 percent more than the actual average revenue for the period). More remarkable is that the removal of total (sector-specific and economywide) interventions would have led to a doubling of the actual average revenue, implying that the indirect impact of exchange rate overvaluation is dominant not only in the price effect (as observed above) but also in the revenue effect. In terms of copra revenue instability, Table 3 shows that the historical case is superior to the sectoral free-trade scenario; however, revenue variability would have been lower if government price interventions were totally absent.

Adoption of the price stabilization scheme would have reduced the average copra revenue relative to the sectoral free-trade scenario (by 14.0 percent); the revenue instability would also have been reduced, albeit insignificantly (by 2.9 percentage points). Table 3 also indicates that in the absence of total interventions, domestic price stabilization would have significantly lowered the average copra revenue (by 31.6 percent) as well as its variability (by 15.0 percentage points).

Overall, it would appear that the free-trade regime without economywide interventions, whether or not the price stabilization scheme is adopted, yields a more favorable revenue effect for copra producers than any of the other three policy scenarios: R_3 and R_5 have higher average and instability values than R_1, R_2 or R_4. With respect to R_3 and R_5, adoption of a variable export tax/subsidy scheme for copra (in the absence of total interventions) is seen to entail a significant tradeoff between average revenue and revenue instability. Whether or not the scheme would have provided a positive net benefit to copra producers depends in part on the value that they would attach to revenue stabilization. Risk averse producers will pay to have the revenue instability reduced, the amount presumably determined also by the accompanying loss in average revenue.

Table 4

Calculated Producer Benefits for Alternative Policy Regimes
(percent)

Policy Regime	Transfer Benefit	Risk Premium	Net Benefit
Free Trade I			
$r = 1.0$	18.4	-9.7	8.7
$r = 1.5$	18.4	-14.6	3.8
Free Trade II			
$r = 1.0$	100.8	2.0	102.8
$r = 1.5$	100.8	2.9	103.7
Price Stabilization I			
$r = 1.0$	1.8	-8.1	-6.3
$r = 1.5$	1.8	-12.1	-10.3
Price Stabilization II			
$r = 1.0$	37.3	6.1	43.4
$r = 1.5$	37.3	9.2	46.5

Source: Author's calculations.

Note: Percentage of actual average revenue in 1970–82.

Free Trade I corresponds to price P_2 and R_2; Free Trade II to price P_3 and revenue R_3; Price Stabilization I to price P_4 and revenue R_4; and Price Stabilization II to price P_5 and revenue R_5.

r denotes the coefficient of relative risk aversion.

Evaluating the Transfer Benefit and Risk Premium for Copra Producers

Representing copra producers as an individual (the "representative farmer") with a von Neumann-Morgenstern utility function of income $U(Y)$,[4] let Y_i and Y_j denote the income variables corresponding to the prices P_i and P_j associated with any two alternative policy regimes. The means

---

[4]In view of this, the distibution of producers' income and their differential aversion to risk are not taken into account in our analysis.

of Y_i and Y_j are $\bar{Y}_i$ and $\bar{Y}_j$, respectively; the coefficients of variation are σ_{yi} and σ_{yj}, respectively.

The monetary benefit to the producers of a change from Y_i to Y_j is given by B in the following equation:

$$EU(Y_i) = EU(Y_j - B) \tag{1}$$

where E is the expectation operator. As shown by Newbery and Stiglitz (1981: 93), using a Taylor series approximation for (1) leads to

$$\frac{B}{\bar{Y}_i} = \frac{\bar{Y}_j - \bar{Y}_i}{\bar{Y}_i} - \frac{1}{2} r \, (\sigma^2_{yj} - \sigma^2_{yi}) \tag{2}$$

where r is the Arrow-Pratt measure of relative risk aversion.

The first term in the right-hand side of (2) represents the "transfer benefit," indicating the increase (or decrease) in average income associated with the shift from one policy regime to another. Table 3 shows, for example, that policy reform toward freer trade during 1970–82 would have produced a positive transfer benefit for copra producers. The second term represents the pure stabilization benefit, or "risk premium," indicating the monetary gain (loss) from a reduction (increase) in income instability. The higher the degree of risk aversion the greater is the relative importance of the risk premium to the total producer benefit from a policy change.

Table 4 presents estimates of the transfer benefit, risk premium, and net benefit for copra producers resulting from a hypothetical change from the historical policy regime during 1970–82 to each of the four alternative policy scenarios considered above. The two alternative values assumed for the coefficient of relative risk aversion, 1.0 and 1.5, are deemed reasonable (Binswanger 1980; Newbery and Stiglitz 1981).

The first point to note is that removal of sector-specific interventions (Free Trade I) would have resulted in a transfer benefit that more than compensates for the negative risk premium, promoting therefore producer welfare. However, application of the variable export tax/subsidy scheme (Price Stabilization I) would have led to a negative net benefit to copra producers; this is mainly due to the large reduction in transfer benefit.

Had all price interventions been removed (Free Trade II), the amount of transfer benefit would have equalled the actual average revenue during the period and the risk premium would have been positive, producing a very substantial total benefit to copra producers. It is striking, however, that adoption of the variable export tax/subsidy scheme (Price Stabilization II) would have reduced markedly the transfer benefit without a commensurate increase in the risk premium, so that the net benefit to copra producers would have declined to less than half of that without the stabilization scheme.

Overall, based on the comparative values of the net benefits to copra producers, it would appear that the historical case is inferior to all but one of the alternative policy regimes. The absence of total price interventions (both sectoral and economywide) would have been the "best" policy scenario for 1970–82. The pure stabilization gain from the variable export tax/subsidy scheme being dominated by the accompanying reduction in average revenue, adoption of the stabilization scheme would have made copra producers worse off.

Conclusions

Copra producers in the Philippines were effectively penalized during 1960–82 by the discriminatory price effects not only of sector-specific policies such as production levies and export taxes, but also and more importantly, of exchange rate overvaluation due to industrial protection and economywide policies. Moreover, government policies did not reduce the variability of the domestic price of copra relative to the border prices; hence, the price stabilization function—often used to justify agricultural market interventions in developing countries—was also not served.

In the absence of either direct or total interventions, application of the variable export tax/subsidy scheme would have substantially lowered the instability of domestic prices during the 1970–82, but at the expense of a much reduced average producer price. In terms of the revenue effects, which are more directly relevant to producer welfare than the price effects, liberalization of sector-specific and economywide policies—with or without the price stabilization scheme—would have led to a higher average revenue and lower revenue instability for copra producers relative to the historical policy regime.

The transfer benefit and risk premium associated with a hypothetical shift from the historical case to each of four alternative policy scenarios indicate again the critical importance of improving the trade and macroeconomic policy environment and reducing the exchange rate overvaluation in promoting producer welfare. Indeed, without economywide policy reform, stabilization around the border price (at the official exchange rate) would have been welfare-reducing for copra producers. Adoption of the variable export tax/subsidy scheme in the context of an unbiased macroeconomic environment would also have considerably reduced the transfer benefit which the increased risk premium would not significantly offset. These findings do not give cause for optimism about the economic benefits of a government-sponsored price stabilization program for copra in the Philippines.

Appendix Table 1
Annual Copra Production, 1970–82 (million kg)

Year	Q_1	Q_2	Q_3	Q_4	Q_5
1970	1,726	1,852	1,973	1,756	1,742
1971	1,679	1,813	1,917	2,055	1,745
1972	2,174	2,413	2,552	1,606	2,399
1973	1,871	2,168	2,324	1,219	2,003
1974	1,424	1,681	1,819	2,759	1,479
1975	2,199	2,575	2,794	2,372	2,453
1976	2,742	3,188	3,484	888	3,130
1977	2,440	2,805	3,061	2,260	2,635
1978	2,517	2,986	3,290	1,140	2,795
1979	1,972	2,375	2,648	3,636	2,159
1980	2,076	2,529	2,787	2,546	2,364
1981	2,316	2,738	3,088	2,859	2,661
1982	2,192	2,505	2,807	2,191	2,486

Source: For data on actual production Q_1, Philippine Statistical Yearbook (NEDA, 1976) and Philippines: A Framework for Economic Recovery (World Bank, 1987); authors' calculations for Q_2, Q_3, Q_4, and Q_5.

Note: Q_1, ..., Q_5 denote quantities of copra production corresponding to the prices P_1, ..., P_5.

Appendix Table 2
Annual Copra Revenue, 1970–82 (million pesos)

Year	R_1	R_2	R_3	R_4	R_5
1970	1,403	1,314	2,549	1,320	1,684
1971	1,192	875	1,932	1,346	1,461
1972	1,050	2,444	1,839	883	1,685
1973	1,895	3,022	2,623	857	1,758
1974	1,985	832	3,887	2,903	1,963
1975	1,088	1,305	2,718	1,478	1,969
1976	1,390	2,084	2,529	457	2,114
1977	1,595	2,232	3,596	1,515	2,359
1978	2,003	3,932	4,217	810	2,705
1979	2,597	1,011	4,954	3,281	2,713
1980	884	905	2,499	1,554	1,776
1981	829	856	2,093	1,474	1,702
1982	686	1,212	1,903	1,058	1,644

Source: Author's calculations.

Note: R_1, ..., R_5 denote copra revenues corresponding to the prices P_1, ..., P_5 and quantities Q_1, ..., Q_5.

References

Bautista, R.M. (1987) "Production Incentives in Philippine Agriculture: Effects of Trade and Exchange Rate Policies," *Research Report 59*. Washington, D.C.: International Food Policy Research Institute.

_____. (1988) "Foreign Borrowing as Dutch Disease: A Quantitative Analysis for the Philippines," *International Economic Journal* 2: 35–49.

Binswanger, H.P. (1980) "Attitudes toward Risks: Experimental Measurement Evidence in Rural India," *American Journal of Agricultural Economics* 62: 174–182.

Cuddy, J.D.A. and P.A. della Valle (1978) "Measuring the Instability of Time Series Data," *Oxford Bulletin of Economics and Statistics* 40: 79–85.

Encarnacion, J. (1962) "Note on an Export Tax as Income Stabilizer," *Philippine Economic Journal* 1: 92–97.

Habito, C. and P.S. Intal (1990) "Macroeconomic Policies and the Coconut Farmer," *Journal of Agricultural Economics and Development* 20: 163–181.

Intal, P.S. and J.H. Power (1990) *Trade, Exchange Rate, and Agricultural Pricing Policies in the Philippines. World Bank, Comparative Studies on the Political Economy of Agricultural Pricing Policies.* Washington, D.C.: The World Bank.

Knudsen, O. and J. Nash (1990) "Domestic Price Stabilization Schemes in Developing Countries," *Economic Development and Cultural Change* 39: 539–558.

Krueger, A.O., M. Schiff and A. Valdes (1988) "Agricultural Incentives in Developing Countries: Measuring the Effect of Sectoral and Economywide Policies," *World Bank Economic Review* 2: 255–271.

Newbery, D.M.G. and J.E. Stiglitz (1981) *The Theory of Commodity Price Stabilization: A Study in the Economics of Risk.* Oxford: Clarendon Press.

Schiff, M. and A. Valdes (1992) *A Synthesis of the Economics in Developing Countries, Vol. 4 of The Political Economy of Agricultural Pricing Policy.* Baltimore: Johns Hopkins University Press.

A Century of Philippine Foreign Trade: A Quantitative Analysis

*Richard Hooley**

The development literature is replete with references to the importance of foreign trade to the pace and pattern of development. What is more controversial is the nature of the linkage between trade, on the one hand, and the rate and pattern of economic growth, on the other. This is particularly true of a country like the Philippines where growth of the domestic economy has been tied to foreign trade throughout the entire period of its modern history.

There have been a number of excellent historical studies of Philippine foreign trade in the eighteenth and nineteenth centuries. Quiason (1966) has given us a good description of trade with the English in the 17th and 18th centuries. And of course there are numerous works giving glimpses of the operation of trading practices and institutions in the work of Bowditch (1962), Bowring (1859) and MacMicking (1967). Legarda (1962) reviewed the growth of foreign trade during the nineteenth century with special reference to its impact on

*Professor of Economics, University of Pittsburgh. Donald Steele assisted in the computations of the database while Anita Tilford took charge of all the editorial aspects. Any remaining errors are the sole responsibility of the author.

entrepreneurship. There are a number of studies of foreign trade in the post-World War II era, including the excellent analysis of Shepherd and Alburo (1991). I know of no studies however, which treat trade development over a century or more as a unit, aside from the Legarda piece already mentioned. One reason is that many writers accept the political watersheds of the War of Independence and arrival of America (1900) and Philippine independence (1946) as also marking distinct economic eras. It is the view of this writer that such a time division does some violence to the facts. In a number of instances the decisive shifts in foreign trade occurred both during the last quarter of the nineteenth century—i.e. before the end of the Spanish period—and during the middle of the American period—i.e. around 1925. It is appropriate to have a time frame which permits examination of long-term trends in trade without prejudice to any particular divisions erected on the basis of essentially political events.

The purpose of this paper is to review the evidence on the growth of foreign trade during the past century and a half, analyzing the major changes and their impact on development. In terms of the time dimension the main focus is on trends during the last one hundred years. The treatment will be quantitative to the extent permitted by the data available. It begins with a review of trends in the latter half of the 19th century and then focuses more intensively on the continuation (or reversal) of these movements in the 20th century. The specific questions to which the paper addresses itself include: How fast has foreign trade grown? How much of this growth was due to price movements and how much to other factors affecting volume changes? What role was played by factors such as alteration in terms of trade, shifts in trade partners' income, movements in relative prices, etc.? What was the impact of government policy—both before and after independence—on trade performance?

The Data

Comprehensive statistical data on foreign trade dated back to 1831. The data prior to 1855 were sporadic and hence required considerable interpolation between reporting dates. They were of fairly low reliability but good enough for establishing broad trends in aggregate exports and imports. From 1855, there was considerable improvement and the reports included annual estimates of exports and imports in the aggregate and for each of the major commodity exports. These data were derived from Spanish customs reports and were summarized in the Census of 1903. Data on individual imports were available from 1885 on, based on annual reports from the Customs Office.

An essential step in the analysis was to separate volume and price movements, and this required indexes of export and import prices. Export and import price indexes were constructed by the author from records of foreign trade prices derived from customs records. For exports, prices were obtained for the major commodities for the period 1855 to 1940. Commodity coverage was high. For each year of the price index, the commodities included in the index accounted for over 90 percent of total exports. Three export price indexes were then constructed—one with 1876 base year weights (for the period up to 1900) and one with 1939 weights (for the period 1901–1940). These were then linked in 1900 to provide an index with 1939 = 100 for the entire period 1855–1940. This index was in turn linked in 1949 to a post-independence period export (published) price index (with 1972 base year weights). The result was one continuous index from 1855 to 1987 with 1939 = 100. Experimentation with shifting base year weights indicated that a fixed base year weight such as 1939 did not introduce large errors into the estimation of overall export price changes. The reason was that the composition of exports over the past century—at least until 1972—had shown remarkable stability. Two commodities—sugar and abaca—accounted for two-thirds or more of total exports for almost every year from 1831 to 1940.

An import price index was constructed utilizing commodity import weights based on data from 1903 to 1940. This was linked to the existing (published) import price index in 1949. For the nineteenth century an import price index was constructed from the wholesale price indexes of the Philippine's major trading partners. Base year weights for 1876 were estimated with data on the country distribution of trade in that year. This index was also constructed back to 1855.[1]

In order to get some idea of the general trends in foreign trade for the nineteenth century, the export and import indexes which began in 1855 were extrapolated back to 1831. In both cases coverage was reduced but it was still substantial. Backward extrapolating of the export price index was based on prices of abaca and sugar, accounting for about two-thirds of exports. On the import side only the wholesale prices of England and Spain were available—but in this case these countries also account for over two-thirds of Philippine imports during this period.

Growth of Foreign Trade

The value of foreign trade increased by approximately 60 times between 1831 and 1940, for an annual average (compounded) growth rate of slightly over 4 percent. There was considerable variation among sub-periods with the most rapid rates occurring during the early years of the nineteenth century and towards the end of the twentieth century. Before 1850 trade volume

---

[1]Major commodity import data are available back to 1885 and a check was made on the error involved in utilizing data by country rather than by commodity. The two series move together fairly closely, and the error involved is relatively minor. Use of import data disaggregated by country rather than commodity makes it impossible to estimate the index for earlier years.

appeared to have grown at an annual rate approaching 10 percent. During the intervening years, it grew by an annual rate of between three and four percent. Between 1950 and 1987 it grew at an annual rate of 12 percent. The growth of exports and imports in constant prices is shown in Chart 1 on the following page. The chart has been presented in semi-log form to facilitate interpretation of trends.[2] From those data six sub-periods can be identified in terms of shifts in the growth rate of real trade volume. Each of these sub-periods will be briefly described here, and discussed in much great detail later.

1.   **1831–1850**. Prior to 1831 the Philippines was restricted to trade carried on in Spanish ships. Although trade was in fact conducted with other countries, the opening of Manila, and shortly thereafter other major ports, to free trade provided a major stimulus to foreign trade. Considering that the founding of Singapore (1820) was the firebell that signaled the entry of Southeast Asia to the expanding colonial trade system, a marked acceleration of Philippine trade at this time is entirely plausible.

2.   **1850–1884**. By the late 1840s Philippine trade had settled down to a rapid pace with sugar and abaca emerging as the leading exports along with several other internationally traded primary commodities such as tobacco and indigo. In addition, there was a small but growing volume of exports in light manufactures (mainly handicrafts) such as straw hats.[3] By the middle of the 1880s the pace of expansion began to slow. The slowdown took place in spite of a substantial depreciation in the value of the silver peso and within

---

[2]A straight trend line on this chart indicates a period during which the growth rate is constant.

[3]A full description of trade composition during this period can be found in Legarda (1954).

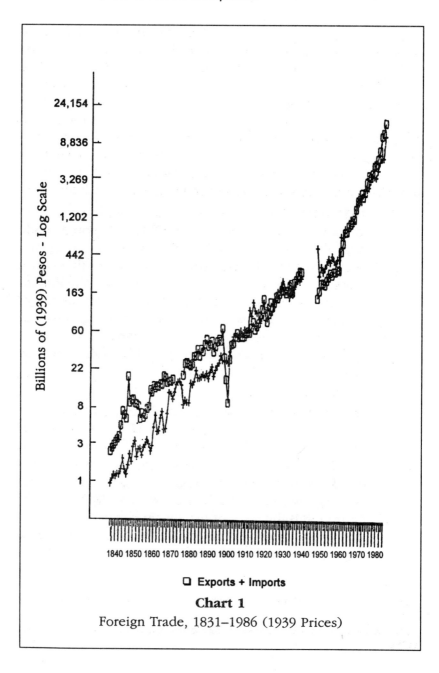

□ Exports + Imports

Chart 1

Foreign Trade, 1831–1986 (1939 Prices)

the environment of a general retardation in the growth of the European and American economies. Conditions during this period will be discussed in more detail later.

3. **1885–1909.** The trend line for this period is considerably reduced from that of the previous period. This is clear from Chart I, particularly when the fall in trade from 1896–1902 during the War of Independence is put aside. Duty-free entry of Philippine products to the American market was not affected immediately after the conclusion of the War of Independence, but awaited passage of the Payne-Aldrich tariff legislation by the U.S. Congress in 1909.

4. **1910–1961.** The year following enactment of the Payne-Aldrich Act witnessed a sharp increase in imports and, shortly thereafter exports, which carried the trend growth of trade volume back to its pre-1885 annual rate of approximately 4 percent. Note that while the opening of the American economy to Philippine exports did cause an acceleration of the rate of trade growth over that obtaining during the last years of the nineteenth century, it did not represent a distinctly new growth path when compared to the nineteenth century as a whole. Trade growth during the first decade of independence (1948–1961) continued at a rate similar to that during the American period, although the volume of trade relative to national income declined sharply in 1950.

5. **1962–1970.** This period saw two substantial devaluations of the peso, reflecting a depreciation from 2.0 pesos to the US Dollar in 1960 to 5.7 Pesos in 1970. A large part of the gain in trade volume during this period represented a redirection of resources from domestic activities to foreign-oriented ones. This was

particularly true in agriculture where export crops were expanded at the expense of domestic food crops after the devaluation of 1962.

6.   **1971–1986.** This final period saw a shift in export composition from traditional primary products to manufactured exports, resulting in a marked acceleration in the annual growth rate. Due to the nature of light manufactured products, both exports and imported (intermediate) products expanded rapidly, producing an explosive increase in foreign trade.

Table 1		
Foreign Trade Growth in Selected Periods, 1831–1987		
Period	Rate of Growth(%)	Foreign Trade as % of GDP
1831–1844	10.30	n.a.
1845–1884	3.95	n.a.
1885–1909	2.99	36.0(a)
1910–1940	4.01	36.5
1950–1961	4.49	18.5
1962–1970	12.20	26.1
1971–1987	13.69	34.2

(a) Based on 1903–1909

Source: Foreign Trade data sources and deflators are described in the text, above. GDP estimates for 1902–1940 are unpublished estimates of the author. GDP estimates for 1950 and later are those of NEDA as published in the *NSCB Philippine Statistical Yearbook 1978 and 1990.*

Summary of Long-Term Trends. A summary of the long-term growth trends in trade volume for the periods set out above is presented in Table 1. To the extent that the data can be relied upon, the period prior to 1850 was one of explosive growth for Philippine trade. For the next forty years the annual growth rate of trade volume was approximately 4 percent. Beginning about 1885 there appeared to have been a reduction of trade volume growth to about 3 percent a year. This is a curious development which requires explanation because this period also marked the first substantial depreciation of the peso, from a value of US$1 to about US$.40 between 1880 and 1900. The reasons for this unusual set of events and its causes will be discussed fully in a later section of this chapter. The volume of foreign trade resumed its earlier annual growth rate of 4 percent with the passage of the Payne-Aldrich Tariff Act during the remainder of the American period. During the first decade of independence, trade continued its colonial growth pattern while real income grew much faster under the aegis of import controls. As a result foreign trade as a percent of GDP fell from one third to about one-fifth. This was by far the lowest level of trade relative to aggregate income recorded in this century. The devaluations of the 1960–1970 period restored some of the balance of foreign trade volume vis-a-vis income as reflected in the fact that as a percent of GDP rose once again to the pre-World War II level of about one third of GDP. Of course, trade composition also changed drastically in this last period—an issue which will be discussed in more detail later.

The Balance of Trade and the Terms-of-Trade

The long-term trends in the volume of foreign trade were much influenced by shifts in relative prices and costs, an area to which attention is now directed. Estimates of the terms of trade are shown in Chart II, along with movements in import and export prices and balance-of-trade. The balance of trade was based on the value of exports and imports in *current* prices and expressed as a percent of exports in current prices. Throughout most of the Spanish period the trade balance was in substantial surplus (excluding the period of the Revolution 1896–1900). The years of deficit were few, mainly 1844, 1861 and 1872. During the American period the trade balance remained in surplus but there were more years of deficit, and the trend of the last decade of that period suggested a

TERMS OF TRADE

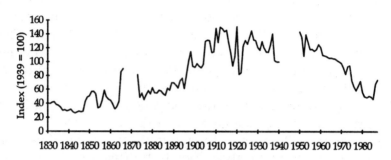

TRADE BALANCE AS PERCENT OF EXPORTS

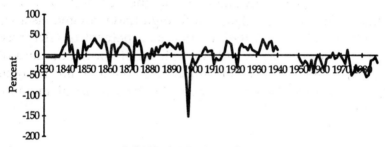

EXPORT AND IMPORT PRICE INDICES

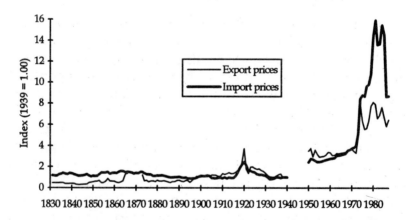

Chart 2

Source: For description of data sources, see text

weakening of the surplus position. In any case, it is clear that the relative size of the surplus was significantly smaller during the American period compared to the last half of the nineteenth century. The trade balance as a percent of exports for the two periods is as follows: 17.25% for the period 1850-1894, and 12.47% for 1910-1940.

I have avoided inclusion of the years prior to 1850 for reasons of data reliability; and avoided the period 1895–1910 which includes the War of Independence and the first years of economic adjustment under the American regime.

In interpreting these figures it should be observed that the trade balance from the 1920s on was heavily influenced by the special preference given to Philippine sugar exports destined for the U.S. This preference was tantamount to an export subsidy of extraordinary size, nearly doubling the price that Philippine exporters would have received for the same sugar if sold on the world market. Without that special treatment the balance of trade figures would have been much lower, and actually in deficit during most years of the second quarter of the twentieth century. The issue of the role of sugar will be discussed in much more detail in a later section of this chapter.

The data on the trade balance shown in Chart 2 may surprise some readers. A widely held view is that deterioration of the trade balance was a post-World War II phenomenon tied to a national fiscal deficit which emerged with political independence. But the data at hand indicate that the trade surplus began to weaken well before independence, and that it was masked by a large subsidy given to sugar exports. That is not to say that the budgetary hemorrhaging which occurred after independence had nothing to do with it. Certainly not. Rather, the evidence suggests that there were other developments which also had a significant impact on the deficit. I now turn to a discussion of some of these other issues.

Estimates of commodity terms-of-trade since the early years of the nineteenth century to the present are shown in Chart 2.

266 Choice, Growth and Development

These were constructed from the export and import price indexes already described in the section on the data base.[4] A long-term trend of improving terms-of-trade began about 1840 with the index peaking in 1920. The improvement was gradual at first, i.e., until about 1882, then accelerated after that date reaching a first peak of 149 in 1909. There was a sharp decline after that date and then a sudden, extraordinary rise to a second peak of 151 in 1920. After that date the terms-of-trade declined but recovered to 145 in 1927. From then on the trend was unmistakenly downward to a level of 100 by the end of the American period.

In the immediate post-World War II era there was a period of almost a decade (1950–1960) during which the terms-of-trade strengthened, at least to the extent that the downward movement evident in the pre-WWII period was temporarily interrupted. This included the years of the Korean War and the sharp, but transient rise in primary commodity prices associated with that period. Between 1950 and 1960 there seemed to be a slight improvement. But looked at from the perspective of the mid-thirties the decade of the fifties was rather like a plateau— a period of no change. By 1960, the downward trend begun in the mid-twenties was resumed. Beginning in 1974 there was acceleration in the fall so that by 1985 the terms of trade were at roughly the same level as in the early 1880s. The net result was that most of the gain achieved in the first 75 years (1840–1909) was erased in the 75 years from 1910 on.

The evidence concerning the break in the long-term trend of the terms-of-trade that occurred in the early years of the nineteenth century is in sharp contrast to the conventional consensus which places this event in the post-independence period. However, the evidence is quite clear and unambiguous

---

[4]Export commodity prices are c.i.f. and import commodity prices are f.o.b. for all years 1940 and before. They are taken from the *Annual Reports of the Collector of Customs*. Data for 1950 and later years is taken from *NSCB Philippine Statistical Yearbook*, various years.

that the deterioration in the trend began in the second quarter of the American period.

What led to this development? In the first place, the export price index for Philippine products rose quite consistently between 1840 and 1920 (Chart II). The sub-periods 1840–1860 and 1898–1920 contain the lion's share of the rise, but throughout these years there was no sustained decline in export prices at any time. Second, import prices were generally falling throughout this period. There was a substantial fall between 1860 and 1914, and they also declined between 1921 and 1940. In contrast, the upward movement in export prices evident in the last half of the nineteenth and first quarter of the twentieth century did not resume after 1921. In fact the trend in export prices was reversed, and export prices actually fell much more sharply than import prices between 1921 and 1940. After independence the weakness in export prices persisted and while there was some improvement with the currency depreciations of 1962 and 1970, it was certainly not dramatic and in fact the rise in export prices was far less than the rise in import prices. Meanwhile, import prices underwent a sharp rise, especially after 1970.

Demand Elasticities for Exports and Imports

The practical and theoretical importance of knowledge about the nature of the export and import demand schedules in the analysis of the growth of trade and changes in the trade balance is beyond question. Perhaps the main focus in some econometric analysis of international trade has been on estimation of price elasticities. Yet income elasticities are at least of equal importance in a growing economy, since income growth in a trading country or its main trading partners may produce either an improvement or deterioration in the trade balance, along with shifts in the commodity composition of trade. In other words, important clues to the behavior of the foreign sector can be found in the magnitude of the parameters of the export and import demand schedules.

The main purpose of this section is to estimate demand elasticities for both exports and imports with respect to income (more precisely GDP in constant prices) and price (defined below). The estimation will be carried out for aggregate exports and imports and where the data permit, for selected commodities. The general approach utilized in exploring foreign sector demand structure in a number of primary commodity exporting countries is described in Leamer and Stern (1970).

In theory the relationship between quantities and prices is simultaneous, i.e., it is a function of both the demand and supply side. However, simultaneous equation models have had only limited success in analyzing international trade movements. Moreover, use of a simultaneous equation model would further constrict the time periods for which estimation would be attempted.

The general methodological approach here has been to utilize a single equation model on the assumption that supply-price elasticities for exports and imports are infinite. On the import side this assumption is certainly realistic in the case for the Philippines. On the export side, it is arguably a close approximation—at least over the intermediate term. For the major primary commodity exports like sugar and coconut products, the country has generally been in the position of being able to increase supply very substantially at existing prices or modestly increasing prices. For example, when the Philippines came under U.S. influence in 1901, total sugar exports amounted to 56 thousand tons. In 1911, with the establishment of free trade with the U.S., they were 209 thousand tons. By 1929 sugar exports had increased to 696 thousand tons (*Statistical Bulletin*). In fact, it was precisely this high supply response which threw fear into the camp of the U.S. domestic sugar industry. The same is generally true of abaca (Owen 1984:49) and coconut products: supply could be increased very substantially at internationally given prices. The high supply elasticity was a result of two factors: the large supply of cultivatable land available and the steady increase in the size of the workforce.[5] Throughout the nineteenth and first half of the twentieth century the Philippines was indeed, a "vent for surplus" economy.

The general approach to estimation of the demand functions for exports and imports is similar in spirit to that used elsewhere and described in Goldsmith and Khan (1985). I have used ordinary least squares to estimate demand functions for exports and imports. Annual observations for all the necessary variables are available from 1902 to the present. Accordingly, demand functions are estimated for the pre- and post-independence periods separately. In addition to the analysis of total exports and imports, an effort has been made to estimate the functions separately for some main commodity exports where feasible. Throughout the analysis I have used double-logarithmic equations because of their generally superior fit and ease of interpretation.

The basic export equation is of the form

$$\ln(X_{pt}) = a_{ot} + a_1\ln(Y_{ft}) + a_2\ln(PX_{pt}/WP_{ft}) + u_t \qquad (1)$$

where X_p is merchandise exports from the Philippines expressed in constant prices, Y_f is aggregate real income (GDP) in the foreign export market, WP_{ft} is an index of wholesale prices in the importing country, t is a subscript indicating time and u is an error term. In this form the demand for real exports is related to real income in the trading partner country and changes in export prices relative to domestic prices in the foreign market. The intent of the ratio (PX_{pt}/WP_{ft}) is to focus on the level of Philippine export prices relative to price of home-

---

[5]Not only the supply of land but its *substitutability* among most major crops was important. For example, land could be converted from rice to sugar production; or from rice to corn, and so on.

produced goods in the receiving country. The use of the general wholesale price index is not ideal, but we have no index of prices of purely competing goods in the importing country (the U.S.).

The import equation is similar to the export equation and takes the form

$$\ln(M_{pt}) = b_{ot} + b_1\ln(Y_{pt}) + b_2\ln(PM_{pt}/WP_{pt}) + u_t \quad (2)$$

where M_p denotes the Philippines' merchandise imports in constant prices, Y_p is real Philippine GDP, PM_p an index of import prices and WP_p an index of wholesale prices of domestically produced goods in the Philippines.

In fitting the export equation, allowance should be made for the existence of quantitative import restrictions on sugar and export restrictions, particularly on sugar. Although there were quantitative export restrictions placed on sugar early in the American period, they were not of any real importance because Philippine production generally fell well short of the limits (Castro 1965). However, passage of the Jones Costigan Act of 1934 resulted in a limit of 1,015,185 tons on Philippine exports to the United States, resulting in a binding constraint on Philippine exports which had already reached that level (Abelard 1947:127). There are two ways to deal with this. One is to include a dummy variable in the demand equations for the years after 1934 until the expiration of the Laurel-Langley Act. Another way is to exclude sugar altogether from the demand equation when estimating demand parameters for the affected years.[6]

Estimates of price and income elasticities for Philippine exports and imports are shown in Table 2. Regressions were

---

[6]With the arrival of American influence in the Philippines the fortunes of the sugar industry became increasingly politicized. In 1902 the American Congress admitted Philippine raw sugar at 75 percent of the duty of 1.685 cents per pound. The Payne-Aldrich Act of 1909 initiated free trade between the two countries but limited the import of sugar from the Philippines to 300,000 tons. This had little effect because at

run on data for pre-independence period (1903–40) and for the post independence period (1950–87). The use of lagged independent variables—income and price—was tried but the results were essentially the same and hence are not reported here. Perhaps if quarterly data had been available the use of lagged variables in the estimating equations would have produced useful additional information. A dummy variable was used however, with the dummy attempting to reflect periods of major quantitative restrictions. On the export side, the dummy is 1 for the period of quantitative controls on sugar exports (1934–1975 while on the import side it is 1 for the period of import controls (1950–62).

In the earlier period, the price elasticity of exports was fairly high—a little over one and statistically significant at the .01 probability level (Eq. 1). Income elasticity is also above unity and statistically significant. No improvement is obtained when the dummy is introduced into either the price or income terms (Eq. 2 and 3). The estimate of income elasticity is similar to the long-term estimate of Birnberg and Resnick, but my

---

(continuation)

that time Philippine exports to the U.S. were well below this limit. In any case, the Underwood-Simmons Tariff (1913) abolished that limit, throwing open the doors to the well-protected U.S. market. By 1920 there were 19 sugar centrals; by 1929 there were 40 centrals in operation. Exports, which averaged 225 thousand tons in the period 1890–95 were destined chiefly for the European and Asian market with only 14.1 percent going to the U.S. By 1929 exports had risen to nearly 700 thousand tons, with 96 percent going to America. After 1930, exports continued in the 1 million ton annual range, with almost all going to the (protected) American market.

The entry of duty-free Philippine sugar to the U.S. market was limited to 800 thousand tons by the Jones-Costigan Act of May 1934. The Sugar Act of 1937 allocated larger quotas to the Philippines. From 1934 to 1961 the quota was 952 thousand tons in addition to 50 thousand tons of refined sugar. From time to time the quota was increased when other U.S. suppliers failed to reach their quota—such as in 1961 when 68 thousand tons of the Cuban quota was added to the Philippines. These quantitative limitations were continued under the Laurel-Langley agreement until 1974, at which time they expired, and Philippine exports once again competed freely in open trade at free market world prices.

export price elasticity estimate of -1.15 is higher than their short-term estimate (-.5) (Birnberg and Resnick 1973). On the import side income elasticity is also approximately one, but price elasticity is much lower—slightly less than -.5 (Eq. 10). These results suggest substantial sensitivity of trade growth to income growth in both countries, particularly the U.S., and a competitivity of trade growth to income growth in both countries, particularly the U.S., and a competitive export market environment. The sum of the price elasticities indicates that the Marshall-Lerner condition is fulfilled, and therefore a change in the exchange rate may be expected to have a substantial (and fairly swift) impact on the trade balance.

In the post-independence period important changes took place in the structure of demand. On the export side there were declines in the magnitude of both the price and income elasticity parameters. In fact, while the price coefficient always takes the correct sign in the later period, it is not statistically significant, even when the dummy is introduced. The income coefficient is generally significant but it is also much reduced from earlier years (Eqs. 4, 5 and 6). These results reflect the much greater degree of trade intervention at the policy level, including quantitative import controls, changes in tariff levels, the impact of the Sugar Act, exchange controls and *ad hoc* interference of a political kind. The dummy variable is not constructed to cover *all* of these items, and hence introduction of the dummy in the regressions (particularly on the import side) is only partially successful in improving the fits.

On the import side during the later period, the elasticity parameters are larger after independence. For example, price elasticity which was -.43 before 1940 was about -.8 after 1950 (Eq. 10–13). In fact, including the price dummy in this period raised the coefficient much higher (Eq. 12). The income coefficient however, remains about the same as in the earlier period.

Regression runs for a few specific commodities are also presented in Table 2. For sugar, the interesting change is the income coefficient declines (Eqs. 7 and 8). This apparently reflects the increased competitiveness of the sugar market in the US during the post-World War II years. The excessively high protection provided to sugar invited competition from a variety of sources. Long before chemical sweeteners invaded the market, other crops such as corn were being used to produce sweeteners, albeit at high cost. This produced increased volatility in sugar prices and, on the whole, much less protection for U.S. (and Philippine) export volume.

The fragmentary data on coconut products indicate that this crop is more like sugar in the early years. The price coefficient of -.5 is not significant, but the income elasticity of 1.5 is statistically significant, and suggests that U.S. income growth is the most powerful element in determining export volume.

To summarize, income and price elasticities for exports were both somewhat above unity in the period prior to 1940. The price and income elasticities for imports were approximately -.4 and 1, respectively. The size of the export and import price elasticities indicated that the Marshall-Lerner condition was satisfied. The policy conclusion to be drawn from these inferences is that income growth and the foreign exchange rate of the peso were the most important elements determining Philippine trade growth in this period. Since the income elasticity of demand for exports was significantly higher than that for imports, income growth in the U.S. was critical in determining the growth of Philippine foreign trade.

During the post-independence period there were significant shifts in the coefficients. Price and income elasticity for exports both declined to around .4 or less. Price elasticity for sugar also declined, reflecting increased competition in the food sweeteners market. This suggests that part of the shift in export coefficients may have been due to changes in export composition. During this same period, the price and income elasticity of imports rose to about -.8 and over 1, respectively. The policy implications for the post-independence period are that while

TABLE 2

Estimates of Demand and Income Elasticities for Exports and Imports

A. Exports Equation: $\ln X_{pt} = \beta_0 + \beta_1(DUM) + \beta_2 + \ln(PX_{pt}/WP_{ft}) + \beta_3(DUMP) + \beta_4 \ln(Y_{ft}) + \beta_5(DUMY)$

Eq. No.	Period	β_0	β_1	β_2	β_3	β_4	β_5	R^2	DW	F
(1)	(1903–40)	8.40		-1.24		1.41		.94	2.04	164.2
(2)	(1903–40)	8.27	-1.86	-1.18	0.41	1.38		.94	1.94	99.7
(3)	(1903–40)	8.18	-1.68	-1.12		1.35	0.26	.94	1.96	99.5
(4)	(1951–87)	15.8		-.267		.357		.99	1.71	131.5
(5)	(1951–87)	16.3	-2.29	-0.47	.31	0.38		.99	1.76	139.9
(6)	(1951–87)	10.35	5.81	-.23		.77	-.60	.99	1.82	131.0
(7)	Sugar	-9.44		-.55		2.66		.85	2.09	86.6
(8)	Sugar	9.89		-1.03		0.28		.87	1.86	29.6
(9)	Copra	-10.9		-.50		1.50		.85	1.63	47.7

B. Imports Equation: $\ln(M_{pt}) = \beta_0 + \beta_1(DUM) + \beta_2 \ln(PM_{pt}/WP_{pt}) + \beta_3(DUMP) + \beta_4 \ln(Y_{pt}) + \int$

Eq. No.	Period	β_0	β_1	β_2	β_3	β_4	β_5	R^2	DW	F
(10)	(1903–40)	.94		-0.43		1.05		.92	2.09	137.9
(11)	(1950–87)	13.13		-.76		1.47		.98	2.07	867.1
(12)	(1950–87)	14.10	13.07	-.78	-2.06	1.26		.99	1.91	865.1
(13)	(1950–87)	13.44	1.59	-.71		1.33	-.56	.99	1.90	865.1

t-values are shown in parentheses.

Symbols:

β_0: Constant

X_j: Exports from the Philippines in constant prices

P_x: Index of Philippine export prices

WP_f: Index of wholesale prices in U.S.

Y_f: National income (constant prices) in U.S.

M_p: Imports to the Philippines in constant prices

PM_p: Index of Philippine import prices

WP_p: Index of prices of domestic products in Philippines

t: Subscript indicating year

DUM (exports): 1 for years 1934–1975. 0 for other years.

DUM (imports): 1 for years 1950–1960. 0 for other years.

Source: Export and import price indexes and aggregate export and import values sources described in text. Additional data on commodity import and export from *Philippine Statistical Bulletin* and *Philippine Statistical Yearbook*, various issues. U.S. national income and wholesale price data from *Historical Statistics of the U.S.*

the level of the peso exchange rate is still important, control of the growth of Philippine domestic income can become more critical in maintaining equilibrium in the country's external accounts.

The Exchange Rate

Throughout much of the nineteenth century both gold and silver coins circulated in the Philippines as currency. The coins took a variety of forms and came from a variety of places— Mexican pesos, Straights Settlements dollars, Spanish pesos, silver rupees, Chinese silver taels, and so on. The Philippine mint was established in Manila in 1861 and coined gold coins in the denominations of four, two and one pesos. The gold peso had a value equivalent to 98.4 U.S. cents. In 1862 the mint began recoining existing silver in circulation into denominations of 50, 20 and 10 centavos. Although the mint in Manila was active, large quantities of Mexican pesos continued to be imported from abroad. In order to better control the supply of money, the Governor General issued a decree in 1877 prohibiting the importation of all kinds of foreign money, but authorizing the continuation of the circulation of all existing Mexican silver coins in the country. However, at about this time the value of silver began to fall relative to gold. This produced two results. First, gold coins, following Gresham's Law, disappeared from circulation while the depreciating Mexican pesos became an ever larger fraction of the money supply. Second, silver coins in ever larger quantities were smuggled into the country.[7] While the exact quantities of each of these currencies in circulation are unknown, an economist who was a keen observer and thoroughly familiar with the

---

[7]The smuggling of silver into the country was a highly organized affair. Silver coins were shipped from Hong Kong in special freighters, which would be landed at a point north or south of Manila. With the connivance of the officials the cargo would be offloaded into smaller boats and taken to vaults in nearby towns, after paying the necessary "squeeze" to the customs agents.

situation in the country observed that the dominant currency toward the end of the nineteenth century and in the first years of the American occupation was the Mexican peso which he estimated accounted for over half of total money supply (i.e. including 3.4 million pesos of banknotes issued by the Bank of the Philippine Islands).[8]

The Currency Depreciation of 1880–1902. Readers unfamiliar with Philippine history may be surprised to learn that the first depreciation of the Philippine peso occurred not in 1960–62 but toward the close of the Spanish regime. As already pointed out, the Philippine money supply moved in the direction of a pure silver standard during the second half of the nineteenth century. From 1875, the value of silver began to decline in terms of gold. The extent of the decline was considerable as can be seen from the data presented in Chart 3. In terms of the U.S. Dollar the Mexican Peso declined from a high of $1.044 in 1870 and $1.00 in 1875 and then to a low of $.3685 in 1903. From there it rose to $0.450 in 1904.

When America occupied the Philippines in 1899 it was necessary to provide for the financing of a force of close to 100,000 troops, including payment of salaries, purchase of supplies, etc. This was a public finance operation of considerable magnitude and a decision had to be made at the outset about the nature of the financial system to utilize. A variety of alternatives were considered. First, the U.S. authorities could use the U.S. dollar for all U.S. Government payments while allowing the local economy to continue using the Mexican peso for local business transactions. This would have resulted in some uncertainty for everyone due to the fluctuations in the value of silver vis-a-vis gold and mirrored in a volatile exchange market. A second alternative considered was that of using Mexican pesos for all local U.S. government payments and receipts. The obvious advantage of this was that virtually

---

[8]Kemmerer (1916) p. 250. The Bank of the Philippine Islands was established by a Spanish decree in 1896.

all business at this time was transacted in pesos—i.e. the Mexican peso was emphatically the money of the country. However, it would have created profits and losses for the U.S. authorities depending on the movements in the Mexican peso/ U.S. dollar exchange rate—something the local military authorities found difficult to deal with. A third alternative was for the U.S. Government to utilize *both* currencies in its transactions, while trying to maintain a stable (dollar) exchange rate for the peso. This was actually the course of action followed for a time until the end of 1901. However, the U.S. Government had difficulty in maintaining the rate chosen—i.e. 2 pesos to $1. The Mexican peso was continually breaking through the limit and depreciating by roughly 10 to 20 percent. This created difficulties for local businessmen who often lost money on the exchange. It also created friction between the local banks and the U.S. Government personnel as the banks were reluctant to maintain the 2 to 1 rate because it involved them in exchange rate losses on their business.[9] This might have been the signal to the U.S. authorities that a rate of ₱2 to $1 represented an overvaluation of the peso in terms of the U.S. dollar. However, this thought never seemed to have occurred to the American authorities or to their advisors.

It is of no particular interest here to follow the arguments brought forth for these different alternative monetary systems. It will suffice to observe that a fourth alternative was devised consisting of a gold-exchange standard. This was embodied in the Philippine Gold Standard Act which was passed by the Philippine Commission in October 1903. This system essentially established a gold-backed Philippine peso with a value of $0.50 without the necessity of gold circulation. The gold exchange fund, created by the Act, was to be used to maintain the 2 to 1 exchange rate. Holders of pesos could, at any time,

---

[9]The private banks were, however, handsomely rewarded in terms of the (for that time) enormous U.S. government deposits held with them at very low interest rates. They undoubtedly exaggerated their "losses" in the whole affair.

apply for redemption of pesos into dollars, which conversion would be supported by the Gold Exchange Trust Fund, held partly in Manila and partly in New York. As the new peso circulation grew in volume, the Fund would also grow and the Fund proceeds were held mainly in the form of U.S. Treasury securities.

The primary goals of the designers of this system seemed to have been (1) stabilizing the value of the peso which at that time had been depreciating continually over the previous quarter century and (2) facilitating the fiscal administration of the new government which had suddenly become a major actor in the local economy. The size of the American fiscal operation from the very start was far larger than anything that had transpired under the Spanish regime. So in August 1898, the American military authorities entered into an agreement with three banks—Hongkong & Shanghai Bank, Chartered Bank and Bank of the Philippine Islands, whereby the banks would agree to exchange U.S. dollars at the rate of 2 pesos to $1. Simultaneously, the banks were given the privilege of importing Mexican pesos as necessary to maintain the rate. This arrangement worked for about two years. Then the Mexican peso began a modest appreciation (around the time of the Boxer Rebellion), but in 1901 resumed its depreciating trend in 1901. These difficulties and the size of the American fiscal/monetary operation led the authorities to consider introducing a new Philippine monetary system. Ironically, the country which was ideologically so close to laissez-faire brought national government fiscal and monetary policy to center stage in the Philippines.

What is of special interest here is the setting of the parity for the new peso. I cannot find any discussion in the literature of the time regarding the appropriateness of the 2 to 1 rate except some offhand comments that this was a round number which made computations simple, would be easily understood by the general public (and by members of the U.S. Congress!), etc. This is curious because setting an equilibrium rate ought to be the chief policy objective in such a situation.[10] The quotes we have for the Mexican peso in 1902 were in the range of 2.40 to $1. In that case the 2 to 1 rate represented an overvaluation of the (new) peso of approximately 20 percent. There was also evidence of a qualitative kind which strongly supported the overvaluation thesis. When the new peso was introduced it was not well received; merchants continued to do business in prices quoted in terms of the Mexican peso, and to accept the new peso only grudgingly. The question was not simply whether or not the 2 to $1 rate represented an equilibrium rate in 1903 or 1904. Since the 2 to $1 rate became fixed in legislation, the question that should be asked was whether it would be an equilibrium rate for the next half-century.

In any case, the general economic situation continued to deteriorate, and by the end of 1902 was being described by observers as one of acute economic distress. The reaction in Washington was to take special measures to get a quick reduction in tariffs to stimulate macroeconomic activity in the Philippines.

> So convinced was the Administration of the seriousness of the universal distress in the Archipelago and the necessity for immediate action, that Theodore Roosevelt on February 27, 1903 sent a special message to the Senate which was then considering the Cooper bill ...the purpose of which was to reduce the existing [tariff] rates on Philippine [export products to the U.S.] to twenty-five percent of the Dingley rates. (Abelardo 1947: 57)

An interesting aspect of Abelardo's discussion is that nowhere does he report discussion in those years which even suggests that the observed economic distress could be due in any way to an inappropriate exchange rate. The immediate

---

[10]In fairness it should be mentioned that the elasticity concept did not appear in the theoretical literature until the early years of the nineteenth century. However, it is somewhat unusual that Kemmerer does not mention the issue in his summary of these events published much later (Kemmerer 1916).

reaction of policymakers of the time was to look exclusively to tariff adjustments for a solution to the macroeconomic stagnation.

The situation could have been rectified by an upward adjustment of the Philippine *domestic* levels of wages and prices which, along with the new exchange rate, would have restored international equilibrium. But this did not happen.

> ...the immediate tendency of the change [in the peso parity rate] was to give the new peso no higher purchasing power as regards retail prices and wages than the old, *and thus to increase prices and wages, as measured in gold values, by the difference between the gold value unit of the new monetary unit and that of the old.* [my italics]. (Kemmerer 1916: 344)

Why was there no adjustment in local prices and wages? The answer seems to be that local prices and wages were extremely sticky, especially on the downside, even in the intermediate term. Again, quoting Kemmerer,

> ...when the new money came to constitute the main part of the circulating medium, prices seem to have been transferred quite generally from the old currency to the new *without any material alterations* [my italics]. (Kemmerer 1916: 345).

The net upshot of these developments is that over a period of a quarter of a century (1875–1902) there was a depreciation of the peso from approximately 1 peso to the dollar to 2.4 pesos to the dollar. Then beginning in 1903 there was an appreciation of the peso to 2 pesos to the dollar with the enactment of the Philippine Gold Standard Act. The appreciation occurred gradually of course, since it took a few years for the new peso to completely replace the old Mexican peso. The available evidence suggests that under the new monetary regime domestic prices and wages rose (in terms of their dollar or international value) with the peso's appreciation, and that the new peso value thus represented an overvaluation in terms of (international) equilibrium prices by as much as 20 percent. This view is founded on the reasonable assumption that the market values of the Mexican peso shown in Chart 3 represent a fair approximation to the equilibrium exchange rate at the time.[11]

What effect did these shifts in the exchange rate have on the volume of trade? First, the depreciation of the peso during the last quarter of the nineteenth century should have had a stimulative impact on exports. That is what one would expect on the basis of the export price elasticities estimated earlier in this paper. It is also what Nugent (1973) argues, i.e., that depreciation of silver in the late nineteenth century was particularly beneficial to the growth of exports of Third World countries which were on a silver standard.

The quantitative evidence at hand does not support this view. The rate of growth of (real) exports from 1885 to the end of the century was a little less than 3 percent, which was the lowest level for that century, at least for the years covered by the available data (See Table 1). The terms of trade did however, improve markedly after 1880, as can be seen from the data in Chart 2. Why was there no significant improvement in the volume of exports in spite of the currency depreciation and the improvement in the terms of trade? One explanation that has been advanced alleges that the demand for primary products was inelastic. While such an explanation might be credible for world demand as a whole, it does not fit the facts for a single country. There were many other areas producing the Philippines' major exports, and demand must have been at least fairly elastic for the major primary exports—sugar and hemp. An alternative interpretation rests on the fact that at this time it was not depreciation in terms of gold which was critical for exports, but depreciation of the peso *in terms of the value of competing countries' currencies.* Many primary exporters were

---

[11]Kemmerer (1916:252-53) argues that the market exchange rates for the Mexican peso represented a small overvaluation of the Mexican peso—i.e. because of (domestic) monetary demand and limitations on importation, the Mexican coins were worth somewhat more inside the country than outside. If his view is accepted, the overvaluation of the new peso in terms of the U.S. dollar was possibly more than 20 percent.

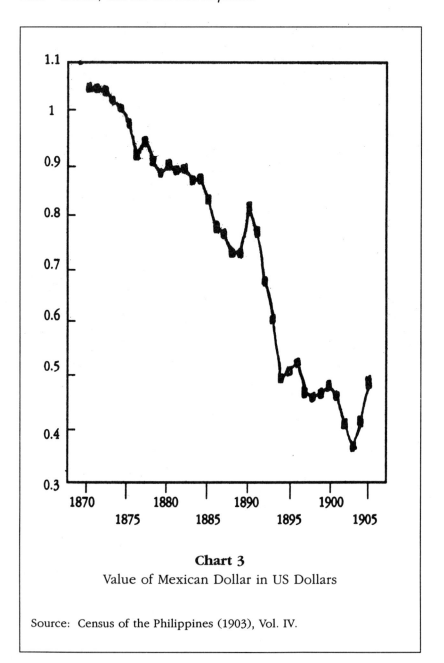

Chart 3

Value of Mexican Dollar in US Dollars

Source: Census of the Philippines (1903), Vol. IV.

on a silver standard. Virtually the whole of Southeast Asia, India, Mexico, and a large part of Latin America were on a silver standard at this time.[12] The depreciation of the peso in terms of gold did not obviously, represent a depreciation in terms of competitive silver-based currencies. Hence the stimulative impact on exports did not take place.

However, there *should* have been some impact on imports since the latter came from the industrialized countries most of which were on gold standard at this time. Some impact apparently did take place judging from the healthy balance of trade surplus of these years in spite of retardation in the rate of export growth. However the impact on imports was damped because western countries were going through a secular decline in prices of industrial goods during this period, estimated as approximately a 30 percent decline in prices (Van der Eng 1993: 16). Thus depreciation of the (gold) value of the peso did not produce the full impact on import prices. That is to say, deflation in the gold currencies of industrialized countries partly neutralized the impact of depreciation of silver currencies such as the peso. So for very different reasons the depreciation of 1875–1902 had virtually zero impact on stimulating exports and only a damped effect on reducing import demand.

What about the appreciation of the peso in 1903–04? Did this have any visible effect on the trade pattern? This is a complex question with several interlocking dimensions. First, it is clear that the balance of trade surplus during the American period was only two-thirds as large as that during the half quarter of the nineteenth century. This tends to bear out the contention that the higher value of the peso, together with

---

[12]The Philippines' leading exports at this time were sugar and hemp. The major competitor in the hemp market was Mexico while in sugar the major competitors were Indonesia and the West Indies—all on a silver standard.

sticky wages and prices, placed a damper on exports and stimulated imports.[13]

The second aspect of this question concerns changes in tariff rates. Insofar as tariffs were reduced during the American period, particularly by the Payne-Aldrich Act, the upward adjustment of the peso would have to be added to the decline in tariffs on imported American goods to get the (new) effective exchange rate for Philippine imports.

The third aspect of this question relates to the trend in foreign trade (i.e. external) prices and the trend in domestic prices over the first half of the twentieth century. The exchange rate established by the Gold Standard Act was a fixed parity rate which was maintained in the next sixty years. Was this rate in conformity with movements in the demand schedules for exports and imports throughout that period? The evidence indicates that it was not, and that the overvaluation of the peso became worse as the years progressed, particularly after the mid-1920s.

The evidence is quite clear. A glance at Chart 2 shows that the terms-of-trade began a long-term decline about 1925. The decline resulted chiefly from a deterioration in Philippine export prices. The deterioration was due to two developments. First, agricultural productivity in the industrialized countries increased rapidly during the last third of the nineteenth century. By the first decade of the twentieth century overproduction (in terms of existing agricultural prices) was the rule in many countries for a variety of primary commodities. This brought about a widespread weakness in prices which became painfully manifest after 1920.

---

[13]Filipino businessmen, represented by Benito Legarda Sr., argued before the Philippine Commission that duty-free imports to the Philippines would hamper industrialization of the country (Schurman Report 1990). What was not made clear at the time however, was that creating a new overvalued currency would also have deleterious implications for local industrial growth.

The second development which caused a weakening in primary goods prices was the advances in modern chemistry which caused a downward shift in the demand for a number of commodities. Indigo, an important Philippine export up to the end of the nineteenth century had its market virtually eliminated in a few years time by the development of chemical dyes about 1900. Abaca, a major export, began to feel the impact of nylon in the late thirties, and lost most of the market to chemical fibers after World War II. The development of chemical sweeteners in recent years has decimated the sugar market.

A third factor is that these developments were partly brought on by the absence of productivity improvement in most Philippine primary production, causing a rise in their prices (relative to industrial goods) which invited research aimed at finding substitutes.[14] In other words, the rise in the price of primary exports in countries like the Philippines which both improved the terms of trade and increased the rate of return on investment in primary production, also sowed the seeds of its own destruction by inviting investment in research and development in industrialized countries aimed at developing substitutes.

It has been argued above that tariff policy was used extensively to compensate for an overvalued peso after 1900. A counterfactual analysis may help to establish the point. Suppose there had been no duty-free privilege for Philippine products entering the American market. What effect would this have had on the balance of trade? I have recalculated the balance of trade for selected periods between 1900 and 1940 on the assumption that sugar entering the U.S. paid full duty. The results are shown in Table 3.

---

[14]There was virtually no productivity increase during the first sixty years of this century in Philippine production of primary exports, with the single exception of sugar. (R.Hooley and V.W. Ruttan 1969).

Table 3

Balance of Trade as Percent of Exports With and Without Sugar Subsidy

Period	Trade Balance With Subsidy	Trade Balance Without Subsidy
1900–13	-3.43	-4.53
1914–20	-0.15	-1.38
1921–25	10.39	-0.63
1926–30	13.92	-4.69
1931–35	21.75	-16.11
1936–40	22.39	0.07
1913–40 Ave.	10.81	-4.54

Source: The observed (or actual) balance of trade is taken from the data in Chart II. The balance of trade without subsidy reflects the value of the subsidy (Peso per ton) multiplied by the quantity shipped to the U.S.

I have made these computations for sugar alone, since the subsidy reflected in the duty-free privilege was much greater for sugar than for any other commodity—indeed than for all other Philippine exports combined. However, I have not adjusted the quantity shipped downward to reflect the impact of lower prices on supply. If this were done the balance of trade would be even more negative.[15] But this is unnecessary. The dramatic impact of the duty-free tariff privilege is clear enough. For the entire period the balance of trade is favorable to the extent of 10.81 percent of exports. But if the sugar subsidy on exports to the U.S. is removed the balance of trade is unfavorable to the extent of -4.54 percent of exports.

The net result of these calculations and the other evidence presented here indicates that the 2 to 1 exchange rate for the peso did indeed represent an overvaluation especially for the

---

[15]An excellent analysis of this general issue can be found in Johnson (1957).

years after 1920. However, *given* the special conditions surrounding the tariff preference in the American market, the 2 to 1 exchange rate may have been close to equilibrium for exports. On the import side the overvaluation would still operate to stimulate imports, which it undoubtedly did. However, careful fiscal management seems to have resulted in substantial private investment along with an expansion of infrastructure far beyond anything seen up to that time. The expansion in public buildings, roads, railroads, communications and also in irrigation facilities (at least up to 1920 for the latter), not to mention improvements in educational facilities and health services along with a substantial inflow of American capital, were all partly made possible by the stable and high international purchasing power of the peso. I mention these accomplishments to preserve balance in the total assessment, although a thorough analysis of their impact is outside the purview of this chapter.

The Currency Depreciation of 1962. When the Philippines emerged from the devastation of World War II, one of the first things undertaken was a stabilization of the currency. The peso was reset at its pre-World War II parity of 2 to $1. At the time no one appeared to have questioned whether, in view of changed economic conditions, this rate was appropriate or not. In hindsight however, reestablishment at the old parity rate involved a further overvaluation of the peso. There are two reasons for this inference.

First, when the Bell Mission (1951) made its investigation of foreign trade trends in the Philippines, they were working with price indexes of exports and imports that were calculated with 1937 base weights.[16] The use of 1937 weights on the import side resulted in a substantially reduced estimate of the rise in import prices compared to the import price index when

---

[16]These were the indexes published in *International Financial Statistics* (IFS) at that time. In later issues of *IFS* (after 1953), the base year weights are shifted to 1949.

computed with post-World War II base year weights. I estimate that use of pre-World War II weights resulted in an understatement of approximately 25 percent in the import price rise between 1940 and 1946.[17] The reason for the discrepancy is that the "basket" of imported items at the outset of the independence period was much more heavily weighted toward food grains and consumables such as textiles, compared to the pre-1940 period where products of iron and steel and similar goods were much more important. For example, in 1940 the weights for food grains and iron steel products were 5 and 27 percent respectively; in 1946 the weights were 13 and 3 percent respectively. But it is precisely in items such as food grains and textiles where price rises were most in evidence after World War II. So, not only were the items of trade weakening, but the shift in the *composition of imports* was placing a heavier burden on the country's external accounts. This fact was not appreciated at the time. I can find no discussion about the shift in import (or export) composition, and the possibility of these impacts on the sustainability of the exchange rate in the Report of the Bell Mission (1951).

A second factor of significance is the nature of the sugar quota. I have already pointed out that (duty-free) tariff policy was used to provide support to the country's external accounts in the pre-independence period. However, when Philippine sugar came under the Sugar Act in 1937, it was under a fixed quota essentially unchanged from year to year. To be sure, small increases in the size of the quota were given at various times, but this did not materially change the quota. Now, when the country emerged after independence, population had

---

[17]The comparison is:

> Import price index 1946/40 (1937 base year weights) = 251.9 (1937 = 100)
>
> Import price index 1946/40 (1946 base year weights) = 314.9 (1937 = 100)

The indexes were constructed from data in the *Philippine Statistical Yearbook* of 1940 and 1946.

grown (from 16.5 million in 1940 to 20.5 million in 1950), and the requirements for infrastructure, consumption, private investment, etc. were commensurately higher, in addition to reconstruction requirements. However, the volume of sugar exports (the country's most important single foreign exchange earner) was essentially unchanged. Nor did sugar prices perform particularly well. In 1951 sugar prices were only a little better than twice the level of 1940; and abaca prices in 1951 were actually lower than in 1940. All of this is reflected in one way or another in the downward trend of the terms of trade (Chart 2).

This is the foreign trade environment in which the country began its drive toward industrial independence. Under the Bell Trade Act the Philippines was forced to continue the overvalued 2 to 1 exchange rate from pre-World War II years into the independence period. It is not surprising therefore, that in spite of substantial once-over foreign aid for reconstruction, the nation was obliged to institute foreign exchange controls in late 1949. Within a couple of years a new policy strategy emerged—that of import substitution.

From a historical perspective, the broad outlines of the independence period policy were not completely new. Rather, it appears to be the policy strategy of the American period "stood on its head". Whereas the pre-independence policy was to compensate for the export-depressing effects of an overvalued peso by use of abnormally low (U.S.) tariffs on Philippine exports, the independence period strategy attempted to compensate for the import-stimulating effects of peso overvaluation by quantitative controls and abnormally high tariffs on imports. Both strategies share a common element: the reliance on interventionist policies to compensate for a disequilibrium exchange rate. What is undeniable however, is that within a short time the new interventionist trade structure created a powerful political dimension of its own—protection of the industrial sector that had sprung up in response to the new regulatory environment. The capital investment in this new sector was generally undertaken by persons different from those who held controlling interest in the export sector. It therefore also made possible a significant rotation of the (political and social) elite structure.

This policy of import substitution was successful for some years, but toward the end of the fifties it began losing momentum. As is now well recognized, the new industries were heavily dependent on imported inputs, putting much additional strain on the external trade accounts (Power and Sicat 1971). In addition, the volume of exports was adversely affected. Because of the high domestic price level relative to export prices, resources in agriculture were shifted from exports to the production of food crops for the domestic market (Treadgold and Hooley 1967). This effect can be seen by referring to Chart 1, where the reduction of export volume is reflected in a decline below long-term trend for the period 1951–1962. This entire period is portrayed in the shape of a distinct "U" which is exactly anchored by the imposition of import controls at one end and the devaluation of 1962 at the other.

In 1962 the peso exchange rate was changed to 3.90 to $1. Currency depreciation was followed by a gradual increase in protective tariffs which continued sporadically until the end of the 1970s.[18] The depreciation of 1962 had an immediate and positive effect on the external accounts. The volume of exports increased almost precisely to the trend level indicated by export volumes during the first half of the twentieth century. In addition, the balance of trade turned around from a large deficit and was either in balance or in surplus for the rest of the decade. This performance is in agreement with my earlier

---

[18]I have treated this important period in summary fashion because there is already a substantial body of literature describing it. For an excellent analysis of the main trade features of this period see Shepherd and Alburo (1991).

inference concerning the fairly high demand elasticity for exports, and the general importance of maintaining an equilibrium rate.

As the import-dependent industrial sector continued to expand, the trade balance once again began to slide into a continual deficit. It was therefore decided to adopt a free-floating exchange rate along with a policy of export promotion of light manufactures. The further depreciation of the exchange rate (by 1987 it was 20 to $1) along with a variety of incentives provided for nontraditional exports, resulted in an acceleration of export volume from 1972–87 to annual rates never before attained by this country. However import volume accelerated even faster, resulting in a growing trade deficit (see Chart 1). Policymakers were forced to address this problem by a sharp contraction in income (and employment) and a further depreciation of the peso to about 28 to $1. The break in the long-term trend in the terms of trade, which I have dated as beginning in 1925 or so, and which accelerated markedly after the early 1960s, contributed very significantly to the deterioration of the trade balance.

While there is no doubt that the terms of trade deterioration was operating in 1970s and 1980s to damp the growth-stimulating effects of trade expansion on the domestic economy, there are two other factors which were also important in this regard. First, it is generally assumed that freeing up the foreign exchange rate and reducing trade barriers will result in a regime of prices and costs conducive to improvement of productivity levels. There is unfortunately, almost no evidence in support of this widely held notion. Philippine manufacturing productivity growth even after trade liberalization has been described as disappointing at best in a number of reports (Hooley 1985).

It is worth special mention that there does not appear to be any stable relation between the expansion of foreign trade and productivity growth in manufacturing. After the devaluation of the peso in 1962 there was a period during the middle 'sixties when manufacturing productivity displayed moderate albeit sustained growth. But peso depreciations at other times have not been associated with the same results. The absence of a linkage between trade decontrol measures and productivity growth is itself nearly fatal to industrialization efforts. Without such a linkage trade growth cannot impact decisively on growth of income and employment. Furthermore, if competitors *are* increasing manufacturing productivity, it is difficult to see how the country can remain competitive and continue to expand trade.

The second factor complicating the new export strategy is the input structure of the export industries. In the period prior to 1960, the Philippines developed a manufacturing sector heavily involved in processing raw materials for export. In contrast, the colonial exports like sugar, copra, cigars, straw hats and so on utilized locally-produced materials in their manufacture. Exports of these products provided large multiplier effects which were dispersed to various regions. Take sugar for example. Value added in sugar milling represents about 25 percent of gross sugar production. However, of the remainder, at least 80 percent of production costs represents value added in agriculture. So total value added (manufacturing and agricultural) of sugar exports represents over 50 percent (probably close to two-thirds) of the gross value of sugar exports. For the current crop of light manufactured exports value added is only about 20–25 percent, and most of the costs involve imported inputs. The result is that the multiplier and linkage effects of these latter industries are far less than most of the "traditional" exports. This issue is often approached in terms of net foreign exchange receipts of the exporting industry. I do not see it as a "foreign exchange problem". However, it does appear that an export drive based on light manufactures of the kind now operating in the Philippines will provide far less growth stimulus to the domestic economy than the export industries (primary commodities and light manufactures) prevalent in the pre-independence period. Although the regional income-distribution may be more equal than that produced by import substitution, it is probably less equal than that produced by the traditional export structure.

Summary and Conclusion

The objective of this chapter has been to review the evidence concerning the growth of Philippine foreign trade during the past century and a half, analyzing the impact of this growth on the tempo and pattern of the country's development. The quantitative treatment perused required a set of estimates of quantities and prices for the major exports and imports. For the post-1950 period there is no problem as published data are available. For the period prior to 1940 I relied on quantities and prices as recorded by the Customs Office, and reprinted in a variety of official documents. Export and import price indexes were prepared for the nineteenth and first half of the twentieth century and then linked together to form one continuous index. Since export and import composition did not undergo major changes until the 1970s, this procedure which consisted of linking three fixed-base indexes together, proved to be a feasible strategy in creating a data base capable of delineating long-term trends in the volume of trade.

There are six main periods of foreign trade expansion. The first period begins with the opening of Manila to free trade in 1831 and extends to mid-century. This period reflects an explosive growth of trade as the country is integrated into the rapidly expanding Southeast Asian trade with Europe following the founding of Singapore in 1820. A second period extends from mid-century to 1885, when trade volume was expanding at about 4 percent per year, a very respectable rate of growth in those years, reflecting the rapid utilization of land resources in a vent-for-surplus model and the increased acceptance of

Philippine products by the international market. Even before mid-century sugar and abaca emerged as the dominant exports while on the import side textiles and, after 1880 rice, became items of particular importance.

A third period extends from 1885 to 1909 and represents a moderate retardation in the trade growth rate. The decline in trade growth during these years can be traced to a variety of developments, including a lower growth rate of real income in European and American markets, as well as the first incursion into primary commodity markets by competing industrialized countries: e.g., chemical dyes which swiftly replaced indigo and dyewood exports from the Philippines. Finally, there was the War of Independence from 1896 to 1900, and a general period of economic readjustment with the entry of America in 1898.

One of the puzzles of the late nineteenth century period is the apparent evaporation of the effects of the depreciation of the peso from 1885 to 1904. The Mexican peso, the main circulating medium in the Philippines during this period, was silver-backed currency. As such it depreciated in terms of the U.S. dollar (and other gold-based currencies) from a level of a little over 1 to the dollar in 1880 to 2.4 to the dollar in 1903, a decline in the value of the peso of over 50 percent. In contrast with the conventional view concerning the stimulating effects of a currency depreciation, including the depreciation of silver at this time, the facts show that in this case currency depreciation produced no stimulating impact on Philippine export volume. There was however, a distinct improvement in the terms of trade throughout this period. This apparent paradox is explained on the grounds that the country's major competitors (in the sugar and hemp markets especially) were also on a silver standard, and hence there was no significant depreciation of the peso in terms of *competitor's* currencies.

A new long-term trend in trade volume began with the American period, which may be taken as the passage of the

Payne-Aldrich Act in 1909 to the early 1950s. During these years export volume resumed its growth rate of approximately 4 percent per year, and the country increased its openness as reflected in the fact that the value of international trade reached 40 percent of gross domestic product.

With the end of World War II and the arrival of independence a new, lower growth trend of foreign trade emerged. There was an absolute decline in the volume of foreign trade for a period beginning in the early 1950s and ending in 1962. This was associated with the policy of import substitution, implemented through the imposition of exchange controls, protective tariffs and a variety of quantitative restrictions on imports. The volume of exports declined as resources were redirected away from international and towards domestic economic activities. Underreporting of exports and imports also occurred, increasing the apparent decline in trade volume. The decline was severe as reflected in a reduction of the ratio of international trade to GDP from 40 percent in 1940 to less than 20 percent by the late 1950s.

The sharp reduction in export volume which occurred during these years was a major reason for the unsustainability of the import substitution strategy of this period. Consequently in 1962 the currency was depreciated from 2 to $1 to 3.9 to $1 while exchange controls and most import controls were lifted. The volume of trade immediately shifted back to its long-term trend of the pre-import substitution era. This situation continued until the early 1970s.

The shift towards an export-oriented macroeconomic strategy, utilizing well-known policy tools such as export zones, etc., raised the long-term trend of trade volume growth not seen since the early years of the nineteenth century. This growth is associated with a shift toward exports of light manufactures. But it is concluded that the impact of this recent high trade growth rates on domestic economic activity is considerably less than if those same rates had been achieved with traditional commodity exports. The reason is that the linkage of nontraditional exports value added with the rest of the economy remains weak. In addition, traditional exports created large income multiplier impacts in a variety of rural areas, while the newer imports have not yet established such links of commensurate strength. There may yet be a strengthening of such linkages, but this will depend heavily on the nature of policy strategies chosen.

A major finding of the research reported in this chapter is that certain adverse developments in the international trade area emerged during the early nineteenth century, and became more serious towards the close of the American period. These issues reappeared and continued to fester during the early independence period, until they finally surfaced in full force by the last third of the twentieth century.

The first of these problems was the overvalued currency. There is substantial evidence that the parity rate of 2 pesos to $1 established by the Philippine Gold Standard Act of 1904 represented an overvaluation of the peso of 20 percent or more at that time. The evidence is both quantitative and qualitative, including comments and observations of some of the best analytical minds of that period. In view of the estimates of export demand presented here, which indicate a price elasticity coefficient of at least unity and probably greater than one, the adoption of an overvalued exchange rate must have had a significantly depressing effect on macroeconomic activity.

The second trade-related problem that emerged during the American period was a break in the favorable long-term trend of the terms of trade. Throughout all the years of the nineteenth century for which there are data, the commodity terms of trade of the Philippines had long been generally improving. Had this improving trend in terms of trade continued throughout the pre-World War II years, the overvalued peso would not have caused much of a problem. But that was not the case. After World War I—actually about 1920—the favorable terms of trade trend broke suddenly and began a long-term decline. There was a marked decline for two decades. After World War II there was a period of sharp year-to-year movements associated with the Korean War boom, but generally the trend was horizontal, i.e., it clearly did not resume its upward trend of earlier years. After 1960 the downward trend reasserted itself with vigor, displaying increasing momentum into the 'eighties.

This development created a policy dilemma for American and Filipino leaders beginning in the late 1920s and becoming ever more poignant during the Commonwealth period. One alternative would have been to float the peso and allow the expected depreciation to restructure export and import price levels. This alternative was not considered seriously because the 2 to 1 rate was defined in legislation creating the Gold Exchange Standard. Instead, the policy tool utilized was the same one chosen to deal with the sluggish performance of the Philippine economy in the opening years of this century i.e., adjustment of the tariff structure. In other words, given the exchange rate overvaluation, the tariff instrument was used. Duty-free entry of Philippine exports was one way of raising the (peso) price of those exports. In the 1930s, putting the country under the Sugar Act quota system was a way of subsidizing exports. It certainly provided macroeconomic stimulation to the economy while at the same time making possible a flow of cheap imports into the country. This satisfied all existing vested interests—the sugar bloc and the importers. The irony of this policy is that the American nation, which was then most closely associated (ideologically) with laissez faire, would end up erecting a trade regime in the Philippines which was a monument to interventionism.

These developments—overvaluation of the peso and the sharp break in the terms of trade, along with a firm commitment to a fixed peso-dollar rate, set the stage for a policy orientation in the direction of trade interventionism which became a permanent feature of Philippine economic history to the present time. A virtual obsession with trade interventionism and tariff policy in particular came to characterize trade policy during the later years of the American period. This policy posture carried over into the independence period. When the development of local entrepreneurship became a goal after independence, the policy tool that the new government immediately reached for was trade intervention—a mixture of an overvalued currency, quantitative import restrictions, and changes in tariff structure. The net result was that trade policy in the first two decades of the independence period exhibits fundamental similarities with the trade policy of the American period.

A full assessment of these policies in the pre-independence period is beyond the scope of this chapter. It would involve a careful evaluation regarding how much of the required macroeconomic adjustment might have been expected from stipulated changes in the exchange rate. Furthermore, account would have to be taken of the benefits of peso overvaluation reaped during the first half of the twentieth century through the adoption of a conservative and far-sighted fiscal policy. Private capital formation was increased and a long list of social infrastructure projects were undertaken—in agriculture, education, health services, etc. providing a solid foundation for future growth.

A balanced evaluation would also have to consider the political repercussions of this policy strategy which cannot be overlooked. Elites learned to use tariff policy to pursue their own special economic interests. The sugar bloc was greatly strengthened and a group of commercial importers with a vested interest in maintaining a particular mix of trade interventionism and exchange rate policy was created. The economic rents associated with the contours of this particular policy mix so strengthened selected sub-groups of the elite that the political and social structure virtually became a hostage to them.

The obsession with trade interventionism, and tariff structure in particular, and the rents that go along with this type of policy, carried over into the independence period. The result is that trade policy in the first two decades of the independence period looks much like trade policy of the American period—but stood on its head.

What factors were responsible for the historic reversal of the terms of trade during the first quarter of the twentieth century? One factor is the lack of any productivity increase in most Philippine primary production which resulted in rising unit costs to industrialized countries, providing an incentive for investment in research and development (in the industrialized countries) to search for substitutes. The high demand elasticity for Philippine export suggests that supplies from competitive suppliers was also taking its toll. An additional factor was that after independence, the Philippines was no longer a true land-surplus economy in the vent-for-surplus mode. It was on its way to becoming a labor-surplus economy. This also was eroding its cost competitiveness in primary production. Finally, agricultural productivity growth had accelerated in many countries in the late nineteenth and twentieth centuries, greatly increasing the number of primary goods suppliers at internationally competitive costs.

Appendix

Computation of Export and Import Price Indexes

The basic data on export and import quantities and prices is taken from *Census of the Philippine Islands* (1903), *Washington, U.S. Bureua of the Census, 1905, Vol. III.* Additional data can be found in Government of the Philippine Islands, Bureau of Commerce and Industry, *Statistical Bulletin of the Philippine Islands* (1920), and also in Government of the Philippine Islands, Bureau of Customs, *Annual Reports*, various years.

The price deflators for both exports and imports are of the Laspeyre type, one for each sub period from 1831 to 1940, i.e.,

$$\sum_i P_{in}Q_{io} \Big/ \sum_i P_{io}Q_{io}$$

where P_{in} is the price of commodity i in year n, P_{io} is the price in the base year, and Q_{io} is the quantity of the ith commodity traded (exported/imported) in the base year.

There is some shift in the composition of exports and imports over the period under study, though the changes in composition are not drastic. For example, sugar and abaca account for at least 60 percent of total export value in virtually every year up to 1900, and nearly half of total export value or most years between 1900 and 1940. However, to better reflect the changes in export and import composition that do occur, three separate sets of indexes employing different base years are used: 1939, 1876 and 1856. This results in an export and import price index for the years 1900-1939 using 1939 weights; an export and import price index for 1856-1900 using 1876 weights; and an export and import price index for the years 1831-1856 using 1856 weights. These indexes were then linked to the 1939 base year index to produce continuous export and import price indexes covering the period 1831-1940 with a 1939 base. Finally, this index was then linked to the published indexes (1972 base year) by extending the 1939 base year index to 1950. Data to extend the 1939 base year export and import price indexes to 1950 were developed from export and import commodity price data contained in the Bureau of Census and Statistics, *Yearbook of Philippine Statistics* (1940 and 1946); NEDA, *Philippine Statistical Yearbook* (1978) and IMF, *International Financial Statistics*, (Sept. 1955).

The weights used in the different indexes were as follows:

1939 Base Year Weights (in percent):

(a) Exports: sugar 35.0; copra 11.5; coconut oil 11.5; mining 20.0; abaca 10.1; tobacco 6.9; lumber 5.0.

(b) Imports: metal products 30.5; textiles 24.8; petroleum products 12.3; food grains 7.7; tobacco products 6.7; paper 4.3; dairy products 4.2; chemicals 3.3; cement 2.3; miscellaneous 3.9.

1976 Base Year Weights:
(a) Exports: sugar 53.5; copra*; coconut oil*; abaca 28.8; tobacco 8.6; coffee 8.1; indigo 1.0. (* = less than 0.1%).
(b) Imports (Weights are used to combine the wholesale price indices of major trading partners): England 60.0; Spain 20.0; China 10.0; U.S.A. 10.0.
1856 Base Year Weights:
(a) Exports: sugar 50.0; abaca 50.0.
(b) Imports: England 70.0; Spain 30.0.

References

Abelardo, P.E. (1947) *American Tariff Policy Toward the Philippines, 1898–1946.* New York: King's Crown Press.

Bautista, R.M. and J. Encarnacion Jr. (1972) "A Foreign Trade Submodel of the Philippine Economy, 1950–69," *The Philippine Economic Journal* II, 2, Second Semester.

Birnberg, T. and S. Resnick (1973) "A Model of the Trade and Government Sectors in Colonial Economies," *American Economic Review.*

Bowdich, N. (1962) *Early American-Philippine Trade: The Journal of Nathaniel Bowdich in Manila,* edited with an Introduction by Thomas R. McHale and Mary C. Mchale. Monograph Series No. 2. New Haven: Yale University Press, Southeast Asia Studies.

Bowring, J. (1859) *A Visit to the Philippine Islands.* London: Smith, Elder & Co.

Brown, I. (1989) "Some Comments on Industrialization in the Philippines During the 1930s," in Ian Brown (ed.). *The Economies of Africa and Asia in the Inter-War Depression.* N.Y.: Routledge.

Castro, A. (1965) "Philippine-American Tariff and Trade Relations," *Philippine Economic Journal,* First Semester.

Goldsmith, M. and M.S. Kahn (1985) "Income and Price Effects in Foreign Trade" in R.W. Jones and P.B. Kenen (eds). *Handbook of International Economics* (V. II). Elsevier Science Publishers.

Hooley, R. (1985) *Productivity Growth in Philippine Manufacturing: Retrospect and Prospects.* Manila: Philippine Institute for Development Studies.

_____ and V. Ruttan (1969) "The Philippines," in E. Shand (ed.). *Agricultural Development in Asia.* Canberra: ANU Press.

Johnson, H.G. *Economic Policies Toward Less Developed Countries.* New York: Praeger.

Kemmerer, E.W. (1916) *Modern Currency Reforms: A History and Discussion of Recent Currency Reforms in India, Puerto Rico, Philippine Islands, Straits Settlements and Mexico.* New York: MacMillan.

Leamer, E.E. and R.M. Stern (1970) *Quantitative International Economics.* Boston: Allyn and Bacon.

Legarda, B. (1962) "Foreign Exchange and the Redirection of Income Flows," *Philippine Economic Journal,* First Semester.

_____. (1955) "Foreign Trade, Economic Change and Entrepreneurship in the Nineteenth Century Philippines," Ph.D. Dissertation, Harvard University.

MacMicking, R. (1967) *Recollections of Manila and the Philippines during 1948, 1849 and 1850,* edited and annotated by Milton Herzog. Manila: Filipiniana Book Guild.

Nugent, J.A. (1973) "Exchange Rate Movements and Economic Development in the Late Nineteenth Century," *Journal of Political Economy* 81.

Owen, N. (1984) *Prosperity Without Progress.* Berkeley: University of California Press.

Power, J.H. and G.P. Sicat (1971) *The Philippines: Industrialization and Trade Policy.* Oxford University Press.

Quiason, S.D. (1966) *English Country Trade with the Philippines.* Quezon City: University of the Philippines Press.

Shepherd, G. and F. Alburo (1991) "The Philippines," in Papageorgiou, Michaely and A.M. Choksi. *Liberalizing Foreign Trade* 2. Cambridge Mass.: Basil Blackwell.

Treadgold, M. and R. Hooley (1967) "Decontrol and the Redirection of Income Flows: A Second Look," *Philippine Economic Journal*, Second Semester.

Van der Eng, P. (1993) "The Silver Standard and Asia's Integration into the World Economy, 1850–1914," paper presented at a Workshop on the History of International Monetary Arrangements. Fundaçao Oriente, Arrabida, Portugal, May 14–16.

GOVERNMENT DOCUMENTS

Philippine Islands. Bureau of Customs. *Annual Report of the Director of Customs*. Manila: Government Printing Office (annual).

Philippine Islands. Bureau of Commerce and Industry. *Statistical Bulletin of the Philippine Islands*. Manila: Government Printing Office (annual).

Republic of the Philippines. National Statistics Coordination Board. *Philippine Statistical Yearbook*. Manila. NCSO (annual).

Report of the Philippine Commission to the President (The Schurman Report). Washington: Government Printing Office, 1900.

U.S. Bureau of Census (1905) *Census of the Philippine Islands*. Washington, DC.: U.S. Government Printing Office.

The Bell Mission (1951) *United States Economic Survey Mission to the Philippines*. Washington.

List of Publications

José Encarnación

"On Ushenko's Version of the Liar-Paradox." *Mind* N.S. Vol. 64, No. 253 (January 1958): 99-100.

"Consistency Between Say's Identity and the Cambridge Equation." *Economic Journal* Vol. 68, No. 272 (December 1958): 287-290.

"A Theoretical Analysis of Investment Allocation Criteria." *Philippine Social Sciences and Humanities Review* Vol. 26, No. 3 (September 1961): 293-318.

"Note on an Export Tax as Income Stabilizer." *Philippine Economic Journal* Vol. 1, No. 1 (First Semester 1962): 92-97.

"A Note on the Stationary State." *Economica* N.S. Vol. 29, No. 115 (August 1962): 280-281.

"Overdeterminateness in Kaldor's Growth Model." *Economic Journal* Vol. 72, No. 287 (September 1962): 736-738.

Review of: J.V. Gragasin, C.A. Espiritu and Z.C. Ellen. "Principles of Economics in Philippine Setting." *Philippine Economic Journal* Vol. 2, No. 2 (Second Semester 1963): 224-225.

"A Note on Lexicographical Preferences." *Econometrica* Vol. 32, No. 1-2 (January - April 1964): 215-217.

"On Multiple Objectives in the Firm and Arrow's Theorem." *Philippine Review of Business and Economics* Vol. 1, No. 1 (February 1964): 1-7.

"Constraints and the Firm's Utility Function." *Oxford Economic Papers* N.S. Vol. 16, No. 2 (July 1964): 213-220.

"Saving and Investment in Agriculture in Relation to National Development Objectives." *Philippine Economic Journal* Vol. 3, No. 2 (Second Semester 1964): 213-229.

"Two-Sector Models of Economic Growth and Development." *Philippine Economic Journal* Vol. 4, No. 1 (First Semester 1965): 1-13.

"On Decisions Under Uncertainty." *Economic Journal* Vol. 75, No. 298 (June 1965): 442-444.

"Some Elements of Economic Theory." In G.P. Sicat et al., *Economics and Development: An Introduction.* Quezon City: University of the Philippines Press (1965): 3-1 to 3-59.

"On Instability in the Sense of Harrod." *Economica* N.S. Vol. 32, No. 127 (August 1965): 330-337.

"A Comment." *Economica* N.S. Vol. 33, No. 131 (August 1966): 346.

"On Independence Postulates Concerning Choice." (abstract) *Econometrica* Vol. 34, No. 5, Supplementary Issue (1966): 81-82.

Review of D.S. Paauw and F.E. Cookson. "Planning Capital Inflows for Southeast Asia." *Philippine Economic Journal* Vol. 5, No. 2 (Second Semester 1966): 386-387.

"A Note on Income Per Capita Growth in the Course of Time." *Philippine Economic Journal* Vol. 6, No. 1 (First Semester 1967): 49-51.

"A Model of Group Decision-Making." (abstract) *Management Science* Vol. 13, No. 10 (June 1967): C-338.

"On the Specificaton of Investment Functions." *Philippine Statistician* Vol. 17, No. 1-2 (March-June 1968): 82-94.

"Comment on Masaru Fukuda's Paper." In *Pacific Trade and Development,* II (ed. K. Kojima) (Tokyo: Japan Economic Research Center, Center Paper No. 11, April 1969): 312.

"On Independence Postulates Concerning Choice." *International Economic Review* Vol. 10, No. 2 (June 1969): 134-140.

"Some Implications of Lexicographic Utility in Development Planning." *Philippine Economic Journal* Vol. 9, No. 2 (Second Semester 1970): 231-240.

"On the Specification of a Social Welfare Function." (abstract) *Econometrica* Vol. 39, No. 4 (July 1971): 63-64.

"A Macro-economic Model of the Philippines, 1950-1969" (with R.S. Mariano and R.M. Bautista). *Philippine Economic Journal* Vol. 10, No. 2 (Second Semester 1971): 131-157.

Review of: J.J. Diamond, ed. "Issues in Fiscal and Monetary Policy." *Philippine Economic Journal* Vol. 11, No. 1 (First Semester 1972): 177-178.

"A Monetary Submodel of the Philippine Economic, 1950-1969" (with A.A. Castro). *Philippine Economic Journal* Vol. 11, No. 2 (Second Semester 1972): 214-230.

"A Foreign Trade Submodel of the Philippine Economy, 1950-1969" (with R.M. Bautista). *Philippine Economic Journal* Vol. 11, No. 2 (Second Semester 1972): 231-248.

"A Production Submodel of the Philippine Economy, 1959-169" (with M. Mangahas). *Philippine Economic Journal* Vol. 11, No. 2 (Second Semester 1972): 249-277.

"A Government Submodel of the Philippine Economy, 1950-1969" (with G.M. Jurado). *Philippine Economic Journal* Vol. 11, No. 2 (Second Semester 1972): 278-288.

"An Economic Model of the Philippines with Projections through 1976" (with R.M. Bautista, M. Mangahas and G.M. Jurado). *Philippine Economic Journal* Vol. 11, No. 2 (Second Semester 1972): 289-332.

"Group Decisions Involving Risk." *Philippine Review of Business and Economics* Vol. 9, No. 2 (December 1972): 1-10.

"Full-Employment Models of the Philippines, 1972-1976" (with R.M. Bautista). *Philippine Review of Business and Economics* Vol. 9, No. 2 (December 1972): 25-32.

"Family Income, Education, Labor Force Participation and Fertility." *Philippine Economic Journal* Vol. 12, Nos. 1 and 2 (1973): 536-549; also in W. Flieger and P.C. Smith (eds.). *A Demographic Path to Modernization: Patterns of Early Transition in the Philippines*. Quezon City: University of the Philippines Press (1975): 190-200.

"An Economic-Demographic Model of the Philippines" (with M. Mangahas, V. Paqueo and P.C. Smith). In *Studies in Philippine Economic-Demographic Relationships* by A. Kintanar et al. Quezon City: U.P. School of Economics (1974): 50-117.

"Some Exercises with the National Economic Council Input-Output Tables." (with G.M. Jurado). *NEDA Journal of [Philippine] Development* Vol. 1, No. 1 (First Semester 1974): 55-79.

"On Appropriate Technology, Saving and Employment." *Journal of Development Economics* Vol. 1, No. 1 (June 1974): 71-79.

"Baumol and Tobin on the Transactions Demand for Cash: A Pedagogical Note." *Philippine Review of Business and Economics* Vol. 11, No. 1 (June 1974): 109-111.

"Fertility and Labor Force Participation: Philippines 1968." *Philippine Review of Business and Economics* Vol. 11, No. 2 (December 1974): 113-144; also in G. Standing and G. Sheehan (eds.). *Labour Force Participation in Low-Income Countries.* Geneva: International Labour Office (1978): 307-326.

"Income Distribution in the Philippines: The Employed and the Self-Employed." In *Income Distribution, Employment and Economic Development in Southeast and East Asia.* Tokyo: Japan Economic Research Center, and Manila: Council for Asian Manpower Studies (1975): 742-775; also in Professorial Chair Lectures, Monograph No. 39, University of the Philippine Press (1977).

"[On The New Household Economics:] Comment," [Philippine] *Journal of Agricultural Economics and Development* Vol. 6, No. 1 (January 1976): 103-107.

"On the Specification of Social Welfare Functions." *Professorial Chair Lectures* Monograph No. 12, University of the Philippines Press, 1976.

"Sectoral Employment, Income Distribution and Consumption: A Macromodel with an Input-Output Structure" (with D.B. Canlas and T. Jayme Ho). *Philippine Economic Journal* Vol. 15, Nos. 1 and 2 (1976): 411-437.

Philippine Economic Problems in Perspective (with others). Quezon City: U.P. School of Economics, 1976 (condensed version: *Performance and Perspective of the Philippine Economy.* Tokyo: Institute of Developing Economies, 1976).

"Unemployment and Underemployment" (with G.A. Tagunicar and R.L. Tidalgo). [Philippine] *Human Resource Development Journal* Vol. 1, No. 1 (December 1976): 5-33.

"[Liberalization Attempts and Consequences:] Comment" in *Trade Strategies for Economic Development: The Asian Experience.* Manila: Asian Development Bank, and New York: National Bureau of Economic Research, 1976: 44.

"On Predicting Subsectoral Outputs and Prices via an Optimizing Model." *Philippine Review of Business and Economics* Vol. 13, No. 1 (June 1976): 89-92.

"Income, Education, Fertility and Employment: Philippines 1973" (with D.B. Canlas). *Philippine Review of Business and Economics* Vol. 14, No. 2 (December 1977): 1-27.

"Population and Development in Southeast Asia: A Fertility Model." *Philippine Economic Journal* Vol. 16, No. 4: 319-340.

"Income Distribution in Manila, Luzon, the Visayas and Mindanao." In H.T. Oshima and T. Mizoguchi (eds.). *Income Distribution by Sectors and Over Time in East and Southeast Asian Countries.* Quezon City: Council for Asian Manpower Studies, and Tokyo: Hitotsubashi University Institute for Economic Research (1978): 319-344; also in Professorial Chair Lectures, Monograph No. 56, University of the Philippines Press, 1979.

"Why Economic-Demographic Models Have Not Been Used in the Philippines." *Philippine Review of Economics and Business* Vol. 16, No. 2 (June 1979): 27-32; also in *Population and Development Modelling.* New York: United Nations, 1981: 113-115.

"A Simple Model of Economic Growth and Fluctuations." *Journal of Philippine Development* Vol. 6, No. 2 (Second Semester 1979): 72-78.

"Fertility Behavior and Labor Force Participation: A Lexicographic Choice Model." *Transactions of the National Academy of Science and Technology* Vol. 1. Manila: NAST (1979): 65-72.

"Relative Contributions of Mixed Variables to the Variation of a Regressand." *Transactions of the National Academy of Science and Technology* Vol. 3. Manila: NAST (1981): 48-53.

"Group Choice with Lexicographic Preferences." *Philippine Review of Economics and Business* Vol. 18, Nos. 3 & 4 (September & December 1981): 104-115.

"Fertility Behavior and Labor Force Participation: A Model of Lexicographic Choice." In *Research in Population Economics* Vol. 4 (ed. J.L. Simon and P. Lindert). Greenwich, Conn.: JAI Press (1982): 287-296.

"An Auxilliary Model for Quantifying the Socio-Economic Impact of a Development Project." In *Essays in Development Economics in Honor of Harry T. Oshima.* Manila: Philippine Institute for Development Studies, 1982 [*Philippine Review of Economics and Business*, Vol. 19, 1982]: 159-174.

"Social Values and Individual Choices." *Journal of Economic Behavior and Organization* Vol. 4, Nos. 2-3 (June-September 1983): 265-275.

"Positive Time Preference: A Comment." *Journal of Political Economy* Vol. 91, No. 4 (August 1983): 706-708.

"Consistency Conditions for Group Decisions." *Transactions of the National Academy of Science and Technology* Vol. 6. Manila: NAST (1984): 183-190.

"Becker on the Interaction Between Quantity and Quality of Children." *Philippine Review of Economics and Business* Vol. 21, Nos. 1 and 2 (March and June 1984): 113-115.

"Lexicographic Arbitration." *Economics Letters* Vol. 21, No. 3 (July 1986): 231-234.

"A Simple Solution to the Strotz Consistency Problem." *Transactions of the National Academy of Science and Technology* Vol. 8. Manila: NAST (1986): 255-258.

"Preference Paradoxes and Lexicographic Choice." *Journal of Economic Behavior and Organization* Vol. 8, No. 2 (June 1987): 231-248.

"Price Decisions and Employment Equilibrium." *Philippine Review of Economics and Business* Vol. 25, Nos. 3 & 4 (September & December 1988): 243-253.

"Consumer Choice of Qualitie$." *Economics* Vol. 57, No. 225 (February 1990): 63-72.

"Portfolio Choice and Risk." *Journal of Economic Behavior and Organization* Vol. 16, No. 3 (December 1991): 347-353.

"Group Choice with Lexicographic Utility." *European Journal of Political Economy* Vol. 8, No. 3 (October 1992): 419-425.

"Optimum Quantity of Money Instability." *Economics Letters* Vol. 42, Nos. 2-3 (1993): 215-218.

"The Source of Time Inconsistency in Optimal Plans." *Philippine Review of Economics and Business* Vol. 30, No. 2 (December 1993): 157-164.

"On Keynes' Aggregate Supply Function." In *U.P. in Search of Academic Excellence: Lectures in Honor of Jose V. Abueva, Fifteenth President (1987-1993), University of the Philippines.* Quezon City: U.P. Press (1994): 87-93.

Index

I

impact of technological changes on income distribution 131
import substitution xxviii, 289, 290, 293, 295
imports 155, 221-223, 226-228, 257-259, 261-263, 265-274, 283-301
imports, composition of 288
income elasticities 153, 267, 271-273
income distribution 105, 106, 109, 134, 135, 143, 147, 293
income inequality/ies 104, 109, 133, 135, 144, 146
indigo 285, 301
indirect utility function 6
Indonesia 78-83, 91-93, 153-155
inefficiency view of share tenancy 175
inequality 77, 87, 88, 90, 94, 97, 103, 104, 107, 109, 132, 134-136, 141, 147, 154
inequality of wages 136
inflation 225, 228, 229, 231, 232
input-output coefficients 42, 46
institutional reorganizations in production, processing and marketing systems 168
internal organization of the firm xiv
internal competitiveness 223, 226-228, 230
international competitiveness 222, 225, 229-231, 299
investment 76, 77, 87
invisible hand 59
inward-looking import substitution policies 86, 94
irrationality xx, 32

J

Japan 58, 66, 73, 75, 76, 78-84, 91-95, 100-102, 105, 136, 147, 151, 161, 163, 166, 182, 187, 223-225
Jones-Costigan Act 270, 271

K

kasugpong 182-188
Korea 77, 79, 81, 85, 91-95, 100, 102, 105
Korean War 266, 297
Kuznets' inverted U-curve 90, 91, 145

L

L^* choice problems, strong 11, weak 11
L^* orderings xv, xvii, xxii, 2, 13, 14, 18, 25-29, 31, 33, 35, 36
labor absorption 154, 157
labor participation rate 80-82
labor-intensive industries 87, 146, 225
labor-saving 142, 146
land diversion from traditional food cereals to new commodities 153
land redistribution 94, 171
land reform 94, 95, 171-175, 180-182, 184, 187-189
landless agricultural laborers 176, 178, 180
large-scale farming 157
Laurel-Langley agreement 270, 271
least-squares estimate 43, 45, 269
levy on coconut production 238
lexicographic

320 *Choice, Growth and Development*

post-World War II 77, 85, 126, 256, 265, 266, 273, 288
pre-World War II period 263, 266, 287-289, 296
preferences 1, 2, 3, 5, 6, 8, 13, 14, 18, 20, 25-29, 32-35, 197, 267 (*see also* lexicographic preferences)
price stabilization 236, 237, 242-245, 271,-273, 281, 296
price elasticities 32, 34, 226, 245, 267, 271-273, 281, 296
price competitiveness 223-225, 230, 231
profit motive 58
property incomes 134, 135, 139
proprietor's profit 134, 139
publish-or-perish xii

R

rational addiction 25, 32, 33
real exchange rate 222, 228, 229, 231
real-valued utility functions xvi, 26, 27, 33, 35
rent seeking 60, 62-65, 67, 68, 96
  litigation 66
  entrepreneur 62
reordering priorities 20
rice 151, 153, 154, 160, 162, 163, 165-169, 172-174, 179, 185-187, 208, 294
risk premium 237, 248-251
risk neutrality 28, 30, 31
risk sensitivity 29
risk aversion 27, 29-31, 124, 178, 247, 249
role of culture 109

rules of the game that determine earnings 65
rules of thumb xiv

S

safety-first 28
sales-maximizing firm xiii
satiation property 2, 3
satisficing xiv, xvii, 2, 3, 5, 9, 11, 12, 20
satisficing choices 5, 8
savings xiii, 88, 89, 95, 115, 118, 136, 199, 222, 223, 231, 232
Say's Law xii
School of Economics, U.P. xxxii, xxxiv
schooling 76, 77, 86, 97, 102, 104, 107-109, 193-199, 200-212, 214, 217, 218
sericulture 161, 163-167
sex differentials 213
share tenancy 172, 173, 176-178
simultaneous-equations 38, 40, 268
Singapore 78-83, 259, 293
social values xxi
South Korea 78, 83, 85, 101, 146
Southeast Asia 146, 152, 154, 168, 169, 176, 187, 283, 293
stabilization, benefits from 249
statistical inference 37-39, 48, 50
steam-driven technology 136, 137
subsistence consumption 32
sugar quota 288
sugar 152, 154, 257-259, 265, 268, 270, 272, 273, 281, 285, 286, 288, 289, 292, 294, 298, 300, 301
Sugar Act of 1937 271, 272, 288, 297